"Howard Fradkin has written a practical and useful guide for the healing of male survivors. His compassionate work is not just another book of survivors' stories or a technical explanation of the process of victimization, but it also incorporates exercises that survivors can use to begin the road to recovery as well as grow to become 'thrivers.'

"As the mental-health expert on the groundbreaking Oprah Winfrey show that featured 200 male survivors, Dr. Fradkin helped explain the effects of victimization to an audience perhaps unfamiliar with this all-too-common experience that affects one in six men. In leading dozens of healing retreats for men, Dr. Fradkin has the understanding born of decades of practice. He has a clear knowledge of the dynamics and issues for survivors, and provides exercises for men to use in a clear and functional way.

"I like this book, and it is a valuable addition to the shelf of any male survivor, loved one, or professional working with this population."

— **Ken Singer, MSW**, author of *Evicting the Perpetrator: A Male Survivor Guide to Recovery from Childhood Sexual Abuse*

*"The title of Howard Fradkin's book, **Joining Forces: Empowering Male Survivors to Thrive**, captures the essence of the healing process for males with a history of trauma: breaking isolation and silence, establishing connection with others, working through shame and developing personal empowerment, and resolving the past in the interest of the future. The use of survivor testimonials is highly effective. The writings of the Silence Breakers are both moving and explanatory; they articulate the struggle but also the gains made in the process of healing. Although this book was written specifically for male survivors to identify their particular issues and needs, female survivors will benefit from it as well. I highly recommend this book for all adult survivors."*

— **Christine A. Courtois, Ph.D., ABPP**, psychologist in private practice, Courtois & Associates, PC, Washington, D.C.; author of *Healing the Incest Wound: Adult Survivors in Therapy* and *Recollections of Sexual Abuse: Treatment Principles and Guidelines;* and co-editor (with Julian Ford) of *Treating Complex Traumatic Stress Disorder: An Evidence-Based Guide* (**www.drchriscourtois.com**)

Praise for *Joining Forces*

"As a co-founder of MaleSurvivor and the co-chair of our Weekends of Recovery program, Dr. Fradkin has helped thousands of survivors of sexual abuse put their lives back together. His skill, compassion, and generosity are evident from the very first words of this book. I am both a survivor of sexual abuse and alumnus of the MaleSurvivor Weekends of Recovery, and I can bear witness to the transformative impact of the wisdom contained within this book. Every year, millions of survivors and their loved ones find help for healing through our website and the practices Dr. Fradkin helped put into place. I highly recommend this book to every survivor of sexual abuse and those people who love, care for, or wish to help support them."

— **Christopher M. Anderson**, Executive Director, MaleSurvivor (**www.MaleSurvivor.org**)

"Thoughtful . . . thorough . . . a must-read for men who may have had an unwanted or abusive sexual experience in childhood or adulthood and for the people who love those men. Howard Fradkin's book will be 'top shelf' in our lending library."

— **Steve LePore**, Founder and Executive Director, 1in6 (**www.1in6.org**)

"For many years Dr. Howard Fradkin has inspired male survivors of sexual abuse to affirm themselves and move beyond the prisons of their childhood trauma. The Weekends of Recovery program he instituted through MaleSurvivor: The National Organization Against Male Sexual Victimization has brought together men from a wide range of backgrounds and experiences and taught them to help one another heal. Now he has written a book that will bring his wisdom to a much larger audience. Men who read it will find their inner strength through exercises, storytelling, and a range of empowering affirmations. It will inspire survivors to heal and move on in their lives. His book is a gift to all traumatized men."

— **Richard B. Gartner, Ph.D.**, Training and Supervising Analyst, Faculty, and Founding Director of Sexual Abuse Service: William Alanson White Psychoanalytic Institute; author of *Beyond Betrayal: Tak[...]* Abuse and *Betrayed as B[...]* bused Men

700040199073

"Howard Fradkin is a leader in recovery for male survivors, personally and professionally. From his extensive experience, he has created a recovery workbook that is a positive contribution to the growing body of literature on male sexual victimization and recovery. In an encouraging and affirming tone, *Joining Forces* offers specific exercises and suggestions of healing activities. Like his workshop leadership, this book will be of great benefit to many men in recovery and those who love them."

— **Mike Lew,** author of *Victims No Longer: The Classic Guide for Men Recovering from Sexual Child Abuse* and *Leaping Upon the Mountains: Men Proclaiming Victory over Sexual Child Abuse* (**www.nextstepcounseling.org**)

"*Joining Forces* is a shout-out for those who identify as survivors, for men who wonder about what was done to them and have had no name for it, and for all who love and support them. Dr. Fradkin provides in his writing what he does so beautifully in his life and work: He creates a healing space for men to understand their experience and to remember who they really were from the beginning. *Joining Forces* not only illuminates one's particular perceptions of what it means to be a male survivor of sexual abuse, but also provides story after inspiring story of men and their partners: their personal struggles, their inevitable challenges, and their incredible triumphs. It is a powerful template for reclaiming what is most essential to any survivor—being a strong, sensitive man who is capable of connecting with himself and others. In so doing, *Joining Forces* will challenge those who read it to take the risk to live more honestly, with greater freedom, integrity, and joy. It is a tremendous gift and an invaluable resource to all of us."

— **Mikele Rauch, LMFT,** author of *Healing the Soul after Religious Abuse: The Dark Heaven of Recovery* (**www.mikelerauch.com**)

"The combination of Dr. Fradkin's years of clinical experience and the personal recoveries of the men and women with whom he collaborated makes for a powerful resource. It provides male survivors and their loved ones with straightforward, practical guidance and inspires hope.

— **Mic Hunter, Psy.D.,** licensed psychologist and licensed marriage and family therapist, and author of *Abused Boys: The Neglected Victims of Sexual Abuse* and *Honor Betrayed: Sexual Abuse in America's Military* (**www.drmichunter.com**)

"Dr. Howard Fradkin's book, **Joining Forces**, is a treasure chest over-flowing with gems for adult survivors of child sexual abuse who are seeking support to begin and continue the healing process, and for those who are ready to reclaim their lives and thrive. The book, based on the powerful and effective structure of MaleSurvivor's successful Weekends of Recovery, is actually an adventure for those who want solid and effective tools for healing—not something to fear or dread, as in facing a long-winded, painful process of recovery. Uplifting in a step-by-step way, this book is a golden toolbox of self-reflective and transformative exercises that naturally help garner positive insights and options for realistic and possible change—change that no doubt challenges the seemingly impossible effects of child sexual abuse.

"This is more than a book; it's a journey, with a clear sense that we are not alone. Included are personal stories of alumni from the Weekends of Recovery, known in the book as the Silence Breakers. Their honest and vivid stories of personal transformation and reclaimed lives are testimony to the possibilities that open up when one does the important healing work offered in this book. Moreover, as in any hero's journey, there's always a guide to help them on their way. Howard Fradkin, a pioneer and leader in this field, offers his wise and safe counsel, giving thousands of survivors the keys to pos-sibilities ahead. We get the sense that he is one step ahead of us, opening the door to each chapter, where he stands at the threshold, shepherding each reader to a room where sunlight and hope reigns, and 'Daring to Dream' becomes a reality step-by-step."

— **Kathy Barbini** and **Simon Weinberg**, founders of Big Voice Pictures and producers of *Boys and Men Healing*
(**www.bigvoicepictures.com**)

JOINING FORCES

Hay House Titles of Related Interest

YOU CAN HEAL YOUR LIFE, the movie, starring Louise L. Hay & Friends
(available as a 1-DVD program and an expanded 2-DVD set)
Watch the trailer at: **www.LouiseHayMovie.com**

THE SHIFT, the movie,
starring Dr. Wayne W. Dyer
(available as a 1-DVD program and an expanded 2-DVD set)
Watch the trailer at: **www.DyerMovie.com**

❀　❀　❀

BEATING BIPOLAR:
How One Therapist Tackled His Illness . . . and How What
He Learned Could Help You!, by Blake LeVine

THE MINDFUL MANIFESTO:
How Doing Less and Noticing More Can Help Us Thrive in
a Stressed-out World, by Dr. Jonty Heaversedge and Ed Halliwell

NO STORM LASTS FOREVER:
Transforming Suffering into Insight, by Dr. Terry A. Gordon

TRANSCENDENTAL MEDITATION:
The Essential Teachings of Maharishi Mahesh Yogi,
Revised and Updated for the 21st Century, by Jack Forem

YOU CAN CREATE AN EXCEPTIONAL LIFE,
by Louise Hay and Cheryl Richardson

All of the above are available at your local bookstore,
or may be ordered by visiting:

Hay House USA: **www.hayhouse.com**®
Hay House Australia: **www.hayhouse.com.au**
Hay House UK: **www.hayhouse.co.uk**
Hay House South Africa: **www.hayhouse.co.za**
Hay House India: **www.hayhouse.co.in**

JOINING
FORCES

Empowering Male Survivors to Thrive

Howard Fradkin, Ph.D., LICDC

HAY HOUSE, INC.
Carlsbad, California • New York City
London • Sydney • Johannesburg
Vancouver • Hong Kong • New Delhi

Copyright © 2012 by Howard Fradkin

Published and distributed in the United States by: Hay House, Inc.:
www.hayhouse.com* • *Published and distributed in Australia by:* Hay House
Australia Pty. Ltd.: www.hayhouse.com.au • *Published and distributed in the
United Kingdom by:* Hay House UK, Ltd.: www.hayhouse.co.uk • *Published and
distributed in the Republic of South Africa by:* Hay House SA (Pty), Ltd.: www
.hayhouse.co.za • *Distributed in Canada by:* Raincoast: www.raincoast.com •
Published in India by: Hay House Publishers India: www.hayhouse.co.in

Indexer: Robert Swanson
Interior design: Julie Davison
T-shirt photos to open Parts I and II; Chapters 1, 3, 4, 6, 7, 8, 9, 13, and 14:
    © 2012 raylavoie.com
T-shirt photos to open Chapters 2, 5, 10, 11, 12, and 15: Mic Hunter

The author of this book does not dispense medical advice or prescribe the
use of any technique as a form of treatment for physical, emotional, or medical problems without the advice of a physician, either directly or indirectly. The
intent of the author is only to offer information of a general nature to help you
in your quest for emotional and spiritual well-being. In the event you use any of
the information in this book for yourself, which is your constitutional right, the
author and the publisher assume no responsibility for your actions.

Library of Congress Cataloging-in-Publication Data

Fradkin, Howard.
 Joining forces : empowering male survivors to thrive / Howard Fradkin.
     p. cm.
 Includes index.
 ISBN 978-1-4019-4134-5 (hardcover : alk. paper)
 1. Male sexual abuse victims--United States--Psychology. 2. Adult
child sexual abuse victims--United States--Psychology. 3. Child sexual
abuse--United States. 4. Self-help techniques. I. Title.
 HV6570.7.F73 2012
 362.76'4019--dc23
                          2012021739

Hardcover ISBN: 978-1-4019-4134-5
Digital ISBN: 978-1-4019-4135-2

15 14 13 12   4 3 2 1
1st edition, November 2012

*To the Silence Breakers and
all the courageous male survivors
who have trusted me with their
stories, and inspired me with
their strength and resilience*

CONTENTS

FOREWORD

One carefully placed raindrop can overflow a dam.

It's funny how you can think you've worked through something, removed yourself from a situation, and then one incident can come along and drag your senses right back into that very moment.

This happened to me on a very normal day. It was a day like any other. I was at home with the dogs, reading. The television was on some news station, but I wasn't paying attention to it until I heard the reporter say something about several young men who had been sexually abused by someone in a church. His words became white noise to me as my senses took me back to my childhood and an awful experience of sexual abuse I endured at the hands of someone in my church. I was listening to this story in shock, but what struck me the most was that even though I was more than 30 years removed from my own abuse and abusers, this story was able to deliver me right back to relive the horror of the violation on such a raw and guttural level. It sickened me to my stomach.

As the day went on, I tried to get the news report out of my head, but no matter what I did, I couldn't. Later that night I was talking to my good friend Oprah Winfrey. I asked her whether she had seen the story, and she responded that she had. I said to her, "You know what would be amazing? If you could make this happen . . . if you could find enough men who were molested as young boys to fill your audience and have them talk about their experiences as adult survivors. I think the world would be shocked at the long-term effects that those moments have had on us."

She said, "I think it would be powerful and life changing for so many men, not only if I did that show, but if you would be a part of it as well."

Now, that threw me for a loop. I thought, *Why would I do that? I am not the type of man who spends time looking in the rearview mirror. I'm very much a forward thinker. I am fully invested in letting the past be the past. So what would be the point in my revisiting those awful experiences?* Over the years I had become comfortable talking about it to friends and loved ones on a need-to-know basis, but I wasn't interested in talking about it in front of millions of people on national television. So I said no. I was past it . . . or so I thought. But here comes that raindrop.

Days went by, and I tried to get the story out of my head. I tried to stop reliving my own nightmare, but the more I tried, the more I realized that I was still haunted by it. As much work as I had put into my own healing, I quickly became painfully aware that whether I wanted to look back or not, it was still looking right at *me,* still affecting my life in many ways. That showed me that there was still a lot of work yet to be done. I also started to wonder how many more male survivors were affected by this news story. I wondered how the victims of the story that I had just been watching were dealing with it. The next day the news ran an interview with one of the young men. He looked to be in his early 20s. I saw the familiar agony in that young man's face, and me being much older than he was, I knew the difficult path that he had before him. So I decided to do the show.

From the moment I agreed to do the show until the day I actually did it, I had so much anxiety, so many questions. I wasn't sure I should do it until the second it was over. I mean, the very second I had spoken my truth, it was as if I had removed a five-ton weight from my chest. I felt as if every bit of evil that these molesters had sewn into the inseam of my soul had been ripped away. I was so glad I did it. I felt so much lighter and freer. I didn't realize how much power lay in talking about it. I didn't know that part of lifting my own shame was in using my own voice. Out of all the years of self-work and discovery, I think that moment was the one that did the most good on my journey to healing.

When it was time to tape the "200 Men" show, and I walked in and saw all these men holding up pictures of themselves at the ages at which they were sexually abused, it moved me inside of my soul. I finally knew I wasn't alone. There was a brotherhood of survivors who had painfully and slowly triumphed. I cried a lot that day. I finally saw myself in all of these men: all races, fathers, husbands, lovers, friends, doctors, lawyers—you name it. We were all represented, and we were all an army standing strong to speak out against the silent suffering.

One of the most impressive of all the men in the room was a gentle, brilliant spirit named Dr. Howard Fradkin. His explanation and care of the journey that all of us in that room had been on was so intriguing to me. For many years I had done so much self-exploration to try to get to a place of healing, and here was this voice describing my climb out of darkness as if he had been the guide who had helped me all along the way. I was hanging on his every word.

I am beyond excited that he has written this book. His kindness of heart, and his way of explaining even the most complicated long-term effects of male sexual abuse, is so revelatory and profound that not only can it inspire those who were abused to heal, but it can also give them a clear and detailed understanding of what has been happening in their lives. He is a brilliant, gifted man, and for him to write this book was a selfless act of sharing.

It is my prayer that as you read this book, Dr. Fradkin's words will do for you what they did for me, and that it will give you the hope and the permission to allow yourself to heal fully. You deserve it. That's what it did for me.

Acknowledging that something happened is tough; realizing that you are still being affected by it is even harder. I applaud your bravery. That is such a difficult thing for most males to do. But you have already made the first step—you have this book.

May every word in this book be marrow to your brokenness and speak comfort to your soul.

God bless,
Tyler Perry

PREFACE

Thank you for picking up this book about male survivors. It is primarily for male survivors of any form of sexual victimization, to help you transform yourself from a victim to a thriver. Although I focus on male survivors because men face unique challenges in healing, which I will detail in this book, any female survivor is also likely to benefit from the tools, experiences, and wisdom shared here. Partners and family members will also find it very useful to understand what a male survivor has experienced and will encounter in his process of transformation. In addition, since loved ones also *need* support in order to *provide* support, I've included a chapter later in the book specifically for them. If you are an ally—an advocate, a professional who works with male survivors, or an educator—I am sure the information will be very useful in increasing your sensitivity, awareness of the healing process, and knowledge about how to help prevent future victimization.

If you are a survivor, or think you might be, I honor the courage it must take for you to simply hold this book in your hands in this moment. Reading a book like this is likely to be very challenging to you for several reasons. Perhaps the biggest challenge is believing that the abuse or assault you suffered had any effect on you at all. It's very common for many male survivors to think, *Yeah, that happened a long time ago, and big deal. I don't have any problems resulting from that.* If you are one of these men, I hope you will choose to read this book, because it's very likely that you will find your story here and will identify with many of the same problems I describe that rob survivors of the possibility of a much happier and fuller life today.

Another major challenge is that although you may admit to having problems, if you are like most men, you were raised to believe you should know the answer to any problem you face and never ask for help because that's a sign of weakness. This is one of the many dysfunctional messages our culture teaches that cause problems for men who have been victimized. I will examine many of these messages in this book and their impact on recovery.

Most often, men who are victimized feel immense shame afterward; after all, as a man, you are never "supposed" to be a victim. You most likely learned that you are supposed to be in control at all times, and victimization is a sign that you did not control your body. These are examples of those masculine-oriented dysfunctional messages. Whether you were a young child or an adult when you were abused, the shame is unfortunately very intense. The most likely result of shame is keeping silent about what was done to you. Many other blocks that men face in healing are discussed in this book. My major goal in writing it is to help you break your silence, heal your shame, and transform yourself from a victim to a thriver.

You may actually know that you have problems, that something is definitely not right, but have not yet remembered any specific details of victimization. This is also common, because survivors can "bury" memories until a time in their lives when they feel safe and stable enough to remember. Your problems may or may not relate to victimization; however, I believe that reading this book will help you put some missing pieces together that are currently confusing you. I will discuss in great detail memories and how they surface.

I chose to write *Joining Forces* now because I've always wanted to share my successful healing techniques and guidance in a book, but I've accomplished that goal only with the support and encouragement of two very special people: Oprah Winfrey and Tyler Perry. Ms. Winfrey honored me with an invitation to serve as a guest expert on two powerful shows she hosted in November 2010. In her final season, Oprah invited 200 male survivors of sexual abuse to be her audience, along with her special friend Tyler Perry, the Hollywood director, producer, actor, and creator of the first African-American–owned movie studio. Just the week before, he had gone public with the story of his own sexual abuse.

The goal of the shows was to break the silence about male sexual victimization and to help inspire hope and healing for male survivors all over the world. As a psychologist and a survivor of sexual abuse myself, I have provided help to more than a thousand male survivors through individual, couples, and group psychotherapy; workshops; and intensive weekend retreats. I was invited by Ms. Winfrey to help her audience understand the impact of abuse and to demonstrate that men absolutely can heal from sexual victimization.

Bringing 200 male survivors and their allies into the studio was a demonstration of the power of joining forces to empower male survivors to thrive. All of us witnessed that power during the show and have observed it ever since. After the show, Ms. Winfrey and Mr. Perry reached out to me and encouraged me to share my knowledge in a book. Up to that point, I had never made the time, but I accepted their encouragement and the support of many colleagues and friends to make this book possible.

A psychotherapist who is a survivor must engage in his own healing if he is to be successful at working with others. However, I started working with male survivors even before I knew of my own sexual victimization. I started my own transformation journey when I attended training for therapists who wanted to learn about working with alcoholics and their families at Hazelden, a world-renowned treatment center in Minnesota. That training began to unearth significant awareness of my own victimization as a child and teenager, and rape as an adult, which I followed up on with years of psychotherapy and various alternative forms of healing, including body-awareness education.

Because of professional ethical boundaries, it's not appropriate for me as a psychologist to share more details of my abuse, but I do want you to know that I understand your experience both as a survivor and as a professional. I have attended many seminars led by the leading authorities in working with trauma survivors, and during those workshops, I had opportunities to both learn important skills and do more of my own healing work. I am also a licensed independent chemical dependency counselor (LICDC), and have undergone years of specialized training to work with people who have all forms of addictions.

I am grateful to the number of healing professionals and colleagues who guided my transformation from a man in denial to one who is now thriving. Many of those colleagues I met while attending training conferences on treating male survivors. At the fifth national conference for therapists of male survivors in Washington, D.C., in 1993, a number of those therapists who were also survivors, myself included, spoke up at the end of the conference and said, "We want more." We decided then to create an organization that was always available and active to support male survivors. A year later, we co-founded The National Organization on Male Sexual Victimization, which later became known as MaleSurvivor: The National Organization Against Male Sexual Victimization. The men and women in that group offer support and encouragement, affirming that healing is possible. Creation of our community was a key step in the history of the male survivor movement. MaleSurvivor is the oldest and most prominent international organization that seeks to prevent, heal, and eliminate all forms of sexual victimization through support, treatment, research, education, advocacy, and activism.

The more self-healing I have done, the more I have been motivated to share the possibilities for healing with both male and female survivors. In 2001, I, along with Boston psychotherapist Mikele Rauch, proposed that MaleSurvivor create Weekends of Recovery, and with a dedicated team of psychotherapists, we began the program. My role as chairperson for the first ten years (and now co-chairperson with Jim Struve, LCSW, since September 2010) of the MaleSurvivor Weekends of Recovery (WOR) formed a large part of my motivation to write this book. More than 850 men and a number of their partners have trusted the MaleSurvivor team of facilitators and participated in a WOR, and this book is a tribute to all the lessons they have taught us.

This book features a number of those weekend alumni, most of whom were also audience members for the "200 Men" *Oprah* shows. I call them the "Silence Breakers." This book would not have been possible without their willingness to share the stories of their abuse and their recoveries.

This book is also the story of the Weekends of Recovery and the combined wisdom of the incredible team of facilitators, including 16 of the most skilled professionals in the field today and some of my best friends. Our team works on a collaborative model to determine how each weekend is facilitated, and in this book, I am excited to share many of the ideas our team has developed over the past decade to help empower men to heal. To date, we've hosted more than 45 Weekends of Recovery all over the United States and Canada. We started the weekends in 2001, because we wanted to help survivors learn new skills and to advance in their recoveries. We believed a group experience would be the most powerful way to help men break their silence, heal their shame, and join forces to build a lasting brotherhood capable of providing a lifeline of necessary support.

In the Introduction, I'll start by helping you understand who a male survivor is and some of the dynamics that create challenges. I'll also address my suggestions for how this book can be most useful to you.

INTRODUCTION

Let's start with who fits the definition of a male survivor. Male survivors have experienced some form of *sexual victimization,* which is a broad term that includes sexual abuse, sexual assault, and rape. Sexual victimization consists of any overt or covert sexual behavior by which the abuser—who could be male or female—*chooses* to take advantage of a power differential with a dependent or vulnerable victim in order to satisfy the abuser's needs without the victim's consent. I emphasize the word *chooses* because it squarely places the responsibility for the abuse on the abuser. I will explore this idea thoroughly in this book.

In most cases, a person knows the one committing the sexual victimization; therefore another very important aspect of the abuse is the betrayal of trust between the victim and the abuser. This is especially true when it is committed by a person who holds some protective role for the victim. Parents, older siblings, or other relatives; babysitters; coaches; doctors; teachers; religious leaders; organizational authority figures such as Boy Scout leaders; and therapists are all examples of such people who should be in the role of protecting vulnerable boys and men.

Whereas in the past *sexual abuse* was a term used to describe victims who were under legal age, and *sexual assault* or *rape* was a term used for adult victims, these distinctions are currently changing. Now it's common to use these terms for any victim of any age. People the victim knows or total strangers can commit rapes. Rape and sexual assault may involve physical violence as well.

Although sexual victimization involves sexual behavior, it is not an act of sex, because sex is a mutually consensual activity. Overt sexual behaviors include any penetration, no matter how slight, of the mouth or anus with any body part of the abuser or any object used by the abuser. Covert sexual behaviors consist of nonpenetration acts and cover a wide gamut, including inappropriate hugging or kissing, showing pornography, taking sexually explicit or erotic pictures or movies of vulnerable victims, inappropriate touching of a victim's genitals or body, and making sexual comments. Covert incest, or mother-son or father-son enmeshment, can also include behaviors when parents make their children into their romantic partners in place of an adult.

No matter what the form the sexual victimization took, all such acts are traumatic, and this book is dedicated to the healing of all boys and men who have had these acts perpetrated upon them. In this book, you will learn about the unique aspects of victimization and male socialization that make the impact of such abuse different for boys and men.

We know from research that at least one in six boys is overtly sexually victimized before age 18.[1] One in every ten rape victims is male.[2] One in ten men have reported inappropriate noncontact sexual activity (covert sexual abuse) by age 16.[3] In summary, one in four men (28 percent) have a sexual victimization history, and most likely this figure is underreported.[4] These statistics prove that if you are a male survivor, you have many other men in your life who absolutely could understand what was done to you and could offer you support.

Beginning Your Healing Process

You have just read about who is a male survivor. Did I describe your experience? What was that like for you to see yourself in the descriptions above? You may be feeling a bit uncomfortable as you hold this book, because, as I mentioned in the Preface, that simple act is an acknowledgment that my topic is important to you and your life. If you are a male survivor of sexual abuse or sexual assault, deciding to read about abuse and how to heal yourself from it is one major step in the process of recovery. I have written this book especially for you, and I hope that in these pages, you will find support, tools for your recovery and transformation, healthy challenges, and an abundance of hope.

You may be a man who does not know whether you were ever sexually victimized or not. Or perhaps you know you were abused, but you believe it didn't hurt you at all. In either case, I invite you to keep reading and trust that your gut is telling you that something in this book will be helpful to you.

If you are a psychotherapist, healer or bodyworker, educator, or advocate, I hope these words will help in your important work. I especially want to acknowledge those of you who may fit more than one of these categories. As a psychologist who is also a survivor of sexual abuse and assault, I am one of those multicategory people myself. To female survivors, your struggle is very similar to that of male survivors, as I touched upon in the Preface, so I trust you will also find the contents of this book useful and inspiring. Partners, spouses, and family members, I hope you, too, will find support here, as well as a deeper understanding of the challenges faced by the survivor in your family as he undergoes the healing process. Toward the end of this book, you'll also find a chapter devoted to what steps you can take to get necessary support youself.

I've titled this book *Joining Forces: Empowering Male Survivors to Thrive* because I want you to have hope that by connecting with other male survivors and allies, and by speaking openly of your experiences, healing will come one step at a time. The sad truth is that most survivors suffer in silence. Although you won't be having in-person interactions with me or the survivors you will meet in this book, my hope is that you will feel our support and, in that way, will be able to join forces with us and the people you are motivated to share your experience with who can assist you in your process of transformation. Through healing, you will be empowered to thrive in all aspects of your life. Hope is necessary for every survivor. When you give yourself permission to hope for and dream of a better future, healing will be achievable. Recovery is possible when you combine support with risk taking. Empowerment is achieved when you allow yourself to see the possibilities for more freedom and happiness. It will require action on your part, and I will support you and guide you each step of the way.

This book will take you through a process, but it's not a race to a finish line. It's okay to read one paragraph, page, or chapter at a time, and to allow yourself time for reflection as you proceed. Speed-reading is neither required nor recommended. Go at your own comfortable pace. Take time to reflect, feel, and speak your truths. I encourage you to "check inside" from time to time so you can absorb the material in a way that best serves you and your needs.

My intention is for you to find this book to be nurturing, comforting, affirming, and, at the same time, challenging. For most male survivors, it will be helpful to have a supportive person to talk to about your feelings and responses to the material as you read. Initially, you may not feel up to the challenge this book presents. That's okay; this is an invitation, not a demand. Know that I care deeply about you, because I have been where you are and have helped thousands of others rebuild their lives.

Visualize me sitting with you as you read, or if you find that difficult, visualize someone else you trust, a person you feel comfortable opening up to, a "recovery ally." In Chapter 3, I will offer guidance in choosing a recovery ally to help you in this process. At this moment, I may be a stranger, but I am also someone who has devoted most of his career to helping men and women heal from sexual abuse and sexual assault. I can't walk personally with each person, but my goal is to help you and as many others as possible through this book by expressing my compassion and understanding, and sharing my proven healing treatments in these pages.

While this book is likely to provide you with a great deal of help, it is intended to be an adjunct to the work you will do with an experienced psychotherapist. During the past two decades, many psychotherapists have been trained to work with male survivors, and you can find a list of them on the MaleSurvivor website, **www .malesurvivor.org**, by clicking on the tab "Find Support." You will find a great consumer's guide there, written by Ken Singer, on how to select a therapist.

It's important that you feel comfortable enough with the therapist you choose. It's natural to feel uncomfortable at first; however, I encourage you to trust your gut sense of the person to decide if this professional feels like the right one for you. You will be sharing some of the most intimate parts of your life with this person, and it's important that you feel safe enough to speak your truth. The qualifications of professionals, including their fields of practice and their degrees, are important, but less important than whether they have the necessary skills to help you. Both male and female psychotherapists can be helpful; however, it's important for you to decide whom you will feel comfortable enough with to share your experience. Know that you can ask professionals questions, including how much experience they have in working with male survivors. You can also ask them how much specific training they have had in providing psychotherapy to male survivors. You will benefit if they have received specific training in helping people resolve trauma in their lives, too.

Anytime you feel uncomfortable with the behavior of a therapist, you can talk with the therapist about your discomfort. If you feel that your boundaries are not being respected, discuss this. It's common for survivors to need to work with more than one provider before they find the right match. Sometimes, you will do one piece of work with one therapist, and then choose another one at a different point in your work to do deeper or more emotionally intense work. If you feel that your needs are not being met, or if your therapist is unable to talk with you about any discomfort you are having in a way that feels respectful of your feelings, remember that you have the right to change therapists.

Healing is best facilitated in a supportive community beyond your psychotherapist. If you can connect with a healing community of men and women, you will be empowered to move forward in your recovery. As you read this book, it's your job—not your ally's or mine—to take care of yourself. I invite you to connect with me or another recovery ally so that you can feel the power of leaving your isolation behind. Shame heals when you allow it to surface. By sharing your feelings with someone you trust, you can move forward to speak the truth and shed your shame.

I will give you opportunities throughout this book to participate in exercises you can practice at home that are titled "Experiment with New Possibilities." You can do most of these exercises alone, but some involve a support person. I encourage you not to just read the exercises, but to *do* them. Many of the answers you are seeking are inside you and will surface as you connect with what lies within. Often, I will ask you to "check in" with yourself. Sometimes I will invite you to try an experiment with me. You may feel silly, but trust me; I am providing you with opportunities to better know yourself and to open yourself to the possibility that you can take further steps to heal and recover.

It will be most helpful if you buy a journal or notebook in which to record your feelings and thoughts as you go through this book. You can also use your journal to record your responses to the many experiments I will offer you. I'd suggest photocopying these experiments, and then you can insert them into your journal along with your reactions to the experiments. If you live with others, it's important that you find a safe place to store your journal because this is your private information.

Being abused may well have caused you to build walls around experiences that are too painful to bear. I will help you take down those walls so that you can feel free to live with your thoughts and feelings. As you expand your ability to connect with your experiences, you will likely become better able to connect with others, too.

Please pay attention to what you are experiencing within yourself as you read. Be particularly aware of your actions as well. If you find yourself doing things that are self-destructive or not in your best interest, you could consider that:

1. You may be reading too quickly. Again, this is not a race to the finish line. It's a healing process.

2. You may be feeling overwhelmed and flooded with emotion. Avoid escaping with old and familiar methods of soothing yourself that may be harmful. Consider that there may be healthier choices available to you now.

3. You may not have enough support in your life or be emotionally stable enough to be ready to read this book, or you may need to address problems with addiction or compulsive behavior

as you read it. It's fine to put down the book at any point, wiggle your toes, or take a walk. My goal is always to help my clients continue to function in their lives while doing healing work, and my hope is that you, too, will do what will allow you to be as functional as possible while reading this book.

4. You have a boy inside you. (You may have more than one boy inside, especially if you suffered more severe abuse, and if so, it will be helpful to get to know those boys. Some of you who have a male identity may also have girl aspects, and if so, know that they exist to help you and protect you.) You may not have any interest in this boy, or you may not yet know about him. It's possible that the boy inside you may be hurting and in need of your attention. Another part of you may want to deny his pain, minimize it, or numb it. You may have disconnected from your younger self a long time ago. By choosing to read, to participate in your own healing and to reclaim you life, you are letting him know that you may be ready to connect with him, if only for fleeting moments at first. If you were abused only as an adult, your boy may have strengths, such as courage and the ability to ask for help and trust others who can help you now, even though he wasn't the one abused.

Each time you read a section and then put down this book, you can engage in healthier behaviors to enhance your recovery. As you are reading and at the end of each chapter, you might find it helpful to:

1. Breathe gently and deeply.

2. Become aware of any feelings, thoughts, or memories that surfaced. Notice if they are still present or if you are blocking them.

3. Keep a journal about your reflections.

4. Remember that recovery is not a 24/7 job. Feel free to take your time and take breaks, too. Put the book down and go play now and then, whether it's exercising, hanging out with friends, watching a game, catching a movie, or just chilling on the weekend.

5. Some men benefit from drawing, painting, playing music, singing, or other creative expression. Consider having a place where you have art paper, pastels, pens or art pencils, or perhaps canvases and paint. Then give yourself permission to use your creative side to express what is going on inside. You may think you need to be an "artist" to do this; however, if you put art supplies in front of you, you may discover a desire to express yourself that will help you externalize whatever process or feelings are inside you; if you are a musician, you might sing or play songs that inspire you.

6. Check in with your recovery ally and let that person know what you felt, thought, and remembered as you read each chapter.

There are 15 chapters in this book, and you are welcome to go directly to the chapters that you believe best apply to you. However, I invite you to read about how I have decided to structure the book, because the order of the chapters is designed to best help you move forward one logical step at a time. The chapters are organized so you learn sequentially the skills necessary to move from one phase of healing to the next. I will share specific skills with you in each chapter in the order in which you will most likely need them. Be mindful that the skills you will learn build on each other, and be aware that all the skills presented here will be helpful if you use them, no matter how far along you are in your own healing.

The book is divided into two parts:

— **Part I** is called "Beginning Your Healing Process." In the first six chapters, I will address some core skills that you can use and some core struggles that male survivors face at the beginning of the healing process. In the first chapter, you will also meet the Silence Breakers, who are fellow survivors—along with some of their partners—who will offer you their wisdom and hope from their own healing experiences.

The first phase of recovery is learning how to be safe inside. Once you know more about how to create internal safety, then you learn about how to create external safety—specifically, how to get support. I will help you consider how it could be possible for you to refuse to isolate anymore, because this is one of the blocks that survivors often inadvertently place in their own way. I will also offer you important guidance for telling your story. Telling your story helps you transform yourself from being a silent victim to being a man who has allowed himself to shed some of his shame and find the support he has always deserved.

For your recovery to move forward, it's also important to know that you are no longer alone and that there is hope for you. In the last chapter of Part I, you'll hear the stories from a number of courageous male survivors about their abuse experiences and where they are today. The likelihood is very high that you will hear your own story here, and that's another aspect of shedding some of your shame.

— In **Part II**, titled "Moving Forward on the Path to Thriving," I will address many aspects of healing that are essential to moving beyond remembering and sharing your abuse. You will have the opportunity to address and resolve blocks to healing, discover how you learned to be loyal to dysfunction, and learn how to be loyal to functionality instead, a core skill needed to move forward. I will also discuss a technique called "sculpting" that can help you become unstuck from the effects of your abuse. In addition, I will help you look at your blocks to intimacy and romance, including questions about sexuality and sexual orientation.

After discussing blocks, I will address with you the controversial topic of forgiveness, and offer you some new ways to think about it that may open you up to consider more about the role that forgiveness could play in your new life. I hope that you will be open to my suggested possibilities for thinking differently, feeling differently, and acting differently in order to transform yourself.

In Part II, I have included a chapter for partners and family members, both because they are an integral part of your healing and need their own support, and because I think it's very important for you as a survivor to understand the challenges your partners and family members can face while providing you support. The last two chapters focus on choosing to be more open publicly about your abuse, and then I'll end with some exciting testimony about how you, too, can transform yourself into a thriving male survivor.

I have begun each chapter title with "Dare to Dream . . ." Recovering from the impact of sexual victimization is an active process that I invite you to participate in as fully as possible. It's common at the beginning to feel very hopeless and helpless. It's normal to have little faith that there is any possibility other than to suffer in silence, shame, depression, anxiety, and loneliness. Each chapter invites you to dare to dream that there are actually other possibilities for your life. Daring to dream is an active step that can open your mind and your heart to make necessary changes that will help you move one more step past the despair and loneliness that may characterize where you are now. "Dare to Dream" is also the theme of the MaleSurvivor Weekends of Recovery.

I have structured this book much like how we structure the MaleSurvivor Weekends of Recovery, a program I have directed or co-directed for 11 years. The structure of the weekends has evolved through the collective wisdom and experience of the facilitator team. At the beginning of each weekend, we invite the participants to dare to dream of leaving their isolation behind. We structure activities so that each participant can pace himself. We begin with the basics, much as I do here, and then move on to the more challenging aspects of the work. What I offer in these pages could not possibly provide the same experience as attending the weekend program. However, I hope that you will benefit from some of the same tools we provide to program participants to help them work through their shame and hurt.

Throughout this book, I have included photographs of some of the hundreds of T-shirts created by male survivors who have participated in a Weekend of Recovery. You can view all of the T-shirts at: **www.flickr.com/photos/malesurvivor**. Many times, healing is facilitated using the creative part of yourself. Many of these T-shirts were made by men who would tell you, "I am not an artist." I'll let you be the judge. What I hope each T-shirt represents to you is one more man who is willing to join forces with you on your journey.

In addition, I will offer you insights and guidance I've developed over three decades of providing psychotherapy to male and female survivors and their families. I have invited a number of our alumni to share with you facets of their stories that relate to each aspect of this book. You will learn more about them in Chapter 1.

PART I

BEGINNING YOUR HEALING PROCESS

"My journey to heal has been based on a very simple truth: I must acknowledge my truth to myself and speak the truth to become free. It is a process, but with support, everyone can achieve it!" *Designer*: Archie Sarafinovski, Toronto, Ontario, Canada.

CHAPTER ONE

Dare to Dream
You Can Join Forces
with a Community
of Silence Breakers

"I have found that connecting with a community of male survivors has been vital to my healing. The Inuksuk symbol on my shirt is a Inuit stone structure traditionally used for navigation. May the guiding stones on my shirt help you dare to dream you, too, can recover!" *Designer:* Archie Sarafinovski, Toronto, Ontario, Canada.

I am honored to be joined in this book by a group of men who are alumni of the MaleSurvivor Weekends of Recovery. Some of their partners have also agreed to share their hearts and experiences with you. Hearing their stories will further your healing process by increasing your awareness of the community of men who have shared your experience and transformed their lives. There is incredible healing power in knowing that you are no longer alone and that others have experienced many of the same feelings and struggles. If you can believe that these men and a whole group of other male survivors stand ready to join forces with you on your journey, you can empower yourself not only to survive your abuse, but also to one day thrive.

While some of these men and their partners have granted permission to use their real names because doing so empowers them, others prefer to use a pseudonym, and I have honored their wishes. All of these men and their partners dedicated months of their lives to answering questions about each chapter. Look for their wisdom woven into each chapter and sometimes in sections of the book called "Silence Breakers' Best Advice."

The Silence Breakers

Now, I will present the 20 alumni who have agreed to share their stories of recovery with you in their own words. Later, I will introduce eight of their spouses or partners. They have agreed to write their stories because they want to be part of your healing, and they want you to join their community. I will refer to them as the "Silence Breakers" throughout the book. I will introduce them to you in alphabetical order.

> *Namaste (a greeting commonly used in India and yoga circles), I am **Alexander,** a 42-year-old black male living in the South. I am that which God is; I do not attend church or claim any denomination, religious organization, religious dogma, or doctrine. I am an author, orator, and survivor of the horror of childhood sexual abuse at the hands of my father, his drug dealer, and two of my male cousins. My abuse started when I was 3 years old and finally ended when I left my hometown at age 18 and moved out of the state. I pray that from what I have to share, you can take love, hope, and a vision for yourself, knowing that you can heal your life and your current situation.*

*Hi, my name is **Bruce**. I am a 45-year-old gay professional man from Toronto, Canada. When I was 13 to 14, my assistant basketball coach, who was also a medical doctor, abused me. I was silent for many years because I feared no one would believe what happened. For such a long time, I lived a confused and dysfunctional life trying to find out who I really was and trying to understand if I was a useful member of society. Today, after dealing with my childhood sexual abuse, I am in the driver's seat for the first time in my life, and it is simply amazing. Life is not perfect or without challenges, but it's moving rapidly in the right direction. You can do it, too, if you just take a chance. The people I have met on this journey have been simply amazing and worthwhile.*

*Hi, I'm **Chris**, age 43. A neighbor some five or so years older than I was abused me when I was between 10 and 12. I've been as close to death as anyone might want to be, but I've continued to push through the pain in order to create a new outlook, one that's not filled with self-doubt and destruction. I am a survivor, and I'm not alone anymore. I'm proud of who I am now, and stronger because of the men and women survivors I've met along the way.*

*Hi, my name is **Christopher**. I am in my mid-30s and have been on the healing journey now for about five years. It took a long time for me to figure out that the root cause of most of my difficulties (anxiety, depression, suicidal thoughts, difficulty forming close relationships) was related to the time when a guy from my neighborhood did that "stuff" to me. I hope you will find help and encouragement in these pages. It's possible to heal and create a life that you never even dreamed possible.*

*I'm **Coach**, a 49-year-old self-employed man living in the western United States and a survivor of early childhood sexual abuse. I started my recovery in my early 20s; however, it has only been in the past couple of years that I have developed friendships with other male survivors. I hope that my perseverance* *and faith in God inspire you as you strive to reclaim soul, mind, and spirit restoration.*

Take a moment now to check in with yourself. Take a few slow, gentle breaths. What feelings are you having? What thoughts are going through your head? If you were in the room with these five men, what would that be like for you?

I have asked each Silence Breaker to offer you hope, because I know how difficult being hopeful can seem in the beginning of your recovery. You've heard from these first five men that they, too, struggled at the start, but each of them is now in a very different place. Some of their abuse went on for years and from a number of perpetrators. Others had only one perpetrator, but the effect was similar.

*Hi, I'm **Gregg**, a 28-year-old gay black man. From the ages of 7 to 16, I was mentally, physically, and sexually abused by "friends" and family members. I also was raped by a police officer as an adult. I am trying to find my way in this world, and it's going slowly and painfully, but before I die, I will get there. It's not an easy road, but you just have to keep putting one foot on the floor, knowing that just getting out of bed each day is 90 percent of it.*

*Hi, my name is **Howie**. I am a married 35-year-old male living in Florida, and I am a survivor of childhood incest. Although the abuse was done "playfully," the effects have had a major impact on my life. While I still struggle, I have been able to work through much of the shame and pain associated with the abuse. I hope to continue my recovery, and I wish for all who are reading this to be able to start their recovery if they have not already done so, or continue their recovery in order to live a happy, healthy life.*

*My name is **Jarrod Noftsger**, and I am a 45-year-old university administrator and lecturer in the Midwest. I am married to my wife of 20 years and have two boys, ages 13 and 15. I* *started active recovery in therapy when I was 42. The ride of the last 36 months has been marked by debilitating lows and exhilarating triumphs. With the help of a skilled professional, I am successfully navigating the troubled waters of my childhood and the sexual abuse that disproportionately shaped my life. I am proud of the fact that I have shed the shame that locked me in isolation for over 30 years, and I'm proud to serve as an example that recovery is completely possible.*

*My name is **Joe Hanbury**. I was born in 1965. I grew up in Los Angeles, where I currently live. I was sexually molested primarily by males but also by females. The first occurrence was when I was 5 years old, and the last occurred when I was 14. Continuing to work through these issues helps me to become more of the open, free-spirited person I've dreamed of being. Instead of expending energy on keeping up a guard, I use that energy to make more and deeper connections with others. Know that there are people who are capable of listening to your story. It really does matter that you tell your story; it benefits you and the people in your life.*

*I am **John Walker**, a retired physiology professor. At age 15, I was sexually abused by my father, a Protestant minister, and one of his friends. I was psychologically and emotionally abused by both of my parents from an early age. As a result, I had no emotional ties to my parents and therefore was essentially an orphan. Because of my abuse, my personal life was a mess. I had low self-esteem. I was emotionally shut down. Alcohol was a problem, and I went through a divorce. I did have a successful professional life as an academic scientist. I repressed the sexual abuse until after my parents died, when I was in my early 60s. I am now emotionally alive and living a joyful life at the age of 79. My message to survivors of abuse is: You are not alone. Recovery is possible, and it's never too late to embark on the recovery journey.*

Recovery can begin at any age. You've heard from hetero-sexual and gay survivors from different ethnic backgrounds. You've heard that some of these men had or have very successful careers or business lives, despite their abuse history. Some have shared their struggles with very serious, self-destructive behaviors as a result of their abuse, and they successfully stopped those types of behaviors. You've read that connecting with others is an important part of healing for these Silence Breakers. And they've told you that it's possible to find joy and happiness through the process of recovery.

*Hi, I am **Jorge**, a 50-year-old gay white-Hispanic man, and an extraordinary individual, as we all are in our own ways. I am a son, brother, nephew, and cousin. I am a partner, friend, and lover. I am an employee, volunteer, mentor, counselor, and leader. I have come to understand that almost none of the emotional disturbances in my life are about the situation occurring in the moment. I am a survivor of multiple childhood traumas, including multiple episodes of sexual abuse. If I and other survivors can step back with a loving and nonjudgmental eye to examine and heal the past, then together we can heal any disturbances that occur in the present day. Here you can, and I hope you do, find that same sense of power over your current struggles and your past experiences that created them.*

*For most of my life, I lived in denial of the abuse. I am **Ken**, a 53-year-old married man living in the southeastern United States. I see myself as being in the ongoing maintenance phase of my recovery. By that I mean that I have acquired the tools to live a full and happy life while acknowledging the impact that the abuse has had on my life. There are aspects of my life that will always bear the tagline of "survivor of sexual abuse," but that does not prevent joy in my life.*

*Hello, I'm **Mike**, and I'm so glad you are reading this book! I am a 47-year-old married white male survivor of childhood sexual abuse. I am so proud to be a part of the survivor* *community because it has made me realize I'm not alone, and even better, I am so grateful for having survivors in my life. I have not met a more real, passionate, caring, loving, and non-judgmental group of people in my life.*

*Hi, I'm **Niall**, a 45-year-old man from outside the United States and a survivor of childhood sexual abuse. I am proud to be thriving in my life today. I hope I can inspire you to believe that healing really is possible.*

In this moment, take a few more gentle, slow breaths. See what you are feeling and experiencing while meeting these additional survivors. You are beginning to learn that men experience a wide range of abuse. Some men were abused only once, whereas others experienced abuse by more than one perpetrator and, often, over a long period of years. Some experienced abuse by a male, others by a female, and some by both. A few of these men are very religious, others identify themselves as spiritual, and some draw strength and faith from fellow survivors and people in their lives who have listened to their stories and believed them.

When I asked these men if they would contribute to this book, every one of them jumped at the chance. You might wonder why they are willing to be so open and take such risks. The answer is simple. These men want to help you recover, to feel supported and more hopeful. That desire outweighs any fears they have about going public with their stories.

*Hi, my name is **Pierre**. I am a 44-year-old Canadian father of two beautiful children, and I am a survivor of childhood physical abuse and teenage sexual abuse. I'm proud to be on my path of recovery, and I hope that through this book and your own path, you will rediscover your inner child.*

*Hi, my name is **Rhett Hackett**, and I'm a 42-year-old white male who is not just a survivor of childhood sexual abuse, but also a champion and a thriver! I live in southern New Jersey with my wife of 20 years and our two children, and*

I work in Philadelphia. I share my story with the hope that it will inspire you to talk about your abuse and to prosper in a life that's greater than you ever could have imagined! With some work, and support, you can achieve it!

*My name is **Rob de la Cruz**. I am 54 years old and was sexually abused by multiple abusers (all strangers) starting when I was 10 years old and continuing until I stopped it in my late teens. I realized late in life that I exhibited some behaviors that were not typical of your average man. Although functional in business and society, I realized after my son was born that I had to examine oddities and compulsions that could prove debilitating if left unaddressed. I think it's important to understand that you should never give up. Continue your search until you find a healing method that works. If you do the work and are honest with yourself, I believe you can find your peace.*

*Hi, I'm **Ryan**, a 49-year-old white marketing manager living in Utah. I live with my male partner and have two grown stepchildren. I'm a survivor of childhood sexual abuse perpetrated by my mother when I was very young. Most of the memory of my abuse was repressed until I was about 35. At one point, I was in a state of severe depression and anxiety, and the thought of even talking about the abuse experience was terrifying. Now I know that talking is healing. I hope that by sharing my experience with you, I can help you understand the extent of healing that can take place, and the joy and freedom that you can experience every day.*

*I'm **Simon**, a 40-year-old man from Liverpool, England. I have struggled to come to terms with my childhood experiences of abuse, but with tremendous support and determination, I have recovered so much of what was stolen. Breaking attachments to the past by reaching out to other men who thrive in the face of abuse has been absolutely vital to my growth. I hope that by sharing my experiences, I will reach you, too.*

*Hi, I am **SJC**. Fifty-five years after my sexual abuse, I am finally dealing with its effects. I almost blew up my family and myself before I was able to find help and hope. It's never too late to get help, or too early either. There are so many resources that address recovery issues from sexual abuse. I am happy to be alive and able to take advantage of these resources. Don't wait for the cancer of abuse to spread; get help now.*

Once more, I invite you to take a few slow, gentle breaths. As you do, let yourself tune in to what is going on in your body. Are you aware of any areas that feel tense? Are you aware of any that feel relaxed and comfortable? If you are tense and willing to experiment, put a hand on that part of your body. And now, see if you can imagine taking a couple of gentle breaths and sending them into your body right where your hand is.

I know this may sound a little weird, but if you are willing to experiment, see if you notice what happens to the tension as you send your breath into your hand and the part of your body that feels tense. Does it feel any different? Do you feel any temperature change? Any easing of the tension? Male survivors often stop paying attention to their bodies, and in the next chapter, on inner safety, I will invite you to learn about a number of tools that can help you become more aware of yours.

You have now been introduced to all 20 of your fellow survivors. Reflect on how you feel after reading just a little of their stories. You've read about men in the United States from one coast to the other and in between, and also men from other countries. You've seen the stories of men in their 20s and men in their 70s. You've read of heterosexual men and gay men, white, black, and Hispanic men. Some have told you they are thriving, while others admit they are still struggling but continuing to feel hopeful. You've read that male survivors can be passionate and caring and loving. Perhaps these qualities are also true of you! You've read a bit about very diverse men, and in every case, they've assured you that your life can be better than you might imagine right now. You've even been provided the hope-filled news that survivors can experience *joy*.

Remember, you can put down this book anytime you need a break. I won't be offended. In fact, if I were with you right now, I would feel honored and want to affirm your choice to listen to your heart and know your boundaries and limits. Reading about abuse is tough at times. Sometimes you may smile and your heart may feel lighter. Other times you may feel sad, depressed, anxious, or overwhelmed. Whatever you feel, I hope you give yourself permission to honor that feeling, and know that allowing your feelings to surface can be empowering. In a later chapter, I will write about the fact that men learn very dysfunctional messages about coping with life, including the message that strength is about *not feeling*. That's a lie, and throughout this book, I will keep giving you permission and will urge you to give *yourself* permission to feel any feelings that surface. Simply put, feeling is healing.

The Partners and Spouses of the Silence Breakers

Next I want you to meet the partners and spouses of the Silence Breakers. These men and women are writing to support you as a male survivor, and also to support the significant people in your life. In a later chapter, these caring individuals will share their strategies and insights for living with male survivors as their partners. They have learned from their mistakes and successes, and now want to share with you so that you can be inspired.

> I'm **Coach's wife**, a 46-year-old educational profession-al. I have been married for 21 years to Coach, and we have three children whom we are successfully parenting. I hope that I will encourage you to support your survivor's journey toward wholeness.

> My name is **Debbie.** I'm a 34-year-old professional mother of two from Florida with an incredible husband (Howie) who also happens to be a survivor of childhood sexual abuse. My hope is that our story inspires many men out there to use their voices and stand up for themselves for their healing and that of

their families. *Just because abuse has been a part of your life doesn't mean it has to <u>be</u> your life. I, as a partner, believe that reclaiming your power from your abuse will make you an even better husband, father, uncle, and friend.*

*Hi, I'm **Lori**. Mike and I have been married for 25 years. I found out in 2003 about Mike's childhood sexual abuse. After 17 years of marriage, I couldn't believe what I was hearing. I thought, <u>Hey, it happened a long time ago.</u> He told me, "Now, let's move on." What I have since learned (and it has taken a long eight years) is that it isn't that easy. Despite all the challenges and tough times, though, I have the reward of still being in love with and married to the most caring and attentive man in the world. I have the reward of watching the man I care deeply for work very hard at getting to the point where he can finally live a joyous life. I know that our marriage can endure anything, because we have already endured so very much together and have remained strong and united.*

*Hi, I'm **Richard**, Jorge's partner. I've been blessed to have two wonderful partners in my life, both abused as children. Twenty-five years ago, I had no idea what it would mean to be in a relationship with someone who had suffered childhood abuse. Now, I realize that it forms much of the core of how these individuals see, function, behave, and relate to the world around them. My partners have been among the nicest, kindest, gentlest, and most giving people I've ever known. That said, relationships are not easy; they take work, like most worthwhile things, if they are to flourish. With all the love I've received, it would have been my great misfortune if I had not seen past their demons and into their souls.*

*Hi, my name is **Sheryl**. I'm the wife of survivor Rhett. We have been married for 20 years and have two children, a son age 26 and a daughter age 16. It was only within the last year and a half that my husband went public about his abuse, but I've known about it since our dating days. My hope is that* telling our stories of the failures and successes we have experienced over the last 20 years may help others understand and accept some of the struggles, thoughts, feelings, and fears that survivors and their partners go through.

Hi, I'm **Troy**, Ryan's partner. Being partners with a male survivor has been a challenge but a blessing at the same time. When I met my partner, we were both in rough situations. He had just started facing his abuse and was trying to come to terms with it. I was just coming out of a 16-year marriage where I was dealing with abuse and torment. I wanted to help him, and he wanted to help me. Life has not been easy, but because we are both determined to make it work, we have a wonderful relationship. Communication has been our biggest challenge. Rewards come in various shapes and forms. Letting the other person take the load once in a while, and giving each other time to feel the pain and for him to heal has also been very rewarding.

If you are new to this journey, please know that there is real hope for healing. I'm **Vicky,** and I am married to a survivor, Ken. His life was torn apart at a young age, and it took him decades to recall the circumstances of his abuse. Once he did recall the experiences, my over-40 gentle husband became a very different human being. He was angry and frightened, and had panic anxiety. But he found help. The adjustment has been hard; I won't lie to you. If you love your partner, hang on during the fire. I am also a survivor. I never suppressed the memories, and they have been with me every day of my life. We all heal differently. No life story is alike. I grew frustrated with the direction his life went for a while, because that wasn't how I did it. With the powerful value of hindsight, he handled it perfectly for himself.

Hi, I'm **Wendy**, Jarrod's wife. One of the rewards of being in my relationship has been seeing my husband enter into social situations with confidence and without anxiety. Before his recovery started, I went to many of these social gatherings alone. Another *reward has been his patience with the family and communicating more openly. His new ability to share this story with others has allowed me to feel less isolated. Once we shared his abuse story with others, we found most people to be extremely supportive, and many have now shared their abuse experiences with us.*

Now, just as you did after the introductions from the men, I invite you to take a moment to reflect on how you feel after reading about the partners of the survivors and their stories. I hope you can hear that they are all grateful for their connections with their survivor partners. I hope you can hear that although the healing journey is often challenging to share, it has also enriched their lives and brought them happiness.

Using Affirmations

At the end of each psychotherapy session, I write an affirmation for my client to reflect on during the week, so it seems appropriate to end each chapter with a few affirmations. In case you are not familiar with affirmations, they are statements you can say aloud while looking into a mirror, or you can recite them to yourself. Some clients choose to say them to a recovery ally. Your goal is to increase your ability to think positively about recovery and to increase your sense of hope for the future.

For an affirmation to work, it helps if you believe it at least a smidgeon. I suggest repeating the affirmation three to five times each week and noticing each time how you feel afterward. What thoughts enter your head when you say the affirmation? Do you hear negative thoughts that might cancel out the positive message? Do you feel tense or more relaxed? Does the affirmation bring any sadness or maybe a sense of pride? There are no right or wrong emotions or thoughts. The goal is to say the affirmation and notice what you experience.

You may choose to write your own affirmation after reading each chapter, and that would be great. Avoid negative words; for example, keep the word *not* out of your affirmations. Why? Our brains tend to cancel out the *not,* and we follow whatever comes afterward. Years ago, a campaign to stop smoking used the slogans "Don't Smoke" and "Don't Light Up." Unfortunately, the campaign didn't work, because smokers' brains canceled out the *don't,* and what they heard was to smoke and light up. You can substitute other words for *not,* such as "I refuse to . . ." or "I choose to avoid . . ."

SILENCE BREAKERS' BEST ADVICE:
Using Affirmations

You will read some familiar themes in this section. One, frequently repeated, is that it's difficult for most survivors to take affirmations seriously. You may have some of the same difficulties, so included here are both the Silence Breakers' reservations and what they have discovered by experimenting:

I was reluctant to use affirmations when I first started my journey. Quite frankly, they seemed hokey and conjured up images of late-night infomercials. Nevertheless, affirmations, or what I refer to as simply "mantras," serve a very important and helpful role in my recovery. In fact, they are pivotal in keeping me focused on getting better and staying positive about my progress. — Jarrod

I thought affirmations were kind of stupid at first. I didn't believe what they were trying to say, because they stated a positive outlook and I felt I was just a piece of crap and worthless. Over time, as I repeated the affirmations, my outlook began to change, and so did my thoughts about affirmations. I was beginning to see the truth, not the pessimism that had always clouded my thoughts. The more work I did, the more the affirmations sank in and the more I believed in myself and the world around me. They now help ground me in times of need or when I'm at odds. — Chris

It's normal to have doubts about the power and usefulness of affirmations. The more these men experimented, the more they found that the mantras did help them improve their self-esteem and their commitment to their recovery. Bruce encourages you to say the affirmation to yourself while looking in the mirror, which is a great technique to help you let go of shame. That's one of the most healing parts of saying affirmations: they help heal your shame. When you look in a mirror, you are looking forward rather than down, as you might do if you felt shame. In addition, by looking in a mirror, you make eye contact with yourself, which will help you feel a connection with the part of you that still holds on to shame. Saying an affirmation to your recovery ally while looking him or her in the eyes is another great way to make your affirmation more powerful and healing.

> *When I started using affirmations, I really did feel silly. They were so foreign to me that saying them was really uncomfortable. I especially would try to say affirmations in front of a mirror, which is really tough to do, but I find it very rewarding. There was a time when I had a really hard time looking myself in the eye when I did this, but it got easier and more comfortable the more I did it. — Bruce*

Christopher does a great job of sharing his struggles with shame, and he writes about how that directly relates to his comfort with saying affirmations and hearing them from others. He also shares the importance of having an ally who believes in him more than he sometimes can believe in himself:

> *Sometimes, the cynical New Yorker in me pops up, and I roll my eyes a little at the earnestness that I feel is behind affirmations. But I know deep in my heart that these messages are really important. A part of my struggle with accepting them is believing that they apply to me or that I am worthy of having such good messages in my life. Maybe it's a foolish pride thing: <u>I've already survived without these. What good can they do me now?</u> However, I am slowly beginning to believe in the positive, loving messages that my wife gives me on an almost daily basis. I confess that it's not always easy to take in her messages of love and support, just as it's not always easy to give myself permission to read the affirmations. — Christopher*

The following are affirmations for Chapter 1. Like the men whose stories you just heard, you may at first feel that these affirmations are silly and stupid. In time, affirmations can play an important role in your healing journey. Write down in your journal any affirmation you want to practice. Consider saying it while looking in a mirror. After you read each affirmation out loud, you might write down your reactions in your journal. As you spend the next week or two repeating these affirmations, see if your reactions to them change. If so, I invite you to write down the changes occurring inside. It can be a great way to mark your progress and to discover where you are feeling the most challenged. Perhaps you'll also get some insight into where your shame resides inside you.

These may be areas to discuss either with your ally or your therapist. I am giving you a number of affirmations so that you will have several to choose from, and it's fine to pick just one to focus on. It may be the one you feel most uncomfortable with right now or the one you least believe is possible for you.

○   ○   ○

In Chapter 2, I will introduce you to some very important skills that you can learn to help yourself feel safer throughout this journey of recovery and transformation. You most likely learned that you should just "know" how to be powerful and safe simply because you are a man, but the reality is that you must learn these skills (which include body awareness and mindfulness techniques) in order to protect yourself. When you do so, they will help you build a strong foundation that will support you as you face the challenging work ahead.

AFFIRMATIONS FOR CHAPTER 1

- *I dare to dream I can leave my isolation behind and join a community of men committed to healing and recovering.*

- *I give myself permission to read this book at my own pace, without judgment.*

- *I can connect with my feelings as much as possible.*

CHAPTER TWO

Dare to Dream
You Can Create Inner
Safety and Be Present

"When I started working on recovery, I realized that there
was something in me that seemed to have been protecting me.
I began referring to it as a gentle warrior, strong and protective,
but compassionate and gentle." *Designer:* Dan Calabria-Russell.

One of the biggest challenges for male survivors is learning
how to feel safer inside and to be "present" rather than disen-
gaged, even long after the abuse has stopped. Many survivors of
abuse disconnect from their physical presence and their feelings
during the abuse. This is a survival and coping mechanism that
provides a way to forget, allowing the survivor to "escape" for the
moment from what is being done to him. Some survivors *disso-
ciate*, which is a more extreme way of disconnecting, where the
individual may be aware that his body is in the room, but he is
consciously separated from it.

It's important to understand that this type of disconnecting is
beyond your choice. Your body does this automatically to protect

you at the time of the abuse. Some survivors talk about floating on the ceiling or focusing on some specific aspect of the room, such as the sound of the air conditioner or a clock ticking, and they don't see or hear anything else. Others survive the attack by singing a song in their heads, counting numbers, or focusing on the pattern of the wallpaper or bed linen.

After the attack, survivors often struggle with how to ever again feel safe enough to be present in their bodies and aware of their feelings in the moment. You may be like those survivors who, afterward, become hypervigilant and obsessively present, unable to ever tune out and relax because of the fear of another attack. You may lack the ability to establish an "off switch," which can result in constant overload from being too intensely present. Perhaps you are like the survivors who learn to be present in the world but never connected to other people. You may identify with the survivor who immerses himself in his career or some extracurricular activity that helps him feel safe. Maybe the only place you feel secure is in that defined safety zone.

The tools provided in this chapter will help you develop the ability to be present and feel safer in your life now. One of your most basic needs as a survivor is to learn how to feel safer in your body. When you do so, you will then be present and aware of what you are experiencing in each moment, and aware of your connection with others.

This is why I want to teach you mindfulness and mind-body awareness. At first, you are likely to feel very uncomfortable with using these skills. However, further practice will enable you to reconnect with the parts of yourself that you disconnected or dissociated from in order to survive.

Being present means being consciously aware of what you are experiencing and feeling in any given moment. I have had the honor of working on being present under the instruction of Dr. Paul Linden, a martial arts educator in Columbus, Ohio. Dr. Linden has shared a lot of his techniques and insights with male survivors in his *dojo*, which is a martial arts school, and at the Weekends of Recovery program.

He has given me permission to share a few of his teachings with you, and he co-authored this chapter to help you understand his exercises. If you want to learn more, you can go to Paul's website and download his free e-book, *Reach Out: Body Awareness Training for Peacemaking—Five Easy Lessons*. It is available in English, Spanish, Portuguese, and German. Peacemaking and abuse recovery require much the same body-awareness skills. Peacemaking is about present threats, and abuse work is about past threats. Paul's website has a number of books and articles about both topics: **www.being-in-movement.com/catalog**.

Breath Control

One of the first tools of safety Dr. Linden teaches is how to breathe. Before I invite you to do your first exercise in this book, I want to review how to take a deep breath. You may be thinking, *Is he kidding?* Here's one of my truths: When I went into therapy for my own issues, I thought I knew how to take a deep breath, but honestly, all I knew was how to take a shallow one. Those shallow breaths saved my life, but just breathing in a shallow way is exhausting. When you breathe shallowly, you breathe into and out of your chest. If you put one hand on your chest and take some short breaths, you can feel your chest lift just a little. Put your other hand on your stomach and see what happens when you take a short breath. You may notice your chest expanding just a little and your stomach actually pulling in.

Now, put one hand on your chest and the other on your stomach again. Take a much slower breath; if you can draw through your nose, do that, but if not, draw through your mouth. Count to two or three before releasing, if possible. Notice how the hand on your chest still moves, but the hand on your stomach moves out more. When you blow the breath out from your mouth, notice how your stomach contracts. This slower breath is a deeper breath that is associated with more relaxation, power, and strength.

Assess what you are feeling right now. Are you more relaxed? More optimistic? Less stressed? I invite you to take a couple of minutes now to practice a few slow, deep breaths. You are worth taking care of. Slowing down and breathing deeply is a key skill for your recovery.

Being Present:
Employing Mindfulness and Mind-Body Awareness

I invite you often in this book to "check inside." Each time, I urge you to be aware of the present moment. Survivors, whether they are currently thinking about their abuse or about some present-day aspect of life, often report feeling distracted by bodily sensations associated with anxiety and anxious thoughts that can keep them detached from the present moment. Use these deep belly breaths to calm any sensations of physical, emotional, or mental anxiety you may become aware of. You may experience anxiety physically—for example, tense feelings in your body. You may notice certain body parts shaking. Notice how it feels to be present and aware of all that's going on with your emotions and bodily sensations.

This skill of checking inside is called *mindfulness* or *mind-body awareness,* and is one of the first skills we teach at Weekends of Recovery. Next, some basic mindfulness practices will be presented, and I encourage you to also read books recommended by the co-chair of WOR, Jim Struve, LCSW, in the Resources at the end of this book.

The practice of mindfulness enhances your ability to be present and aware of your thoughts, feelings, sensations, and energy in each moment. If you are to feel safer wherever you are, it's very important to be present. Imagine how difficult it would be to protect yourself from any external threat while remaining unaware of your surroundings or feelings.

Your brain is only capable of one thought at a time. In each moment, you can choose whether to be present or go somewhere else in your mind. In this moment, take three deep, gentle breaths, and "check in." How are you feeling as you read this chapter? Are you focused on what you are reading? Do you find yourself drifting away? Are you aware that you are reading a book to help yourself heal from abuse? Take a moment to notice what you experience in your body. Can you feel tension? Do you feel more relaxed and at ease in some areas than others? Think about how safe you are feeling now. Chances are the more relaxed you are, the more likely it is that you are feeling safer. On the other hand, the more tension you are experiencing, the less safe you likely feel. Remain aware of your breath and use this controlled breathing to relax yourself no matter where you are and no matter what the situation throughout this process. The advantage of this skill is that you can use it without anyone else knowing that you are taking care of yourself.

EXPERIMENT WITH NEW POSSIBILITIES: Creating Internal Safety with Six-Directions Breathing

One of the breathing techniques taught at Weekends of Recovery that many survivors find helpful originated from Paul Linden. It's called "six-directions breathing." In this exercise, you stand and, with your eyes open, focus on feeling your feet on the floor. Wiggle your toes, raise the front half of your feet for a moment, and then put your weight on the front while lifting your heels off the floor. Now let both feet relax on the floor.

In this exercise, you will practice breathing out in six directions.

1. Take a gentle, deep breath in through your mouth or nose, and exhale through your mouth. On the exhalation, think of sending the breath down through the soles of your feet, six feet into the ground.

2. Now, take a soft second breath in through your mouth or nose, and on the exhalation, imagine directing the breath six feet up through the top of your head.

3. Take a relaxed inhalation, and on the exhalation, send your breath six feet out in front of your chest.

4. After breathing in again, exhale and imagine directing the breath six feet out from the middle of your back.

5. After taking another breath, exhale and imagine directing your exhalation six feet out from the right side of your body.

6. Take one more breath in, and on the exhalation, feel that you are sending that exhalation out six feet from the left side of your body.

Now for the final challenge, take in one last breath, and on the release, feel that you are breathing out of your body in all six directions at the same time.

Congratulations! You may now feel like a human wind machine, but there's a healing purpose to Paul's breathing exercise. One of the effects of abuse is that survivors "smallify" themselves: they mentally diminish their presence as a protective survival measure. One of the goals of this exercise is to counteract that by helping you experience feeling bigger and taking up more space. You can challenge yourself as you are breathing in and out in all six directions by taking a few steps. Notice what it feels like to take up six feet above you, below you, in front of you, behind you, and to the right and left of you. Any feeling you have is okay. At first, this might feel uncomfortable. However, the more you practice, the safer you will feel inside and the more powerful.

I created another meditation exercise to help you be present and feel safer. I know that for some of you, this imagery may work great, and for others, it may feel too "New Agey." If so, please revise it to fit your beliefs, or just use the six-directions exercise and skip to the next section on using a body cue. I created this meditation based on my core beliefs, including the following:

I believe that there's an infinite amount of healing energy in the world, which enhances my sense of safety because I know I don't have to compete with anyone else to access healing energy. I imagine that this infinite source of healing energy is stored at the core of the earth. I envision that every time I breathe out, that energy travels to the core of the earth. I imagine that every living being also contributes to this infinite supply of healing energy with every exhaled breath.

I find it healing to imagine that the core of the earth is capable of transforming all the energy it receives from every exhaled breath into healing energy. Since we are all breathing in and out constantly, this core transformer is working 24 hours a day, continuously receiving and transforming all exhalations into healing energy that is available to each of us every time we draw a breath.

This meditation may be more powerful if you choose to see this energy as a beam of light or energy in any color that you believe will bring healing to you. If it fits with your spiritual beliefs, you may choose to imagine that the Higher Power of your choice is the engine driving this transformer. If you do not believe in a Higher Power, you may imagine that this transformer is powered simply by the energy it is receiving.

Imagine that the healing beams of colorful energy from the core of the earth have two vital qualities:

1. The first quality is that the beam of light and energy is capable of being breathed into your body, and like a magnet, it can attract any unnecessary negative, self-defeating, pain-filled energy, feelings, or thoughts that you want to let go of. Imagine that as it travels through your body from your feet to your head, it attracts all of the energy you want to let go of. And when you breathe out, you will send that negative, pain-filled, self-defeating energy back down to the center of the earth, where it will be transformed into healing energy.

Please note: You may not be able to imagine letting go of all of your negativity or all of your anxiety or pain. You may feel that it's necessary to hold on to your awareness of the real forces in this universe that are negative and destructive so that you can continue to be vigilant. In this exercise, then, practice letting go of some of the negativity you carry around, and see how that feels for you. Hold on to whatever you believe is necessary to hold on to at this moment. Only let go of what you are ready to truly let go of. Think how carrying around less negative energy may impact your ability to feel safer in your body.

2. The second quality that I imagine this energy to have is the ability to bring nurturing, encouraging, and healing energy to your body. It can bring calm, peacefulness, compassion, and relief from pain and suffering. So each time you breathe in, you can imagine drawing on this positive form of energy to help you feel safer and calmer. Consider how much safer you may feel in knowing that you can draw on as much positive healing energy as you need anytime you need it.

Now you have a picture of how this "transformer" works. I invite you to experiment with this meditation.

EXPERIMENT WITH NEW POSSIBILITIES: Feeling More Present and Safer

Start by sitting in a comfortable chair with your feet on the floor. Allow yourself to feel safely supported by the chair and the floor. Take a few gentle breaths, keeping your eyes open or closed.

I invite you to take a deep breath and imagine that breath originates at the core of the earth. As you take in that first gentle breath, allow yourself to see what colors are reflected in the energy and light as it travels from the core of the earth toward you. Take a few seconds to allow the energy to enter your feet, and see the energy traveling through your body, attracting any unnecessary negative, self-defeating, or painful energy to it, until it's all gathered up.

When you are ready, release all of that unnecessary energy in a big arc back down to the center of the earth. As you breathe it out, imagine that you can feel a little safer inside. Imagine all that energy being transformed into healing energy that is accessible to anyone who needs it.

Take in a second deep breath. Picture that you will be receiving a beam of positive healing energy; picture the colors reflected in that beam of energy and light as it leaves the transformer and travels through the core of the earth until it arrives at your feet. Allow this healing, nurturing, and encouraging energy to enter your feet. As it travels through your body, imagine that it deposits pockets of peacefulness, calm, compassion, and a sense of safety anyplace in your body it seems drawn to. Then, breathe out, releasing any leftover energy and sending it in a big arc back down to the center of the earth. Imagine the energy you exhaled being transformed into healing energy that is accessible to anyone who needs it.

Now you are ready for the third breath. Imagine that the energy traveling to your body can attract negative energy to it while depositing pockets of calm and safety throughout your body. Allow this dual-purpose energy to flow through you and attract all the negativity you want to release. At the same time, allow healing, nurturing, and encouraging energy to spread throughout your body.

Now, breathe out, releasing any remaining positive energy, as well as all the negative energy you gathered as it passed through your body, and send it all in a big arc back down to the center of the earth.

Using a Body Cue to Relax Anywhere

I invite you to "check in" as you finish the preceding experiment. If this is a feeling you want to access anytime in the upcoming week, I'd suggest you place your dominant hand (the one you write with) somewhere on your body that feels comfortable to do in a public place. For example, you might put your hand on your right or left leg, and just rest it there for a minute. Tell yourself that anytime that you want to feel this same sensation of peacefulness and calm, you can do it just by placing your hand on your leg in this same position. This is called a *body cue.* You could also use this at the end of the six-directions breathing exercise. It's useful when you are in a stressful situation, because it can help you be present and calm, and know that you are connected with a powerful healing energy in the universe that can help you. This body cue can also help you when you are feeling unsafe, by reminding you to take a breath and become grounded and relax.

Notice that in three breaths, you have given yourself two opportunities to let go of the negativity that prevents you from being present and safe, while also taking two opportunities to create positive energy that enhances your ability to be present and calm and safe. You can do this breathing exercise anytime and anywhere. In addition, by practicing a body cue, you can create this same sensation of peacefulness to your body in a matter of seconds.

Once you have practiced the breathing exercise and the body cue for one week, you can consider whether this is a skill that you want to carry with you at all times. Every additional tool in your self-awareness/mindfulness toolbox will help you to feel safer inside.

Being Mindful and Present by Slowing Down

Being present also requires slowing down. You may have learned to cope with the stresses of your abuse by speeding up, keeping busy, and distancing yourself from your feelings and experiences. When you are running at full speed, do you feel safe? Usually that's not the case. When you are cut off or numbing yourself from feeling and experiencing, you make yourself feel insecure and more vulnerable, because you are less in touch with your surroundings and the information and warning signs that help protect you.

The easiest and quickest way to slow down is to take a gentle, deep breath. You might slow down by breathing three breaths as we did in the previous experiment, or you might also practice breathing using Paul's six-directions breathing exercise. Consider also practicing using the body-cue method in the preceding exercise. As you breathe, you might also visualize comforting words floating in front of your eyes, such as *calm, peaceful, safe,* or simply *breathe.*

Our Weekends of Recovery also offer mindfulness walks and mindfulness meals. In both cases, it's important to have silence and to slow down from your usual pace. For example, if you are hiking, instead of making distance a goal, make mindfulness the focus for each step. Tune in to all of your senses, and be aware of what's going on. Listen, observe, smell, and feel all that is around you. Do this for at least 15 minutes, knowing that it may feel like an hour if you are one of those fast-paced guys. Go ahead and try it. Take a chance. Value yourself enough to experiment with slowing down. If you take this opportunity, also "check inside" and see how safe you are feeling when you are tuned in to your environment, compared to when you are moving faster. You may notice that you feel much safer when you are using all of your senses.

EXPERIMENT WITH NEW POSSIBILITIES:
The Four-Pebbles Meditation

As part of our Weekends of Recovery program, participants go on morning meditation walks, which our co-chairperson Jim Struve ends with the Four Pebbles Meditation adapted from a similar exercise developed by the renowned Vietnamese Zen Buddhist monk Thich Nhat Hanh. To do it, you'll need to gather four small pebbles. The meditation is designed to help you know that you can live happily and free from fear and suffering. Each pebble can remind you to reflect on a different aspect of yourself.

Take a few deep breaths, and then pick up the first pebble and hold it in your left hand. Breathe in and say to yourself, *I feel fresh.* Breathing out, say, *I am a flower.* Do this three times, and then switch the pebble to your right hand, again repeating the sayings for each inbreath and outbreath. The first pebble is "flower," and it reminds you that you are like a flower that enjoys the freshness of the air, is beautiful, and needs to be fed and nurtured to stay alive. Put down the first pebble.

With the second pebble in your left hand, breathe in as you say, *I feel solid,* and then breathe out, saying, *I am a mountain.* Do this three times, and then transfer the pebble to your right hand, and repeat. The second pebble, "mountain," invites you to reflect on the stability and solidity you can offer to the people in your life. Like a mountain, you can be solid and stable, steady and confident. This pebble also reminds you to reflect in this current moment on your thoughts and emotions. Now lay down this pebble.

Pick up the third pebble, "water," with your left hand. Breathe in and say, *Water, stillness.* Breathe out, saying, *Reflecting.* Do this three times, and then repeat with the pebble in your right hand. Imagine a still lake in your mind that, when you look at it, reflects on its surface all that is around it. Water reminds you to reflect on what is clear and true in your life, and invites you to reflect on your own wisdom. Now, lay down this pebble.

Pick up the last pebble, "space," in your left hand. Breathe in as you say, *I feel space inside and around me.* Now breathe out, saying, *I am free.* Do this three times, and then repeat with the pebble in your right hand. This pebble reminds you to reflect on how everyone needs space and how you can offer space to those who are close to you. Also, by creating more space inside you, by letting go of what's troubling you in this moment, you can create space for happiness to enter your heart, body, and mind. This pebble also invites you to explore your capacity for freedom and curiosity.

If you'd like to watch a video of the meditation, a good one is available on YouTube: **www.youtube.com/ watch?v=TXJs9bdcnXw.**

The "eating mindfully" exercise is a great slowing-down technique that we also share during the Weekends of Recovery. To do this exercise, you can use a raisin or one piece of Life Saver candy. Your task is to enjoy it by eating it as slowly as possible. Take a minute or two to savor the taste of the raisin or Life Saver. Note your feelings as you do this. Typically our participants report sensations, tastes, and textures they were not aware of in the past. You can expand this exercise and do it during an entire mindfulness meal. For one meal at WOR, we eat as a group, but you, of course, can also eat mindfully by yourself.

The key components are eating silently and with the intention of enjoying your food as fully as possible. The goal is to use all of your senses as you eat. Maybe you normally eat as fast as you can to get on to the next activity, or you may be one of those guys who pay little attention to the taste of food because they are multitasking and doing several other activities while eating. In mindfulness eating, the goal is to have a full experience with your food.

SILENCE BREAKERS' BEST ADVICE: Using Mindfulness Techniques

I have asked the Silence Breakers to talk about real-life applications of mindfulness techniques that help them cope. As with the other techniques in this chapter, you can use these tools throughout the day to make your life a little more manageable, and hopefully you will experience a greater feeling of self-love and acceptance. You will also notice how much safer the Silence Breakers say they feel when they employ mindfulness techniques.

Mike shares an experience of using mindfulness to bring him from a very negative thought spiral into calmness. As you read this, consider how much safer you might feel while driving if you were not obsessed with shame, worry, guilt, or anger.

Last summer, my wife and I were driving down the road, when she said something to me that triggered an onslaught of thoughts, and in my mind I was going down quickly. I then reached into my mindful-awareness toolbox and started counting the cars on the road. All of a sudden, I noticed all these trees, so I started counting them and then road signs, and the next thing I knew, I was out of that negative thought onslaught. — Mike

---

Bruce has had a number of experiences where employing mindfulness has helped him slow down. He admits that at first it's very uncomfortable to be silent. He and Chris share how much more of their lives they enjoy by employing these techniques.

It's amazing how much awareness is gained by being silent and present, and focusing on myself. It is really a moment where I come to a screeching halt and am more aware of everything: nature, other people, water, planes in the air, wildlife, and myself. All in all, I have discovered that I am a pretty great person to spend time with. — Bruce

I am so much more mindful now because I've become more grateful. I've learned to enjoy my food more, nature, the presence of others, and my friends. I feel the bark on trees, sense the wind blowing across my skin, or hear it in the leaves. I also find myself choosing the slow lane in traffic, because I make the time to get up earlier. Petting my cats and hearing them purr is such a pleasure, as well as laughing and hearing laughter. — Chris

Rhett describes how he has employed mindfulness to help him cope with his abuse. He explains in detail how he used to get overwhelmed when he allowed himself to experience the feelings connected to his abuse. Picture yourself driving while in the state of mind that Rhett describes, and you can see how unsafe he felt—and was. When he employed mindfulness, he became much more at ease and was a much safer driver.

When I was first introduced to the concept of mindfulness, I thought I would never be able to connect with it, because I've lived my life in fast-forward. I knew that whenever the trauma from my abuse came closer to the surface, it was better to keep moving. In some cases, recalling the tragic events of my abuse put me into a panic. I was mindful of my body reacting with a tighter grip on the steering wheel and sweat accumulating under my shirt.

Then I learned how to employ mindfulness techniques, and I became much more at ease with these thoughts and the process. I was able to take control and direct my body to release the energy by focusing on the parts of my body being affected. — Rhett

Another benefit of mindfulness is that it really allows you to reawaken inside yourself some of your sensitivity and the awareness you may have shut down to survive your abuse. Ryan describes his first experience on a mindfulness walk and how he came to understand that he had numbed out to survive.

During my first weekend retreat, I attended my first mindfulness meditation. We silently walked along a path in nature and concentrated on what we saw, heard, and felt. Suddenly, it seemed as if all the colors were in Technicolor. Sounds and my sense of touch seemed to be amplified. It was as if I'd lived until then in a world where my vision had been distorted by a gray screen and my senses had been numbed by something similar to the static that comes from a TV screen with no signal.

During the mindfulness meditation, any distortions to my senses were suddenly lifted. I felt an overwhelming sense of gratitude to my Creator for that moment of healing as I realized that when I was a child, my senses had been muted, and my mind had been "carried away" and protected while the worst parts of the abuse were happening. Suddenly I realized that God had protected me from the moment the abuse had started until the present day. I felt enveloped with a warm sense of nurturing love and light, and so full of gratitude that the tears flowed freely. — Ryan

Learning How to Become Grounded and More Powerful with Mind-Body Awareness

When you were abused, you probably had a normal reaction, which is to tighten up, retract, pull in, become smaller, and, in some cases, disappear or at least to try to disappear. Some men react by seeking to seem intimidating to others and being defensive, by becoming larger and more powerful. The normal reflex reaction is to constrict the body to create power. In addition, men in our society typically learn that the way to fight is to clench the fists and tighten the whole body. It's common to constrict and get smaller in an attempt to get larger.

Another way to get smaller is to collapse, often in resignation or defeat. Tightening or collapsing actually makes you more vulnerable, because you restrict your ability to move your body, which is essential if you want to protect yourself from an attack. It's also true that if you are limp and collapsed, you cannot move well.

I did not understand how I could become more vulnerable by tightening up and puffing out my chest, until martial arts expert Paul Linden demonstrated. I am a muscular guy who works out several times a week. Paul, on the other hand, is a shorter, much leaner guy, so I figured, *No problem.* I thought, *If he tries to push me over, I can easily stop him.* Paul said that if I tensed up my body and puffed out my chest to demonstrate the results of all those bench presses, he could push me over with just one finger on my chest. And he did it! My first thought was *What a weakling I am.* I felt ashamed that I wasn't strong enough. This shame reaction is normal, especially if the other guy is smaller and we perceived him to be weaker. Men typically feel even more ashamed if they lose to a woman.

Unfortunately, in most cases of abuse, the perpetrator is stronger than the victim, or the abuser may be a weakling who has learned to prey on the vulnerable. Paul was able to push me over because I didn't really understand how to balance and protect myself. I'll describe in the next exercise how Paul teaches men in a few short steps how to achieve a protective and powerful stance.

EXPERIMENT WITH NEW POSSIBILITIES:
Two Body-Awareness Exercises

One of my favorite exercises from Paul is the Kleenex toss. For this exercise, you will need a partner. This person doesn't have to know anything about this book or why you are reading it. Just say you need help for an experiment.

Ask your partner to stand six feet away. Give the person a piece of Kleenex and ask him or her to wad it up. Then, tense up your body, puff out your chest, and make your legs tight.

Keep your eyes open. Now ask your partner to hurl the Kleenex at your chest. Ask him or her to notice what you do with your body and your face, and see what *you* notice about your reaction. Many people act startled, closing their eyes or blinking; they might tense up even tighter, even though this is a simple, harmless wad of Kleenex.

Why? The brain codes the Kleenex as an intruder, and we do what we have learned to do when we fear an attack; we tighten up. If you didn't tense up, you could ask the person to come closer, maybe two feet away, and hurl the Kleenex with more intensity, perhaps with a scowl on his or her face. Again, notice what you experience and ask your partner to give you feedback. You might be less likely to tense up in subsequent efforts because I have reminded you that it's just a Kleenex, but some people do still tense up or close their eyes even after being reminded.

No judgments need be made about how you perform in this exercise. The point is that we can't protect ourselves effectively when we tense up and close our eyes. So how do you get yourself in a protective and more powerful stance? Maybe you have guessed: You do the opposite of what you did before. You consciously choose to relax your body.

Paul describes the process in a few steps: First, let your tongue be loose in your mouth. Next, let your jaw relax. Then, allow your belly to become softer or more relaxed. (Let your six-pack abs go soft; no one is watching!) You can also soften your knees. Paul adds one more step, which may sound funny but seems to work: "let your balls hang loose." In this much more relaxed body posture, invite your partner to again hurl the tissue at you from one foot away. If that's too close for you, have the person move back.

This time, thanks to the more relaxed posture, chances are you maintained your stance. You didn't withdraw, getting smaller or tighter. Perhaps you laughed, knowing how silly it is to have someone toss a Kleenex at you.

Next, try the finger-to-the-chest exercise that Paul did with me. Adopt a relaxed body posture and have your partner push one finger against your sternum in the middle of your chest. Resist the push while remaining relaxed. Notice how much stronger you are, how it's difficult for him or her to move you.

Now tense up, raise your eyebrows, keep your abs tight, and puff out your chest. Invite your friend to push against your sternum in the same place with the same amount of pressure.

What position were you stronger in: the more relaxed posture or the tighter, more "muscular" one? You might also notice whether it's easier to breathe in the more relaxed position or in the tighter one. Most people feel stronger when they assume a relaxed position. Most also notice that they can breathe much deeper when they are relaxed.

It's impossible to be relaxed and tense at the same time. Tense your hand and make a fist. Now let the tension go and relax your hand. Now try to tense and relax your hand at the same time. Impossible, right? You are likely thinking, *This is a trick question.* No, it's not. It's not possible to tense and relax your hand at the same time, and that is true of every other part of your body, too.

Remember the two experiments we did with deep breathing? Puff out your chest and then see if it's possible to take a deep breath. Go ahead and try. Can you feel yourself straining? Now let your shoulders go, drop your arms to your sides, and try taking another deep breath. Notice as you do this experiment that your chest also relaxes and softens. Which breath is deeper? Most likely, it's the second breath, where you relaxed.

Feeling protected and safe comes with relaxation. You are stronger when you breathe slower and deeper. Unfortunately, when you were assaulted and abused, you probably had no training in this. If you had any training in defending yourself, most likely it was not from a martial arts practitioner, but rather from a family member or teacher who taught you to "be tough," which probably translated in your head as *Tense up, Muscle up,* or *Get tight.*

EXPERIMENT WITH NEW POSSIBILITIES:
The Power of Words to Help You Feel Safer

Your thoughts and feelings also impact your sense of safety. Let's try an experiment in which you use your breathing and your thoughts. First, think of the word *tense*, and repeat it five times without saying it aloud and while breathing as deeply as you can. Now think the word *calm* and repeat it in your head five times while breathing as deeply as you can.

Pay attention to what your body does even as you simply think the words. Did you notice it tensing when you said the word *tense?* Did you notice it relaxing and letting go when you mentally said the word *calm?* Was there any difference in your breathing? Hopefully, you saw that you could breathe easier and deeper when you said the word *calm*.

I assure you that Paul's mind-body awareness program goes beyond teaching relaxation techniques. For our purposes, though, it's important to understand that softening and opening the core of the body are the first steps to rewriting your past. Paul's next steps include teaching you postural strength and stability to help you deal with challenges effectively. Along with that goes using kindness and compassion as power sources for self-protection. He puts it all together with role-playing exercises that reenact abuse and apply the lessons in body awareness plus self-defense measures to change the outcome.

When survivors, through their own efforts, create safety within themselves precisely where they had been powerless before, they experience joy and freedom. This is a step-by-step process that Paul teaches in his free book mentioned earlier. All I ask is that you take your time with it. This is not a crisis, even though you may feel very uncomfortable right now.

Silence Breakers' Best Advice:
Developing Your Ability to Achieve Internal Safety
Through Mind-Body Awareness

I asked the Silence Breakers to share their advice about achieving internal safety through mind-body awareness techniques. Sometimes these concepts are hard to translate into real-life applications, so I am sharing with you some real-life examples of how the alumni of the Weekends of Recovery put their learning to use.

Bruce shares how he used Paul's techniques when he was testifying against his perpetrator, a situation that would be stressful for anyone. I think one of Paul's greatest contributions is teaching men to relax in order to be stronger.

I worked with Paul before testifying against my perpetrator. Paul taught me the art of staying very calm and focused when I am in conflict with an opponent. This allowed me to be more in control than if I were upset and unfocused. Paul taught me how much energy I was wasting by being angry and upset, rather than calm and focused, and "in the driver's seat," which is ultimately a much safer place to be. Testifying after Paul's training was very different from other times I had testified. I was much calmer than I had been in the past. — Bruce

Chris shares about a confrontation with a co-worker, and how he employed Paul's relaxation methods in order to be more confident in the situation:

I think about taking full breaths, and picture the air moving in and out of my lungs, which helps me when I feel anxiety. Shaking out tension from my muscles, wiggling my jaw, and opening my mouth to lessen the tension in my throat help as well. I also remind myself about posture while sitting and listening. Relaxing during a confrontation with a co-worker helped me stop to think and make the right decisions. I didn't engage physically, as I might have done in the past. I was calm and ended up walking away. Paul's work has become a part of me, and I often don't have to think his methods through; they just happen automatically. — Chris

Simon describes one of the most troubling sensations for survivors, having body flashbacks. During a flashback, your body "remembers" what was done to you and how you responded at the time. Your mind and body can block out such memories until a time when you are much better prepared and able to remember and process the feelings connected to what was done to you. Simon describes using Paul's mind-body awareness techniques to help him with these disturbing sensations:

I have learned to better tolerate some very disturbing bodily sensations, including uncontrollable jerking and a sickening feeling that there's a poison in my body. I have been able to understand that the trauma I endured as a child can sometimes make me feel that my body is being taken over by an "abusive force," like a demon. Paul's techniques helped me to accept these feelings as a form of body flashback, and I know now that I am not powerless to respond, as I was as a kid. I now can reassure myself that I'm having a flashback and that I can cope. — Simon

Internal Safety and Sleep

Sleep presents a threat to the sense of security of many survivors who have trouble getting a night's rest. Like them, you may associate going to bed with being abused. You may be like others who have grown up in chaotic homes, where bedtime was when your parents started arguing and yelling at each other. Remember, we can't be relaxed and tense at the same time. If you associate being abused with a bed, it's likely that when you go to bed, you will feel tense. The association with a scary time in the past may lead you to have more trouble sleeping.

As a boy, I was expected to wait up for my drunken father to come home from the bars. I came to associate staying up late with being there for my dad, which was my responsibility. Even after he was long dead, I still sometimes stayed up late, as if I were waiting for him to arrive home safely.

How can you create an internal feeling of safety in your bedroom? The key is to bring a state of relaxation to your sleeping area. You may need to put your imagination to work. Some survivors imagine a security guard outside the door. Chances are that in your boyhood, you had a favorite superhero like Superman, Batman and Robin, the Green Knight, Ant-Man, Astro Boy, Captain America, or one of the Fantastic Four or the X-Men. Some of you may have preferred a female superhero like Wonder Woman, Elektra, or even the Bionic Woman. They all make great imaginary guardians.

You may prefer to use tension-releasing exercises and breath control. Before you go to sleep, you are in a prehypnotic state of mind, which means that you are much more open to suggestions. You can give yourself relaxing suggestions that can help facilitate your sleep. For example, you could say to yourself, *When I put my head down on my pillow tonight, I will be able to fall asleep with ease and get all the sleep I need.*

Like affirmations, you can help yourself relax with your thoughts prior to turning out the lights. Make sure to deploy positive phrases and avoid negative ones. For example, an ineffective suggestion would be *I won't have any trouble sleeping tonight,* because your brain will hear *I will have trouble sleeping tonight* (remember, the brain tends to cross out the *not*). If you have trouble letting go of negative thoughts, you might use this suggestion: *Every time I breathe in and out, my eyelids will become heavier and heavier.*

Paul would add another element to the process of feeling safe for sleeping, and it has to do with another aspect of safety: external safety. One way to feel more relaxed when you are in bed is to practice self-defense techniques that are effective against the danger you experienced in your past. Reassuring yourself of your abilities to defend yourself can help you feel more secure and comforted as you prepare to sleep.

❀ ❀ ❀

In the next chapter, I will introduce you to skills you can use for "external safety." These skills will help you to determine who is safe enough to emotionally share your feelings and thoughts with, and will help you affirm your right to ask for what you need to feel with others.

AFFIRMATIONS FOR CHAPTER 2

- *I can create a sense of inner safety.*
- *I can learn to relax and slow down.*
- *I can be present right now.*

❋ ❋ ❋ ❋

CHAPTER THREE

Dare to Dream You Can Co-create Trust and a Sense of Safety in Communicating with Others

"There is an ache for protection that, I think, all survivors long for. They want to feel the security of a safe embrace. The quote is from Leonard Cohen's song 'Anthem.'" *Designer:* Kevin, Hope Springs Weekend of Recovery, 2011.

Trusting people and sharing intimate information in conversation is a common problem for survivors of sexual abuse, so in this chapter I present several strategies for increasing the trust and intimacy in your life. By *intimacy,* I am referring primarily to intimacy in communication—not physical intimacy, but the sharing of personal information, whether in a budding friendship or with a work colleague, an ally in your healing, or a person you might want to date. I refer to co-creating trust because all relationships are two-way streets. You can only control your side of the street;

however, it's important to understand how your behavior impacts another person's ability to trust you. Let's begin by looking at methods for feeling safe enough to take the first steps in intimacy.

External safety has to do with how folks treat you emotionally, physically, verbally, and spiritually. You might also be aware of the vibes, or energy, another person communicates. Everyone has "gut" feelings that affect first impressions. I believe gut feelings are often reliable measures, but traumatic experiences can make people unwilling to trust their own judgments, especially people who have been abused or neglected by someone they'd loved or trusted.

Survivors of abuse may no longer trust even their own instincts regarding the people they meet. Having once fallen prey to someone they trusted, they may no longer find it possible to trust that they are safe and secure in any situation.

In the previous chapter, I discussed the importance of creating an internal sense of safety, and helped you understand the connection between being present and mindful and being safe. These steps will take you a long way toward feeling better able, and more comfortable and secure in your safety. During the MaleSurvivor Weekends of Recovery, one of the first things we do is the "safety exercise." In this brainstorming exercise, we ask all the guys in the room to tell us what would make each of them feel safe enough to participate as fully as possible.

For many survivors, this is a difficult question. Many have never considered what they need to feel safe, because they have spent so much time feeling unsafe and guarded. Yet once a survivor hears others share what would make *them* feel safe and secure, he can usually come up with his own suggestions. In our sessions, we generate lists of what every person in the room needs to feel safe.

The following is a list of common "safety" suggestions. Look it over and consider which of these items might help you feel safer and more secure when you first meet someone, such as a psychotherapist, physician, massage therapist, co-worker, friend, or boss.

The goal is to find methods that help you feel safe and unthreatened. The test question you might ask yourself is: *What will it take to help me feel secure if someone asks personal questions or casually touches me during a conversation?*

Participants in WOR agree to meet with a group of strangers in hopes of restoring their ability to trust their instincts and also to trust those whom their instincts identify as trustworthy. We invite each participant to take the risk of identifying what he needs to feel secure in such situations. Would any of these items be on your list if you were meeting someone new?

- *Don't touch me at all.*
- *Don't touch me without my verbal permission.*
- *Don't touch me from behind.*
- *Don't call me names.*
- *Don't yell at me.*
- *Knock before you enter my room.*
- *Don't give me advice unless I ask for it.*
- *Don't tell me what to do.*
- *Let me cry without handing me tissues.*
- *Offer a hug if I seem to need it, but wait for me to tell you it's okay.*
- *Don't label me.*
- *Please be as present as you can be.*
- *Respect my courage even when I am afraid.*
- *Be willing to take risks with me, and I'll take risks with you.*
- *Accept that I may need something very different than you need to be safe enough.*
- *Be honest with me.*
- *Be compassionate with me, but don't feel sorry for me.*
- *Don't assume that because your story is similar to mine, we are "brothers."*
- *I need permission to be angry.*
- *I need permission to cry.*
- *I need permission to speak.*

- *I need permission to be silent.*

- *I need permission to leave the room if I feel too uncomfortable.*

- *I need to know that it's okay to say no.*

- *I need to know that it's okay to say yes.*

Now consider these questions:

- As you look over the previous list, what feelings arise for you?

- Do you feel any sense of relief that other survivors need the same types of things you do?

- Do you feel any fear that other survivors need the same types of things you do?

Sometimes it feels good to have someone relate to you and experience feelings similar to yours; other times it can feel threatening, as if someone knows you too well and could get too close and then hurt you as people did in the past.

In seeking to restore your ability to trust others and to feel secure in the company of strangers, you might find it helpful to think in terms of "safety layers." At the top, or superficial, layer, you allow yourself to share only basic information about yourself with a new acquaintance. Pay attention to whether the individual you've just met shares his or her information at the same level you do. Generally, matching levels of disclosure is a safe bet. As you build trust over time, you likely will both share more in increments.

I am not suggesting that you launch into your abuse history at this point. Typically, that kind of personal information should only be shared once you are feeling deeper levels of trust. Match your information sharing with the other person's as long as you feel comfortable doing so. If the other person doesn't share as deeply, I encourage you not to go any deeper, as clearly that person is sending a message that he or she is not willing to be as intimate or personal as you may be inclined to be.

Sharing personal information is a first step in creating intimacy, and I see it as a gift you give someone. When you give a gift, you want it to be appreciated. If it's not welcomed, then I'd suggest slowing down your sharing or holding off on future exchanges.

In the case of psychotherapists, supervisors, bosses, or personal physicians, it's typically not appropriate for them to share much personal information with you, especially the deeper types of information. If they do share a lot about their personal problems, especially early in your relationship, it's a sign that they do not have good boundaries. I would encourage you to be cautious about what you share, because this person may not be worthy of your trust.

A Signal System for Sharing and Trusting

As I've noted, I myself am a survivor, and I've had to work on my own methods for overcoming trust and security issues. When I meet someone new, I keep the image of a traffic signal in my head. I may have the gut sense with this person that I have a green light and it's okay to get closer. For others, I may sense some warning signs, which I experience as if they were a flashing yellow light. Then there are those interactions where I'll clearly sense a red light.

Your gut sense can help you determine the color of the traffic light. When you are a child, your instincts may not be as highly developed, and as a result, you tend to be more trusting. That's why it's possible for perpetrators—who often are in positions of authority or have worked to win your trust—to take advantage of your vulnerability. Once your trust is betrayed and your body violated, you protect yourself by building a wall: withholding trust and suspecting everyone. Any gut instincts that tell you to trust someone may be overridden by past experience and powerful survival instincts.

I invited the Silence Breakers to share with you their experience with green-light, yellow-light, and red-light relationships. Listen to their experiences, and reflect on your own experiences and whether this method would help you feel very safe, somewhat safe, or not at all safe with other people.

I then invite you to do an experiment to identify who in your life falls into each category. I hope reading the experiences of the Silence Breakers helps you find ways to build trust and a sense of security with people you meet.

SILENCE BREAKERS' BEST ADVICE:
Creating Green-Light Relationships

Simon says that creating a level of comfort is important when meeting someone. He also reminds you that even in a green-light relationship, the other person may not be perfect or meet all expectations.

It's important to recognize that it can be hard work to create fulfilling relationships. A green light for me is when I feel relaxed enough to not focus on the intense feelings all the time, but can be comfortable enough to have fun as well as open up emotionally. Sometimes I have to manage my expectations and realize that one person cannot give me everything I need. When I accept that a person may not understand everything about my feelings, but is great company in other ways, then I can enjoy what we can share. I sense a green light when I can calmly communicate with someone and the person is open to hearing how he or she may have impacted me if I feel hurt. — Simon

Ryan shares an example of a green-light relationship characterized by a gradual process of building trust over time, equality in sharing, respect for boundaries, and a sincere interest in each other's well-being.

When I think of green-light, or safe, friendships (other than my intimate relationship with my partner), my friend Jim comes to mind as a good example. I know I'm safe with Jim in our friendship because I've "tested the waters" with him over several years. Our friendship started out on a more superficial level and became closer as we gained trust in each other over time. He's never betrayed my confidences. As time has gone on, I've felt safe enough to share more personal things. Jim is equally self-disclosing, indicating his trust in me. Jim has always been careful to respect my personal boundaries regarding my comfort level with touch and the ways we show affection. This is

---

absolutely vital in any relationship. Jim and I have "been there" for each other through good and bad times. Jim is compassionate, listening closely and checking in with me at times when the going is rough.

Another part of green-light relationships is evaluating what happens when you set boundaries. When setting your boundaries with others, just be direct and kind, and stand up for what you need. If the person is a good friend or someone who properly respects you, he or she will respond according to your wishes, and that represents a green light for me. — Ryan

Rhett, like Ryan, writes of developing green-light relationships as a process. He describes the types of questions he asks the other person in order to determine whether he feels safe enough. He also relies on his gut sense, as does Alexander, whose thoughts are provided after Rhett's.

I believe relationships take time to build, although there are people in this world you just hit it off with instantly. You share common interests in more ways than most, and that's what starts the green-light process. Knowing that we have interests in common and asking questions help me to determine how to proceed. The questions I ask are about the other person's family and childhood, and whether he or she has children or is involved with children at all. I like to ask if the person is involved in organized clubs or sports. When asking the questions, I make sure the person doesn't feel as if I'm conducting an interrogation, but rather I angle it in a friendly way. This allows me to surround myself with positive people and keep the negative ones at a distance. — Rhett

Always listen to your gut and train yourself to listen to that inner voice that tells you to go left instead of right, no matter how "off" it may seem. If the behavior of the person is of a loving and kind nature, go with it. Trust yourself enough to know that all people are not the same and you don't have to judge others based on your past experience. — Alexander

John found that other male survivors and their partners were easy for him to categorize as green-light people. His list of the qualities that engender trust and security includes empathy, being a good listener, and asking questions that encourage sharing.

The person has to make eye contact and be present. By being present, I mean that the individual has to be an active listener. The person has to hear what you are saying, respond with open-ended questions, and display empathy. I find that most of the hospice staff I interact with are green-light people. In my experience, the best place to find green-light people is in the male-survivor community, including, often, partners of male survivors. — John

Howie relates to people through humor and is more interested in how they feel about themselves than what they possess:

I've always been attracted to people I can joke around with. I'm sure this is just my way of coping, but I feel much more relaxed when I'm able to laugh with someone. The relationships I feel most comfortable in are those where people are very comfortable being themselves and not focused on material things. — Howie

The Silence Breakers have shared what helps them establish green-light relationships, and I hope their comments help you think about what you need to feel about someone in order to establish a green-light relationship. I invite you to also reflect on how often you offer these behaviors in a developing relationship. How much do you relate to the challenges mentioned? As you think about the people in your life, whom might you include on your green-light list? Later in this chapter is an exercise to help you identify green-light behaviors of your current friends.

Before we move on, though, I want you to check inside. Do you need a break?

❀   ❀   ❀

Now I want to focus on yellow-light relationships that could become green-light relationships or, on the other hand, transform into red-light relationships. Caution is the rule here. I have again asked the Silence Breakers to share some of their experiences with yellow-light relationships. Take some time as you read their descriptions to see how much you identify with the survivor and how much you identify with the friend who is practicing yellow-light behaviors. Pay attention to the behavioral warning signs that make each of the Silence Breakers cautious. You will find that most pull back when they sense a lack of respect for boundaries, feelings, and thoughts.

In Alcoholics Anonymous and other 12-step programs, it's often said that participants should not "take another person's inventory." The idea is to discourage participants from being judgmental toward others and to be accepting instead.

SILENCE BREAKERS' BEST ADVICE:
Identifying Yellow-Light Relationships

Being open and accepting of others is a great thing, but survivors of abuse usually feel that they don't have that option—and for good reason. Their ability to trust others has been damaged by perpetrators and nonprotectors, and must be restored over time. To trust, you need to learn to feel safe enough to create, maintain, and make known the boundaries with which you are comfortable in conversations and other social interactions. Ryan notes this next, while admitting that the ability to "trust your gut" can be difficult to restore for a survivor of sexual abuse.

For me, a big "caution" signal is when people ask questions that feel inappropriate or act in ways that are too invasive for a casual friendship. For example, I knew a woman who liked to approach me while I was seated and massage my neck and shoulders. At first, I made the error of feeling obligated to go along with it. I thought that because no one else would consider this inappropriate, I shouldn't object. Then I realized that if it made me feel uneasy, it <u>was</u> inappropriate. I asked her to stop, and she replied, "Oh, you mean I'm invading your boundaries?" I replied that she was. She stopped, and our friendship continued on a more comfortable level. — Ryan

Rhett, on the other hand, realized that he had become more cautious and guarded with people as soon as his abuse began, and has carried this defensive demeanor throughout his adulthood. He knows this lack of trust is tied to his own sense of self and self-worth.

Looking back, I can recall that from the moment my abuse began, I instantly went into yellow-light mode and proceeded with caution. Initially the caution was all about someone finding out (about my being abused) and getting me into the supposed trouble I was told I would get into if anyone ever found out. As I matured into a young adult and then into adulthood, the yellow-light status remained, because I worried about trusting anyone with what little there was left of my sense of self-worth, love, and overall being. This cautiousness developed into an almost instinctive way of reading people. — Rhett

As you read Rhett's comments, you may have been tempted to think such cautiousness would be helpful to a survivor. The truth is that it could help him carefully pick whom he is vulnerable with. The problem with this stance is that it could also create a major block to any intimacy or support, as the yellow-light mode can be interpreted by others as a red light: *Don't get close to me.*

Mike shares some very specific examples of what he regards as yellow-light comments that instantly make him cautious. Most of his examples reflect how others disrespect him or discount his experience. I believe many people don't know how to respond to disclosures of abuse. They may be well intentioned and yet say some very hurtful things. The key to whether it remains a yellow-light relationship is to see how the person responds when you tell him or her that you feel hurt. If you encounter defensiveness, then you may need to change this relationship status to red light, because you deserve to have your experiences and feelings respected.

One of the things I have learned is to be very careful about to whom I speak about the details of my abuse and its aftereffects. People can be so careless in their responses to you, even though they think they are helping you. Someone might say, "You're strong; you will be fine." But inside, I'm thinking anything but that. I will not talk about my issues with anyone who wants to give me a pep talk. People who hold me to Superman standards don't understand that I am trying to compensate for what I really feel inside. I have been a star in this game of life, but now I am playing with an injury; that injury has finally taken over, and I just can't bandage it enough to play at those levels anymore. If someone tells me to "man up," that person just doesn't get it or doesn't take the time to get it, and I need to put the brakes on that relationship. — Mike

Another form of disrespect occurs when someone tries to use you, take advantage of you, or manipulate you. SJC describes how a friend tried to use him in his career and how negative that was. He describes how he has come to the insight that he was used by his incestuous family, who had manipulatively treated him as special, which set him up for a lifetime of being suspicious of anyone who might try to use him.

> *I actually had a friend who, without my permission, announced to his law firm that they would be getting my company's business because of his friendship with me; we became more distant friends after that. My position in my company actually exacerbated my inability to get close to others. I worried about being used, because that's what happened when I was a child. I was the golden child, the mother-enmeshed son who was fondled. I didn't realize it, but I had been inculcated into not trusting, worrying about betrayal, and keeping a safe distance from anyone who wanted to get close. — SJC*

In relationships, it's as important to know how to say no as it is to say yes. If you are unable to say no, it will be much more difficult for you to say yes. There are many qualities for you to look for that could help you say yes or "maybe" to a possible relationship. It's also important to know when to say no, especially at times when you need to avoid a relationship altogether, and when to say "no more" and stop a dysfunctional relationship.

During your abuse, you may have felt that you didn't have the right to say no or "no more." For many of you, there was no choice except to endure the pain until the abusers were done with you. Other survivors may have felt it was their job to do everything for everyone else, and that neither their feelings nor their safety mattered.

It may be especially difficult for you to say no to a relationship, because you don't want to appear disloyal. Some people are not comfortable standing up for themselves in such situations. My goal is to help you learn how to say no and "no more," and to give you support if you choose to set this boundary.

SILENCE BREAKERS' BEST ADVICE:
Identifying Red-Light Relationships

The Silence Breakers offer examples of their own experiences in identifying red-light relationships. Note that they write about heeding their instincts and paying attention to their own behaviors in the relationships.

Simon describes his red-light signs for ending a relationship, including feeling unsafe, unheard, ashamed, worn down, and abused. He also points out the need to look at the coping strategies employed in the relationship. It was a real red-light sign that he started engaging in addictive or compulsive behaviors to stay in a relationship.

> If I feel that I cannot manage my feelings safely without using poor coping strategies, such as addictions or attacking myself, then I have to consider ending the relationship. If a person is unable or refuses to listen to how I've been impacted, then it's time to call it a day, because I am very open about my feelings and this has to be a two-way street. If the relationship makes me feel as if there's something wrong with me a lot of the time, then it's not healthy. I ended a relationship once because my partner constantly monitored me and made frequent accusations about my feelings toward other women. It was not right to tolerate such abusive dynamics because I was left feeling like less of a man. I had to give up some very loving aspects of that relationship, but it was the right thing to do in the long run. —Simon

Ryan agrees with Simon, as he discusses the importance of analyzing whether a relationship enhances your life or causes great problems. He has been a career rescuer and has "given until it hurts," as if that were his only choice. It was not until his recovery that he developed his own criteria for ending an unhealthy and unbalanced relationship.

> It's important to ask yourself if a relationship is good for you and enriches your life, or is a cause of anxiety and stress. Many of us are programmed to "give until it hurts" or to chronically rescue others in relationships. We may feel it's the "Christian" thing to help others at the expense of our own sanity. If others consistently betray confidences, if they don't "have your back" in social situations, or if they stomp all over your personal boundaries, I believe it's time to reevaluate or end the relationship. — Ryan

Christopher describes what should have been his red-light signs, and shares how, in his efforts to avoid hurting himself or his ex-wife, he actually wound up hurting both of them more:

> *It took years of being with my ex-wife for me to see that we didn't have a sustainable relationship. I wish I'd had the courage to deal with it before it all exploded and I lashed out in ways that hurt people more than was needed. Not walking away from a bad situation can lead to explosively disastrous results and hurting other people unnecessarily. What I should have seen far earlier was that I was sharing a life with someone who had little desire to share more than a superficial life with me. Anytime someone disregards or disrespects your wishes or feelings, it's time to seriously think about separating yourself from that relationship. — Christopher*

When I discussed establishing green-light relationships earlier in this chapter, I mentioned the importance of pacing yourself and recognizing that healthy trust always takes time to build. Rhett points out that for him, it's a red flag when another person moves way too fast, and he gives some good examples for you to consider. Alexander discusses the importance of being aware of how the person acts toward others. If that person shows signs of disrespect or is abusive, then likely he or she will disrespect you, too. I invite you to see if any of these descriptions are accurate for you, because it could be very important information that helps you see why you may be struggling with intimacy.

> *An instant red flag to me is what I call "too much, too soon." For example, if I have just met a person and, in the course of the conversation, am told every personal, negative aspect of the individual's life—or private items you would normally only tell someone you have known for years—it's an indication that this is not my kind of person. Additionally, if someone comes on too strong in wanting to do things together, do things for me, or lend things quickly, it's a sign that this person may be too "clingy" and expect too much of me. — Rhett*

> *A lack of common decency and respect tells me to run. A lack of respect is more than some big dramatic fight. A person who will not respect you concerning the little things will never respect you around anything big. If there's any sign that your presence is a burden or unwelcome, it's time to release and let go. — Alexander*

I wrote a lot in the green- and yellow-light sections about trusting your gut. This is just as important in assessing potential red flags. Mike gives an example of a red flag he encountered with a fellow survivor he had hoped he could trust:

> When I am in relationships with other survivors, I keep an eye out for behaviors that look suspect. For instance, I was in a workshop where I shared that I struggled with acting out, and later in the day, a participant approached me about my problem, but my gut said he was trying to hook up with me. That was a big red flag. — Mike

Pierre points out another important aspect of red-light relationships: the failure to take responsibility for problems. You have the right to have people in your life who will be honest with you. If you confront them, and they are unable to apologize and make amends, that's a serious red flag.

> Dishonesty—there's nothing like lying to me to make me go away. I severed a long friendship that had started when we were teenagers, because that person had lied to me and when I confronted him about it, he lied some more to dismiss or explain the first lie. As important a part of my teen years as that friend had been, including helping me survive, I decided that we had since taken different paths. — Pierre

EXPERIMENT WITH NEW POSSIBILITIES:
Identifying Your Own Green-, Yellow-, and Red-Light Relationships

It will be helpful to make a photocopy of this experiment. I invite you to list in your journal or notebook any new friendship or relationship you have formed in the last few months. Reflect on how safe you feel with this person, and in your journal, name the person and assign a traffic-light color that reflects how you feel about sharing more about yourself with that individual.

Next is a list of qualities I have discussed as being important in identifying how safe you are feeling with a potential new friend or intimate partner. After reading the first column, put a check mark in the second column next to any quality you tend to offer in relationships when you want to get closer (for example, green-light behaviors). For example, when you come to "Accepts me as wounded" in the first column, ask yourself, *Do I accept others as wounded?* If that applies to you, put a check mark in the second column. At the top of the additional columns, write the names of the people you listed in your journal, and then check off which qualities each person offers you or is likely to offer you as you get closer. Hopefully using these lists can help you make healthier decisions about getting closer to others.

Quality	Me	Friend 1	Friend 2
Reciprocity			
Trust			
Treats others with respect			
Honors boundaries			
Willing to go slowly			
Able to offer support			
Able to offer constructive feedback			
Able to risk conflict			
Expresses interest			
Shares common interests			
Shares common values			

Accepts me as wounded			
Offers empathy			
Good sense of humor			
Keeps confidentiality			
Honesty			
Admits to mistakes and is able to take responsibility for his or her part of a problem			
Compassionate			
Passionate about life			
Able to verbalize needs			
Honors my needs			
Manages anger without taking it out on others			
Has healthy self-esteem			
Absence of manipulation			
Consistency			
Ability to listen and hear			
Absence of active addiction			
Actively recovering			
Positive view of asking for help or being in therapy			

Once you've completed your checklist, you might want to see if you are offering enough green-light behaviors to others so that they can get closer to you. Consider the behaviors your friends offer you, and check in with yourself to see how you feel about what each person offers you. Remember, all of these qualities are ones you can practice more. Think about what steps you might need to take to exhibit more of these green-light behaviors more often. I will address many of these behaviors and the blocks to being healthier in the next few chapters.

The following statements will help you affirm that you can identify what you need in order to begin forming healthier relationships. But maybe you believe that isolating is preferable to risking getting closer to others. In the next chapter, I will address many of the myths I have heard from survivors about isolation. Chances are you will hear traces of yourself in their words, and I hope you will open yourself to the possibility that those beliefs are holding you back from getting the support you need and deserve.

AFFIRMATIONS FOR CHAPTER 3

- *I have the right to protect my vulnerability today by sharing at my own pace and as I desire.*

- *I dare to dream I can create a green-light relationship with a person who can help me recover.*

- *I give myself permission to ask for what I need to feel safe enough in a new relationship.*

CHAPTER FOUR

Dare to Dream
You Can Leave Your
Isolation Behind

"Four simple clauses—*I matter, you matter, we matter. Survive!*—
as a message to myself and my brothers of the importance
of connecting with each other." *Designer:* Jesse Potts.

One of the greatest barriers to healing is isolation. You may be like many survivors who have learned that by isolating themselves, they can feel safe, or at least they can convince themselves that they feel safe. So far, we've looked at ways for you to feel safer by making internal adjustments and by using methods to increase your sense of safety with others. Now I'd like you to consider that you can find support, which is ultimately much safer than isolating yourself.

I have heard many stories of survivors who found hiding places to avoid their abusers, sometimes in their homes, a garage or attic, a forest or park, or other places away from home. When these survivors went into hiding, their perpetrators could not find them. So they actually *were* safer than they would have been in their own rooms in their own homes—which should have been safe places for them.

Sometimes they created hiding places by dissociation—mentally leaving their bodies and floating off—so that they didn't have to be present during the abuse. During the 2010 show in which Oprah Winfrey invited 200 male survivors to be her audience, special guest Tyler Perry described his childhood as "a living hell." He said he felt he had "died as a child." He talked about what he had done to feel safe: "Some of it was so horrific that I found a way I could leave myself and go to this park that my mother and aunt had taken me to. And all the boys were there playing, and so I am running and playing, and it was such a good day. So every time somebody would be doing something to me that was horrible, I could go to this park in my mind until it was over."

It's a tragedy when a child has to hide to be safe. The long-term consequence is that he learns that hiding is safer than interacting with others. He also buries the truth about his abuse, in effect hiding it from his consciousness. When you hide from that truth, you shut it out and make it impossible to heal, essentially putting yourself in a deep freeze. Survivors who hide their abuse become loyal to isolation as a survival mechanism. It's also true that most survivors only let go of one coping mechanism when they feel comfortable and competent with another. My goal in this chapter is to help you develop the ability to comfortably seek support instead of isolating yourself. To do that, you must let go of the belief that isolation is truly safe.

I am not suggesting that asking for support is risk-free. There is risk involved in seeking it, but isolation involves much *more* risk over the long term.

Myths about Isolation

Let's look at some of the myths about isolation that survivors often subscribe to. After each myth, I have provided testimony from the Silence Breakers regarding their own experiences with that myth.

Myth: *When I isolate myself, no one can hurt me.*

Truth: Although this myth seems true on the surface, all of us have to interact with others, and if we remain emotionally isolated, we are much more vulnerable to being hurt from not having practiced any emotional coping skills, or learning to engage in healthy conflict or setting boundaries, except for the absolute boundary of "leave me alone." Listen to Pierre as he shares how misunderstood and alone he felt as a teenager. Although he says he felt safer being alone, you can hear his pain.

> *As a teenager, I was a loner. I always thought of myself as the round peg in the square hole, so it was easier to keep to myself and to my books than to try to fit in. I never understood the other teenagers, nor did they understand me. I realize today that I shut down a side of myself, and as a result, I could not be a "normal teenager." I was afraid to try to fit in and felt safer being alone.*

Next, John shares his insights on how this myth hurt him terribly, even though it was supposed to protect him. It even left him feeling worthless after he became an internationally renowned scientist.

> *At an early age, I became a nonperson, because my parents used me to fulfill their needs instead of allowing me to develop my individuality. As a faceless person, I was isolated, because no one recognized me. I took on the attitude that no one could hurt me; after all, I had suffered and survived. To ensure that no one could hurt me, I remained a faceless person, living behind impenetrable boundaries and remaining emotionally shut down. Because I so completely suppressed the abuse, I didn't even know I was keeping a secret. However, I was always hiding my low self-esteem and couldn't take credit for my accomplishments, which were not trivial, considering that I had earned a Ph.D. and had garnered an international reputation as a scientist. I attributed my accomplishments to luck.*

Myth: *By isolating, I'll protect myself by keeping my abuse a secret.*

Truth: What if by sharing your secrets, you allowed another person to give you support and acceptance? Many survivors have received support when they shared the truth about their abuse, even though they were afraid. While it's possible that someone might use the knowledge of your abuse against you, it's much more likely that others will become closer to you. It's quite possible that they will respect you rather than reject you. Listen to Howie's experience after he appeared on *Oprah:*

> *I usually feel that people will judge me differently if they find out about the abuse. The truth is, ever since I was in the "200 Men" audience on* <u>The Oprah Winfrey Show</u>*, I've told many friends about the abuse, and I'm still in shock when I realize that most of my friends know and nothing has changed.*

I hope that by hearing these stories, you will be able to challenge the part of you that keeps lying to you and that holds you back from receiving the support you deserve and need. Rhett had an experience in which he challenged this myth. As a result, he was rewarded with support and friendship.

> *The greatest misconception I ever had was that when I isolated myself, no one would know my secrets and therefore couldn't use them against me. This misconception was challenged roughly a week after my very first therapy session: I had to drop off something at my best buddy's house. We had the usual conversations, but in the back of my mind, I wanted to tell him what had happened to me as a child and reveal to him the journey on which I was about to embark. As I look back now, I realize that he was more alarmed at how I stumbled over my words than at the actual message. As I disclosed my secret to him, I was cautious but honest, without going into detail. I waited for his reaction, feeling as if I were standing on the edge of a cliff. For so long, I had played out in my head what reaction I'd receive if I revealed my secret. His response took me by*

complete surprise. He recited his cell-phone number and told me that if I ever needed to call him, I should do so. In my head I was like, <u>What? Where are the comments about how dirty I am? I deserve them!</u> Telling him also helped me to realize that if his reaction had been different, then I probably wouldn't want him in my life anyway.

Myth: *I'll do no harm to myself by isolating.*

Truth: Isolation prevents you from taking any risks. It's harmful because it makes you much more vulnerable to depression, suicide, and anxiety. Unfortunately, survivors often believe they are comfortable practicing isolation, when instead, that's what is most familiar to them, and the truth is that it's not at all comfortable. Risking discomfort will help you heal and receive the support you deserve.

I honor that you learned to avoid risks to feel safe. I honor that you learned that being a curious and trusting boy made you vulnerable and, unfortunately, led to your wrongful abuse due to the fact that perpetrators seek boys and men who are vulnerable. You may have concluded that the only strategy to be safe was to shut out others. You may have taken the huge risk and told someone, but the person didn't believe you or, worse, blamed you. Again, you may have learned that the best strategy for your safety was to remain isolated. But here is an important thing to remember:

Truth: All men who are abused or assaulted deserve support and understanding.

As he notes in the next paragraph, Chris chose isolation, and his experience mirrors those of many other survivors who become depressed and suicidal. You will learn how to avoid this dangerous road, and it's important to hear how others have found a new, safer path.

Much of my 20s and 30s were marked by isolation and limited risk taking in order for me to feel that I could survive. Hiding in the apartment was my safety net, because no one

65

could hurt me there. No one could learn my secrets. My decision to avoid any risk taking was very regimented, bordering on oppressive. Phone messages, if I checked them, would be returned days later if at all. Trips to the supermarket were done only when nothing was left in the fridge or when trips to fast-food restaurants became too expensive. Other than work, trips to a store or restaurant were sometimes my only attempts at socialization during my deep and debilitating depression. Isolation only reinforced my depression, resulting in continual suicidal thoughts, which eventually led to self-admission into the psych ward at a local hospital. In my mind, I created my own reality based on past experiences, assumptions, and false truths. I didn't trust or share with anyone, so I began to create a safe world that was not truly a reality. I thought that no one was trustworthy and that I was unlovable, worthless, and broken. I created a defeatist, self-fulfilling prophecy.

To heal, you can manage your feelings and risk being uncomfortable by leaving your isolation behind. Next, Joe discusses taking one risk at a time, starting small:

I can take risks and be safe at the same time. I start by taking small risks. Then, I repeat them, possibly increasing the size of the risk each time. As I learn that it's safe to take risks, I gain confidence and then am willing to take slightly larger risks. A sense of relief increases my motivation to increase my risk taking. Getting out of the comfort zone requires my being uncomfortable.

Rob shared an important myth that he says is one of the catalysts in his current recovery:

Myth: *I cannot tell a woman what I am suffering from or how I am suffering inside.*

Truth: Intimacy is risky and can be scary. By holding on to your fears that no woman (or if you are gay or bisexual, no man) could possibly understand and be supportive—or that it would just be too threatening for you to speak your truth because surely you would be rejected—you may risk discovering, as Rob did, that the opposite is true.

> *In one case, a lover and I went to see* <u>Brokeback Mountain,</u> *and on the way home, she asked me if I had ever been with a man. I pondered this question for a moment and then decided to tell her about the abuse. I didn't share all of it with her, but I shared enough, and she offered me support and under-standing. This conversation was the catalyst for what has, so far, been a four-year search for a better standard of emotional well-being.*

Here's Simon's experience with this myth and what he learned. He shares a common experience with some male survivors who are unfaithful to their partners and always looking outside their relationships for comfort and support.

> *I kept the identity of the person who abused me from my wife while we were married, and ultimately this led to the breakdown of the relationship. I had been led to believe that what my dad did to me when I was a child wasn't that bad and that it would destroy my family if I reached out to any-one on the outside. As a man in my mid-20s who was getting increasingly confused and depressed, instead of turning to my loving wife, I "ran off" with another woman, who offered me what I thought was an escape from the fear of telling my wife and the rejection I anticipated. When I shared my story with this new woman, it was emotionally explosive. I now see that if I had taken the risk of sharing my story with my wife, then the turbulent feelings might have come to the surface in a safer way because we had already built up enough trust through the struggles of everyday life.*

Myth: *Men are scary to get close to, because most likely, they will judge me for being weak. I was also abused by a man, so all men could potentially hurt me, just as I was hurt during my abuse.*

Jarrod describes next all the contributing factors that led to his difficulty in making male friends. He describes what underlies his fears of men, because he both fears their judgments and fears that they might actually understand him and see right through him, and then he couldn't hide from his pain anymore.

> *I was always curious and a bit sad about having so few male friends. My wife would joke that I needed "some dudes." I discovered in therapy that the idea of having male friends frightened me: I simply did not feel comfortable. In groups, I usually end up congregated with women. However, this left me feeling isolated, odd, and weak.*

Truth: It makes great sense that as a male survivor, you could find other men threatening to get close to for all sorts of reasons. *Grooming* is the behavior perpetrators engage in to secure the trust of their victims by treating them as "special," such as by giving them gifts, taking them on trips, giving them opportunities other boys would not get to experience, offering money, or providing access to alcohol and drugs that would appeal to a younger man or boy. Former Penn State football coach Jerry Sandusky was reported to have engaged in many of these grooming behaviors with the ten boys he abused. If you are a man abused by men who initially gained your trust—and perhaps even your family's trust—through grooming, it makes great sense that the wound of that betrayal makes the thought of being close to any other man unacceptable to you.

If you have hidden from your truth and pain, it makes sense that you wouldn't want to be in a room with another male survivor who might see right through you and know your pain. Even if he is accepting, you may believe that he'll judge you more harshly than you already judge yourself: thinking you are weak, sick, perverted, and maybe even dangerous and unstable. If your perpetrator was not a woman, it also makes sense that if women in your life have been "safe," you would seek out women for support instead of men.

Alexander shared another myth that kept him isolated and, worse, essentially led him to feel that he was walking through life with a "signed and sealed death sentence":

Myth: *Nobody cares about me.*

I took everything upon myself, because I believed nobody cared about me. I stopped socializing and interacting with co-workers because I thought nobody cared about me. Self-pity is the most debilitating act you can thrust upon yourself. You become the walking dead because your life is empty and isolated. Without some purpose, life has no meaning and you have no reason to live. This is why, for me, the "Nobody cares about me" myth is basically a signed and sealed death sentence.

Truth: You will hear Silence Breakers often tell other survivors, "You are more cared about than you can imagine, and more worthy of care than you give yourself permission to feel and accept." Male survivors, in my experience, are some of the kindest and most sensitive men walking this planet. If you can acknowledge that your friends think of you as a caring person, then hopefully you can accept that they also care about you. If they care about you, then telling them the truth about your experiences will probably make them care for you even more. If you asked them (which is really hard to do when you feel so worthless) to tell you why they are your friends, you might be amazed at the long list of good qualities they see in you.

Niall discovered how important it was to stop believing these myths:

My whole healing journey can be defined in terms of leaving my isolation behind. When I first started dealing with the abuse, I confided my story only to a friend, which was the most liberating act of my entire life. Then, I chose to share my story with trusted professionals. But over time, I felt a deep hunger within my soul to reach out and share my story with other survivors. Ending my isolation has required courage and allowing myself to be vulnerable. However, I have generally found immense reservoirs of acceptance, respect, and support from the people with whom I have shared my story.

Bruce shared his myth, which stopped him in his tracks:

Myth: *Eventually this sexual abuse stuff will go away on its own. Time heals all.*

Truth: Your emotional wounds from sexual abuse will heal only when you take active steps to promote healing. Waiting for time to heal you will prevent you from reaching out for the vital support you need to heal your shame. Refuse to wait for the clock. Your time is valuable. The fact that you are reading this book is evidence that you know you are worthy and deserving of healing.

Chris shared another myth that kept him isolated, what I call the "I can't" myth:

Myth: *I can't. I can't risk socializing. I can't risk going to a party. I can't risk a job where I have to socialize instead of sit at my desk alone. I have to keep believing that my isolating is protecting me.*

Truth: Chris saw many others enjoying their lives, taking risks, dating, going on trips, and socializing. Eventually he began to think, *Why can't I?* instead of continuing to think, *I can't.* In Alcoholics Anonymous, there's a saying: "Sometimes you have to get sick and tired of being sick and tired." Chris describes how he grew sick and tired of living such a limited life:

> *I was often asked why I didn't want to come to a party or why I didn't talk to the girl who was clearly interested in me. I told myself countless times, I can't. But in order to participate, I needed to begin taking some risks. These situations are what prompted me to start questioning the myth that taking no risks would continue to protect me. Life was passing me by. I was*

tired of being alone and not enjoying all the life around me. I was no longer safe, because I didn't take risks. I had to begin taking risks again to save my life, because for me, isolation would have led to suicide. And I decided and believed that this was not the path I was destined to take.

Pierre relates another myth that isolated him:

Myth: *I am unworthy of being helped.*

Pierre describes how he believed his mother always had his best interest at heart and how he had to challenge this belief to see a larger truth. This is really tough for survivors who believe they must always be loyal to their mothers and fathers. Like Pierre, they must learn that they are worthy of help.

In my case, since my mother wouldn't believe me, I wondered why someone else would. If my mother didn't want to help me, it must have been because I didn't deserve to be helped. As an adult, I realized that my mother didn't help me because she couldn't deal with what I had told her, not because I was worthless. That was when this myth stopped being true for me.

Truth: We are worthy of all the help and support we need. It's a painful truth that for many of you, your abusers and non-protectors (the people whose job it was to protect you who failed you, including parents, other relatives, teachers, coaches, administrators, and doctors) did not want you to be helped. Some may have wanted you to suffer so that you would blame yourself and not hold them accountable. Some who refused to protect you couldn't face the pain you were experiencing. Some made the choice to doubt your story rather than face their guilt for having failed to protect you. They may not have been able to stop the abuse when it was done to you, but they could have helped you heal by getting you the help you needed and deserved.

After your abuse, you may have believed the lie of the perpetrators that it was your fault, that you wanted it or deserved it. The fact is that that's a lie, and you are absolutely worthy of support and help. You may be afraid to ask for it. Some survivors believe the macho lie that asking for help makes you weak, but the opposite is true. Asking for help is a sign of strength.

Where to Turn for Support

To believe that you can ask for support, you have to believe that it's absolutely possible to get support and that there are people out there who do offer it. In 1994, I helped co-found the organization now known as MaleSurvivor, the oldest of its kind dedicated to helping male survivors and their allies heal and find support. MaleSurvivor has an extensive website, and provides conferences and the Weekends of Recovery program. In our organization, there are many male survivors, allies, and trained professionals willing to support you. These men and women can be reached through their postings on our Internet bulletin boards and in our moderated web chat rooms. Our moderators are trained to assist you and to keep the online conversations as safe as possible. More than 850 men have participated in our WOR program. Most are willing to share valuable experiences and insights. Many have chosen to build on their weekend experiences by starting local peer-support groups, which are also listed on the website.

There are many other international, national, and local groups that sponsor websites where you can find additional support. I've listed some in the Resources section at the back of this book. One other website that I highly recommend is **www.1in6 .org**. The mission of 1in6 is to help men who have had unwanted or abusive sexual experiences in childhood live healthier, happier lives. Their mission also includes serving family members, friends, and partners by providing information and support resources on the web and in the community. I hope that being made aware of these resources will encourage you to reach out for the support you deserve.

With any connection you make on the Internet, you can choose how much you want to share regarding your identity. You can use pseudonyms or just your first name. There are plenty of ways to protect your privacy and still reach out to learn how others cope with the many challenges you are facing as you take steps to recover. A safe way to start is by going on one of the bulletin boards and reading some postings that you are drawn to. Most likely, you'll find someone whose story is similar to yours. Someone will be sharing the truth you have kept inside for a very long time. It's my hope that you will be encouraged and empowered to share your truth, too.

If you find someone you connect with, you can respond to that person's posting with even a simple "Me, too." That signals the end of your isolation. You can choose to connect with those who have struggled just as you have.

It takes more courage to go into an Internet chat room, but remember that you have the option of just observing. Everyone in the chat room will see that someone else is there, but they will only see the name you post. They may or may not ask you questions. If someone asks you a question, it's fine to say, "I'd rather just observe today."

Everyone will understand. So even if you choose to simply witness what others are writing in the chat room, you are still making a connection and taking a step to end your isolation. You also have the choice of asking questions of others in real time. Often people report that one of the key advantages of the Internet is that people feel safer sharing their stories because of the relative anonymity.

Be mindful that if you go to the Internet for support, you may find yourself comparing your experience to others, which can be reassuring or, in some cases, may make you feel worse. Some survivors minimize their abuse when they read or hear the horrific tales of others. Remember that abuse is abuse is abuse. If you believe everyone else is farther along in their healing, there's still reason to be hopeful. Most of them were once where you are. I encourage you to share whatever feelings you have. Refuse to keep them to yourself, because it's highly likely that someone else has been in your shoes and is probably willing to help you.

Remember, too, that the Internet is just one resource. It's also important to reach out to people you know. If, for now, you have no one to reach out to, then use the Internet to help assure yourself that there are others who care enough to help you and that you are worthy of their care.

The Difference Between Isolating Yourself and Taking Healthy "Alone Time"

Know that spending time by yourself can be very valuable as long as it isn't simply an effort to avoid others out of fear or guilt. There's a big difference between choosing to be alone and isolating yourself. Choosing to be alone gives you an opportunity to reflect on what you are learning. It also can give you time to journal, exercise, read, watch television, listen to your favorite music, or do artwork.

Some people are naturally more introverted and need quiet time to recharge. For them, this is a healthy and necessary choice.

Be aware, however, that you may be simply isolating yourself out of fear or guilt if you choose to be alone because of any of the myths debunked in this chapter. There are better options that are healthier than isolation in the long run, even though they may be uncomfortable in the short run.

Warning Signs That You Are Isolating Instead of Engaging in Healthy Alone Time

The Silence Breakers offer a few clear warning signs from their experiences:

> When I am choosing to isolate, I become unproductive.
> — Alexander

My key indicator is to just be aware of how I feel. If I am feeling crappy and want to just be alone, this sets off a red flag that I am isolating. — Bruce

For me, isolation is usually associated with dysfunctional behaviors, such as ruminating on the past, getting lost in fantasies about the future, or engaging in addictive behaviors. — Simon

I am isolating when I turn to one of my coping mechanisms, like eating, watching TV, sleeping, or—here we go— Internet porn. Yup, I admit it. I have addictions that still play a part in my recovery. — Chris

Rhett proposes considering positive and negative isolation. He pays special attention to the frequency with which he engages in the behavior. He also checks in with himself to see how he feels while engaged in the behavior and afterward.

I prefer to classify isolation as either positive or negative. For me, there's nothing wrong with any kind of positive isolation, provided there are some basic characteristics. The first indicator is frequency. No matter how positive it may be, if the frequency of your taking alone time is such that you are disconnecting from those around you, then you are using positive attributes in a negative way. The other main consideration is to examine what exactly you were doing when you chose to isolate yourself. For me, this becomes a method of checking in with myself by determining how I felt prior to, and what I did during, the chosen period. If the selected activity was beneficial to my health, both physical or mental, then it would be acceptable.

EXPERIMENT WITH NEW POSSIBILITIES:
Breaking Out of Your Isolation

For the next week, I invite you to keep track of the times you are isolating, the times you are choosing to be alone, and the times you risk reaching out for support. Anytime you isolate, spend five minutes listening to the thoughts and feelings you are having. Then spend five minutes more considering what other options you might have instead of isolating yourself, such as writing down challenges to yourself to affirm your worthiness of support. Anytime you choose to reach out for support, spend five minutes afterward checking how you felt about the amount of support you received. During that time, give yourself permission to explore the behaviors that invited support and the behaviors that might have given the message that you didn't want or need support.

Include your answers to these questions in your journal:

- What thoughts and feelings do I have as I isolate?
- What can I remind myself of to help me break out of my isolation?
- What new possible activities could I risk engaging in now?
- How do I feel about breaking out of my isolation? What were the results?
- What behaviors did I engage in to invite support?
- What behaviors did I engage in that gave the message that I didn't need support?

Hopefully by now, you have effectively challenged the part of you that believes you are safer when you are alone, and have gained some awareness and skills to help you feel safe as you begin taking risks to get closer to others. Affirm these beliefs, and in the next chapter, I will address what, for most survivors, is the scariest part of this whole process, namely, telling your story to others. I hope that the next chapter will help you address the many fears you may have and that through my suggestions and the wisdom of the Silence Breakers, you will find the courage to begin to break your silence.

AFFIRMATIONS FOR CHAPTER 4

- *I can choose to be alone when I want to replenish myself.*
- *I can grow now to believe that reaching out for support is safer for me than isolating.*
- *I dare to dream I am worthy of all the support I need now.*

CHAPTER FIVE

Dare to Dream
You Can Tell Your Story
and Find the Support
You've Always Deserved

"I felt so much shame about my sexual abuse story, yet
I felt compassion, understanding, and forgiveness for other men's abuse
stories. My work now is to rediscover how to be a compassionate witness
for myself. With the gracious love and support of my fellow survivors and
my healing heart, I feel I can." *Designer:* JPR, Toronto, Ontario, Canada.

Telling the story of your abuse is a key part of your recovery. There are many considerations for this critical step, including why to tell, whom to tell, how to tell, when to tell, and what to share. Keep in mind that this is a long process, not a brief, one-time occurrence.

You might wonder why you shouldn't just keep the traumatic experience to yourself. Many survivors choose to keep the abuse secret out of fear, which is understandable. In most cultures, men are expected to always be in control and to never be victims. From an early age, boys learn this masculine stereotype. The misperception is that if a male of any age is abused or assaulted, he is less than a man. So, if a man chooses to tell his story, he is likely to risk being thought of as weak and damaged. Some who are uninformed or insensitive may criticize him for not protecting himself or for allowing the abuse to happen. So it's important to be selective in sharing your story, and in this chapter, I will give you tools to do that.

Some survivors keep their stories to themselves, because they honestly can't see any good reason to tell them to anyone else. They have lived with holding their secrets inside for many years. Most believe that they can take their stories to their graves and that until then, life will be just fine. In most cases, however, there are substantial advantages for survivors to tell their stories, and the Silence Breakers will confirm this message.

Far too many survivors suffer because they keep their secrets and never receive the support and counseling that can greatly improve the quality of their lives. The consequences of never talking about sexual abuse often include self-imposed isolation, depression, anxiety, difficulty with intimacy, addictions, poor self-esteem, suicidal urges, and overwhelming feelings of insecurity and unworthiness.

A sense of shame underlies a lot of these symptoms, and many survivors talk about living with that painful feeling for long periods before they sought help. Shame is, simply put, the feeling *I am not good enough*. There are many compelling reasons to tell your story. Disclosing the secret of your abuse will help you let go of the shame once you feel safe enough to tell your story. Disclosing your experience gives you the opportunity to connect with other survivors and to learn that others have survived similar abuse. There is significant healing in knowing that you are not alone.

Telling your story gives you the opportunity to receive understanding and empathy, which is another powerful salve for the suffering you have endured. I believe that all survivors, including you, deserve support and encouragement. Sharing your story with people who care about you helps you end the "death sentence" of your isolation and begins your healing process. It also gives the child inside you who experienced the abuse (if you were abused as a child)—or your adult self who was assaulted—an opportunity to have the truth acknowledged. This is necessary for the abused part of you, which may live in darkness and be desperate for the light of hope.

EXPERIMENT WITH NEW POSSIBILITIES:
Exploring Reasons to Tell Your Story

Take out your journal or notebook, and write at the top of a page "Reasons to Tell My Story." Then take a moment to list those reasons.

At the top of another page, write the heading "Reasons to Keep My Story to Myself." Then make a list of any reasons you have for doing so.

When you have completed both lists, ask yourself, *What am I feeling inside?* How does it feel to read the list of reasons to tell? How does it feel to read the list of reasons to keep it to yourself? Be aware that these lists may well change as you read this chapter and learn about the experiences of survivors who have chosen to share their stories.

Next I share with you the Silence Breakers' best reasons for telling their stories instead of keeping them secret. As you are going along, ask whether their reasons and outcomes resonate with you.

You may think, *I'd like that as an outcome.* And you may think, *Wow, that's how I have felt, too* or *I'd like to feel that way after telling my story.* Remember, these men are just like you, so if you hear yourself saying, *That's fine for them, but I'm different,* I invite you to challenge that idea with tools I will provide you in the pages ahead.

SILENCE BREAKERS' BEST ADVICE:
TELLING YOUR STORY

Jarrod and Bruce share several very powerful reasons for telling their stories: love and support, freedom, strength, and more fulfilling relationships.

For 30 years, I firmly believed that telling anyone my story would mean that terrible things would happen. I was never exactly sure what the terrible things would be, but I was convinced that my world as I knew it would end and that I might even die. When I actually told my story to a wider audience of friends, family, and my community, I was most struck by the reality that bad things did not happen. In fact, almost every reaction was of love and support. This was the most free-ing experience of my life. It became clear to me that the premise I lived under most of my life had been a lie. The 30 years of fear, anxiety, and pain of living with my dark secret were over. — Jarrod

Telling my story has been extremely important in my recovery. It has made it more of a "story"—and less horrific for me. I have found a massive amount of strength in telling my story when it might comfort someone else. Perhaps most important, it has made my relationships with friends, family, and others much stronger and more fulfilling. — Bruce

I trust that you will enjoy learning about the following rewards Chris, Ken, and Mike discovered, because these rewards led them to contribute to this book. Their rewards include feeling freer and reclaiming power from the perpetrators and putting the shame on them, where it belongs.

Initially I told my story of abuse because I wanted to explain to others I trusted why I had trouble dating, why I didn't approach women, and why I no longer felt confident. I needed to get across that I struggled with things like trust, being hurt, intimacy, anger, and the like. After sharing the first few times, I began to feel liber-ated, and then came empowerment the more I challenged myself to share. The weight that has been lifted from me through sharing has allowed me to thrive in a manner that I couldn't have anticipated. By letting go of the secret, I become stronger. The power the perpe-trator once had over me is now becoming rightfully mine. — Chris

Telling my story was an important part of realizing that the shame I felt was not mine. It was amazing to me that when I spoke of the abuse, I was never asked, "Why did you let that happen?" When my story was a secret, the shame was always all mine. Refusing to keep the secret enabled me to place the shame where it always belonged: on the shoulders of the abusers. — Ken

The best reason is to get it out. Telling someone is very freeing, even if it doesn't go perfectly. Keeping it a secret only protects the "perp," not you. Another great reason for telling your story is that you will find people like you, and that's worth its weight in gold. — Mike

Christopher, John, and Gregg echo the previous comments about feeling more powerful after ending their silence. In addition, they say that telling their stories has increased their ability to be more connected and intimate with the important people in their lives.

Speaking the truth of what happened to me reduces its power over me. Every time I have told my story in one form or another, a little more of the shame flakes away. I wish I could say that once you tell it, all the shame disappears, but that would make the act of sharing the only thing needed in order to heal. Obviously it takes so much more. Telling my story in the right place (by "right place," I mean a place of healing, with a supportive and receptive audience) opens me up in a healthy way and gives me the experience of connecting in a healthy and healing way with others. — Christopher

I tell my story to inform people about the lifelong deleterious effects of abuse. By sharing my story, I demonstrate that I have gotten beyond the shame of being abused and that you can, too. I also tell my story to say to abuse victims that they are not alone and that recovery is possible. I now lead a life that is vastly improved over my pre-recovery life. — John

I just had to get it out! I was so angry. I was a kid who constantly got into fights, yet I was a good kid and played sports. The trouble is, I grew up on a diet of sex and violence. I told two relatives at the time of my abuse, and nothing ever happened. I discovered that telling my story does free me up, even if people don't understand fully because they've never been through it. I am working to change the perception of me as the icy-cold guy, which is how I can come across. I want people to get to know me as a warmer and friendlier guy, and telling my story is an important part of that process. — Gregg

In the case of SJC, he makes it clear that keeping his story to himself was his major "undoing." He offers a powerful list of all the things he cheated himself out of by not telling his story.

Keeping my story a secret was my undoing. Pretending or deceiving myself that it was all no big deal was the equivalent of putting my head in the sand or in some other dark place. Telling my story enabled me to hear others' stories, feel others' pain, seek therapy and other help, feel my pain, learn about all the information available to deal with the trauma—childhood mislearning, enmeshment, boundaries, intimacy, and the list goes on—learn about MaleSurvivor and all that it has to offer, begin the process of healing, eradicate the shame, and "man up"—stand up and speak out against the epidemic of abuse in this country. There's no healing in hiding. — SJC

Factors That Can Make It Easier to Tell

Whom do you tell? As you reflect on this question, consider especially the people to whom you gave a green light on your list at the end of Chapter 3.

As you think about telling the story of the abuse you suffered, how does it feel to consider sharing it with these green-light people? Consider how they tend to respond when you share a problem or concern with them. If, in general, you have felt safe, affirmed, and nurtured by them in other discussions, it's likely that they would be safe people with whom to share some aspect of your story.

If you have no green-light people on your list, you may need to choose a professional person or consider someone with a yellow-light designation. In the case of a yellow-light person, I'd suggest experimenting with less risky content to see how the individual handles less sensitive disclosures.

A professional person, such as a psychotherapist or a clergyperson, may also be a good choice; however, feel free to take your time in revealing your story. If you can identify another survivor who is willing to listen, that person can be very helpful as long as he or she is on a healthy path of recovery.

EXPERIMENT WITH NEW POSSIBILITIES: Whom Would You Like to Tell?

Make a list in your journal of any person who you believe may be a safe audience for sharing your story. Just as in Chapter 3, you may want to create a green-light list and a yellow-light list. How does it feel to read over this list of names? Allow yourself to picture each person, and to trust that every person on the green-light list is actually willing and able to hear your story and to give you the support you deserve. What is it like to think about where you are now and where you might be if you were able to receive all of this support?

Next, the Silence Breakers share with you their experiences in deciding whom to tell. They have suggestions for distinguishing between those who are safe enough and those who may not be so safe.

SILENCE BREAKERS' BEST ADVICE: Deciding Whom to Tell

Alexander suggests using caution, especially with regard to your privacy, because he believes it can be empowering:

I believe that sharing your story, although a very empowering experience, must be done with tact and caution. Always seek to share with someone who has a healthy morality and a strong sense of self-worth. This is a person who recognizes that there's a time and place to share information or discuss certain topics. This person has a clear understanding of the differences between acquaintances and friends, and acknowledges that not all information is to be shared with everyone. This person fully understands that secrets between friends remain between friends so that you won't have to worry about your information coming back to you through a third party. — Alexander

Rhett has had many positive experiences, first in telling just a few people and eventually in disclosing his abuse on national television. Each positive experience gave him confidence to tell the next person. It helped that he started with the people who were closest to him.

Deciding whom to tell is like no other decision I have ever made. It wasn't like shopping for a car or some other item. In the early stages, the perception that you will be shunned is so at the surface that you really debate yourself about whom to tell.

I told my girlfriend, who became my wife, because I decided I wanted to be in a relationship instead of running from one as I had done previously. She was the very first person I ever told. I decided to tell my best friend, because I had just entered into therapy and was proud and scared of what I was about to do; since I knew him so well, I knew I could trust him. I told my parents when I was about to file paperwork against my abuser, because it was in the township where it happened and that was where my parents still lived. Eventually, I told many people, because I was about to disclose my abuse on national television and didn't want people to hear it from another source before hearing it from me. [Rhett was featured telling parts of his story on the Oprah "200 Men" episode, which he'll describe in more detail in Chapter 14.]

By the time all of that happened, though, I was above the feeling of shame and was quite confident that I had nothing to be ashamed of, because I was, in fact, just a little boy at the time all of that happened. — Rhett

Christopher writes that deciding whom to tell is about getting himself ready and being clear about motivations:

> *Too often, I would open up too quickly. If I believed I could trust someone enough, I told my story, believing that I had to explain why I was a little odd. This was not a good strategy. Soon I learned that most people simply don't know how to accept or process that information. Later, I learned that it's important to share in the right place at the right time.*
>
> *The right place is one with one or more receptive and support-ive listeners. The right time is when space for this story has been made. It does little good and can sometimes harm a survivor to share too much, too soon. The motive behind sharing one's story should be to get help, not to simply unburden one's secrets onto someone else. I think it's really important for survivors to know that just telling someone your story doesn't necessarily mean that you are doing healing work. — Christopher*

Pierre, like Christopher, writes about checking inside to determine whether he feels safe enough to tell. Howie writes that he had to feel safe and trusting enough to tell. He relates that telling his story sooner might have helped him stop abusing himself.

> *When I decided to tell my wife, it was during the Weekend of Recovery. I realized that it was something I needed to do. It just felt right: the right time and place. I gave her a few requests to help me, and off I went. The second time, I was meeting a fellow survivor who needed someone to talk to other than his wife or therapist. While we were having coffee, he started asking me questions and finally asked me if I would tell him my story. It felt safe and natu-ral, so I did. I knew that I had my wife waiting for me at home if I needed her. I also checked in with myself to make sure I was ready and willing to do this. — Pierre*
>
> *I first told my wife (girlfriend at the time). She was the first woman I really got to know well. Once I felt that I could trust her and open up, I told her. It was an amazing relief and one of the few times when I completely bawled as an adult. I then confronted my*

abuser and told my parents. Years went by without my telling any-one close to me (except guys I'd met through MaleSurvivor). I told another friend here and another friend there, and finally I decided to go on the Oprah show. I then felt compelled to send an e-mail to most of my friends. It's hard to say that I "decided" to tell. It was just time, and I couldn't hold it in anymore. I wish I had told my story years ago instead of continuing to abuse myself in my head. — Howie

Preparing to Tell Your Story

How can you decide when in the recovery process to tell your story? As I said earlier, telling your story is not a one-time occurrence. And you probably will find that each time you share it, you will tell it differently. Since we have established the advantages of telling your story, it's likely that telling your story is a good idea throughout your recovery process. For the first telling, it's important for you to have identified as safe a person as possible. Also, you should negotiate with the person to set aside a block of time (at least an hour) and find a place where you can feel as safe as possible.

Since your abuse left you feeling powerless, it's very important that you are in control of how, when, and to whom you tell your story. For most men, this means telling your story in a private place where distractions are unlikely to occur. Be sure you've both turned off your cell phones. Pick comfortable chairs to sit in. Decide how close you want the other person to sit, but make sure you can maintain eye contact and be heard without straining.

EXPERIMENT WITH NEW POSSIBILITIES:
Getting Emotionally Ready to Tell Your Story

I'd encourage you to take some time in advance to consider how you will tell your story. During the Weekends of Recovery, every man is assigned to a small group of seven participants and two facilitators. Before the actual storytelling sessions on Saturday morning, we assemble all the groups and brainstorm to help each man prepare to tell his story. In any brainstorming exercise, all answers are right, because each is a reflection of the person's truths and experiences.

Next is a series of statements for you to complete to help you assess how prepared you are to tell your story. The statements will help you identify the things you are most concerned about. They will also help you think about what you need from the person to whom you decide to tell your story. No matter how carefully you have picked the person and how ready you think you are to share, some stress is normal.

The first few statements are designed to help you think about your fears and your coping mechanisms. Then you'll be asked to complete sentences that are specifically about telling the story of your abuse. I recommend writing your responses in your journal so that you can refer to them later.

- *When I'm afraid, I . . .*
- *When I feel safe, I . . .*
- *One way I've coped with stress in the past was . . .*
- *One way I deal with stress that I find helpful is . . .*
- *Letting people see the real me means . . .*
- *Letting people know me feels . . .*
- *Telling the story of my abuse means that I . . .*

- *If I tell you the story of the abuse I experienced, I . . .*
- *What most pisses me off about telling my story is . . .*
- *What really hurts about telling my story is . . .*
- *The way I'll most likely protect myself when I'm telling my story is . . .*
- *The way I might try to hide when I'm telling my story is . . .*
- *The reaction I'm most afraid I'll get when I tell my story is . . .*
- *If I remember to breathe, I will . . .*
- *Knowing that I'm in a safe place as I tell my story means . . .*
- *The reaction I most hope for when I tell my story is . . .*
- *I want my witness to know that when I tell my story . . .*
- *After I tell my story, my inner child will most likely . . .*

Use these statements if you have told your story in the past:

- *When I have told the story of my abuse in the past, . . .*
- *What I learned from telling my story in the past that I want to remember this time is . . .*

After you have completed each statement, take a moment to reflect on what you are aware of feeling in your body, in your mind, and in your emotions.

Remember, anything you are experiencing is okay to acknowledge, explore, and learn from. If you like, you can write your observations in your journal.

Next I will describe the suggestions we give to the men at the Weekends of Recovery for telling their stories. Keep in mind that during these weekends, they each tell a group of six other guys. You can use these same ideas as you prepare to tell one person in your life who doesn't yet know the story of your abuse. I'd love for you to have the experience of telling your story at a WOR or in some other setting with a group of survivors. But before you can be ready to tell your story in a group, the first step is to tell your story to one person at a time.

On Saturday mornings, right after our brainstorming exercise, each man goes to his small group and tells the story of his abuse. In WOR, we give each man 12 minutes to do so. It's interesting to hear the reactions when we set the time limit. Some think that's entirely too long, while others say it's impossible to tell their stories in such a brief period. We've conducted more than 40 weekends and have found that 12 minutes is enough for most beginners.

During the storytelling, we suggest that no one ask questions, and I'd recommend that strategy to you as well. Taking questions tends to throw off most of the men who are trying to tell their stories, and some just shut down if interrupted. You can offer to respond to questions once you are done, but you always have the right to decline to answer any of them. After you tell your story, you may want to share additional information, especially if the response is positive and supportive. Setting a time limit helps you structure what you say, and makes the experience less intimidating.

We also tell the guys it's okay to use all 12 minutes or less time. Ask your witness if he or she would be willing to keep track of the time for you. For many men, they like to have a two-minute warning that the time is nearing an end. Just holding up fingers is usually enough of a warning. At the 12-minute mark, your witness can simply say, "Thank you; your time is up." If you have a lot more to share, you can choose to add to your story after processing what you experienced in the initial disclosure, while also giving your listener an opportunity to process his or her reaction as well.

Here are the instructions we give each man:

1. This is your story. There's no right or wrong way to tell it. The story can have many components, including:

- How your life was prior to your abuse
- What was done to you, who abused you, how long it lasted, and how many instances of abuse there were
- How you felt during and after the abuse
- The impact of the abuse on your life
- Whether or not you told anyone about the abuse
- The steps you have taken to heal from the abuse

Here are a few other tips:

- Monitor your breathing to stay as relaxed as possible while you tell your story.
- Take as many breaks as you need.
- Be aware of your feelings as you tell your story.
- Give yourself permission to pause, be tearful, or feel your emotions, including anger. That's expected. It's your right, and it's entirely human.

2. Be prepared for inner alarms that tell you to stop sharing. Part of you may be holding on to the belief that the perpetrator is still a threat or even still deserving of loyalty and protection. You may also have doubts that your listener wants to hear your story.

3. After each man tells his story, we invite him to look around at the other survivors and the facilitators in the room. For many, it's very hard to look into the faces of their listeners after they tell their stories. I usually suggest that they do that, and I suggest you do that, too. Looking into the face of your listener after he or she hears your story is important for several reasons. First, it can

help you release some of your shame. Second, most often, men see compassion, warmth, and acceptance, rather than the dreaded rejection and disgust they expect to see, which is a huge relief.

4. When you are finished, take time to check how you are feeling. Before answering any questions, you may want to take a few minutes to relax your breathing and reestablish your sense of inner safety. You may want to express your gratitude to your listener and invite him or her to offer thoughts and feelings about your story.

As for how much physical contact you want after sharing your story, this varies tremendously from man to man. Do what's most comfortable for you. Your listener may want to hug you, but if that makes you uncomfortable, feel free to say so. Many men feel very vulnerable after they have shared their stories. Some experience flashback emotions of fear and shame, and the desire to isolate themselves as a protective measure.

Even if this is the case for you, I'd encourage you to make eye contact with your listener and to remind yourself that telling your story is part of the healing process. Then take a minute to feel good about yourself. It takes courage to make this big step! Ask yourself what additional support you need right now. Some men feel the need to go for a walk and be alone. Some want to do some type of nurturing activity, like journaling, listening to music, or being creative.

SILENCE BREAKERS' BEST ADVICE:
How to Prepare to Tell Your Story

The Silence Breakers share their thoughts on the steps that they believe will help prepare you to tell your story to someone other than a therapist. As you read, you will notice that they have received positive, negative, and neutral responses to telling their stories. They want you to be prepared for the full gamut of possibilities.

Earlier in the book, I discussed the importance of establishing inner and external safety. Here, Bruce and Rhett describe their methods for establishing a sense of inner safety.

It's very important to ask yourself why you want to tell a specific person. If the reasons are comfortable for you, then go ahead. Remember that people who have not been through abuse may not respond as you would like. Maybe they don't understand, are shocked, or don't know what to say. Be prepared for a not-so-supportive reaction. I have told my story to people who had almost a nonreaction, because they were simply trying to process it in their heads. I needed to respect that they needed time to figure it out. — Bruce

Before I choose to tell a person about my history of abuse, I assess how this person is connected to me. I prepare myself for how I feel that this person will react. The first 15 seconds of any uncomfortable conversation is the worst part of it. After that, it does get easier. I believe that even more important than preparing to tell someone is being prepared for how you may feel afterward. I make sure to take a moment for myself to collect my thoughts and think about how what I just shared benefits me. — Rhett

Christopher and Rob write of honoring your truth and all the feelings connected to the truth. Christopher also describes how to be compassionate and kind to yourself. Rob reminds you that your goal is to become free.

First, respect that a part of you has been deeply hurt, and honor that part of yourself. The child or man inside you who was harmed in the past will continue to struggle with the pain until you give yourself permission to honor that pain in this present moment. Understand that you can set the limits for what you want to share, at your pace. The important thing is to continue, when the time is right, to try to tell someone you trust (besides a therapist) the whole story. Reward and treat the brave child inside you who comes forward to speak the truth, no matter how painful. — Christopher

Acceptance—once you have accepted that you are ready to venture into this brave new world, accept that it will be at alternate times joyful, sad, painful, and morose. Then realize that it will ultimately be liberating. Keep in mind why you want to heal, to fight through the pain; despair; anger; grief; and myriad other emotions, feelings, and events that you've experienced over the years. The goal or desire should be to live life in a free and unfettered fashion. You deserve nothing less! — Rob

Howie offers great advice for recognizing that while you may fear your friends' reactions to your story, those fears are usually not grounded in the reality of how they respond.

In my mind, I imagine, when I tell someone about the abuse, that that person will run away after finding out who I really am, or be unable to handle it. When I let people know of the abuse, it shatters all of the walls I have built up around me. Realize that your (good and true) friends are your friends, and they are compassionate human beings, complete opposites of those who abused you. They will be there for good and bad, and it's usually never as bad as you think it will be. On the other hand, in my experiences in talking with family about the abuse, I usually encounter a "get over it" type of response. That's usually the hardest to deal with. — Howie

I want to assure you that you can have all the support you want and need, and that you deserve to fully recover. Telling the story of your abuse can absolutely help you to no longer feel alone.

EXPERIMENT WITH NEW POSSIBILITIES: Next Steps in Telling Your Story

Think about the people to whom you have told your story, and write down their names. Then make a list in your journal of any additional people with whom you want to also share your truth. Take your time, inviting them one by one to join you for an hour so that you can become closer and let them know you better. Journal your reactions after each disclosure.

Each time, check in with yourself about the level of shame you are feeling. My goal is to help you feel less and less responsible for any abuse that was done to you, and more and more deserving of all the support you receive.

Next, two Silence Breakers share how they have successfully told their stories. Learning from them can be a key aspect of your own successful disclosure. As you read these successful sharing stories, you will find some listeners reacted in ways that were not what the survivor wanted to hear. It's significant that the survivors needed to take time with the listener to process the experience of sharing and hearing the story.

SILENCE BREAKERS' BEST ADVICE:
Successfully Telling Your Story

First, read about Bruce's experience of what helped him, what shocked him, and how even a good experience still left him feeling somewhat frustrated:

> Telling my parents my story of abuse was interesting. I went to their house, sat them down, and told them what had happened to me and what was going on now (criminal charges against the perpetrator, a huge legal battle). My mother said, "We thought something happened with that coach-doctor." I reacted very strongly and was upset and angry. As it turns out, my parents had been afraid to confront the perpetrator, because he was such an influential person in the community. They decided not to ask me about it, because they didn't know what to say.
>
> I told them that this was a big mistake and that I wish they had sat me down and tried to connect with me. I don't know if I would have been able to tell them, but I would have remembered their trying rather than doing nothing. Later in the conversation, it came out that a clergy member had sexually abused my father when he was a boy. My mother had no idea about this and was shocked. My father said

that it happened years ago and he had just tried to forget about it and "get over it" on his own. Considering that my father had always had aggression issues and had been physically abusive to us kids, it really explained so much about his behavior over the years. When I left my parents' home, I was relieved to have told them and wished I had told them years earlier. I did, however, feel frustrated and annoyed that they had held these suspicions and not done anything about them. — Bruce

Ryan offers his own testimony to the power of speaking your secret, even though you may fear a disastrous outcome. As often happens, Ryan feared he might be challenged or criticized, but instead he was encouraged and supported.

When I first started to confront my issues of childhood sexual abuse by my mother, intense feelings of shame made me hesitant to tell anyone. I had a false belief that if I even shared my story of abuse with my family, I would be met with hostility.

When I decided to talk openly to my dad, he and my mom had been divorced for a couple of years. My dad knew I'd been seeing a counselor, but he didn't know why. One evening, I summoned my courage and explained that I had been recalling disturbing, repressed memories that had thrown me into a state of clinical depression. I described how the repressed memories brought me back to when I was five or six, when my mother had begun to perpetrate sexual abuse. He listened closely and responded that he was glad I told him. He explained that he'd been concerned but hadn't wanted to pry. He said he "could see how something like that could have happened." He described a couple of occasions when my mother had said odd and inappropriate things about my appearance or my body.

At that moment, a flood of feelings rushed in, but first and foremost, I'd gained a new advocate, someone who could relate to me. Second, it was a relief to hear firsthand that my memories and anxious feelings were not imaginary. In short, it felt risky to share my story with my dad, but in the end, it strengthened our relationship, provided a new source of support, and helped me believe I had someone I could confide in. — Ryan

Take time now to affirm your right to get support when you share your story. For the next chapter, I invited all of the Silence Breakers to share *their* stories with you. This may be one of the toughest chapters in the book, which is why I have presented you with a number of skills you can use to help yourself cope with hearing the details of their stories. Most likely, you will find something of yourself in the upcoming stories, and if so, remind yourself that you have support and someone who can understand your experience. I hope you will hear in these stories the message that healing is absolutely possible for you.

AFFIRMATIONS FOR CHAPTER 5

- *I am worthy of sharing the story of my abuse today and letting go of my shame.*

- *I dare to dream I am worthy of receiving all the support I need as I tell the story of my abuse.*

- *I am much more than the story of my abuse: I am a strong and courageous man now.*

CHAPTER SIX

Dare to Dream You Can Learn From the Experiences of Other Male Survivors

"At the age of seven or eight, I was sitting with a small group of adults, including my parents, when I had the distinct feeling that I was wearing a mask and no one could see me. I have gone through life wearing a mask until I finally realized what I was doing. This shirt is the result of that insight."
Designer: John Walker, Silence Breaker.

This may seem unusual, but I advise you to be selective about which of the Silence Breaker stories you read in this chapter, because some are quite disturbing. You might even want to take several days and read the chapter in sections so that the material doesn't overwhelm you. I advise against reading the entire chapter straight through in one sitting. You will again read about the men who have agreed to share the stories of their recoveries. I wish I had room for all of their stories; however, I will share enough details about all of them to convey the courage they've shown in their efforts to reclaim their lives.

I asked them to write a few sentences about what they hope you might learn from each of them. You might use these introductions to help you decide which stories you want to read. Please also see my warning just below so that you can choose whether to read graphic stories or skip over them. I've added my own comments to help you learn and benefit from their experiences and insights.

As you read their stories, remember all that I have shared with you about establishing a sense of inner and external safety. Decide whether you want to read a few stories, many of the stories, all the stories, or perhaps none at all. It's totally up to you whether you read any of them and how you do so. What's important is to monitor your response and feelings as you read. Remember to relax your breathing.

Warning: Many of these stories are very graphic, and I have chosen to empower the contributors of this book by allowing them to explicitly tell the details of their abuse. You will likely have strong reactions to these stories. Please be gentle with yourself. It can be very disturbing to read another survivor's story, especially if you relate strongly to it. In reality, any story of sexual abuse or assault is graphic. However, many of these contain explicit details. I want you to feel empowered to decide if you want to read them. You have permission and every right to put down this book and stop reading at any time. You may want to pause now and then to take some centering breaths or do six-directions breathing as described in Chapter 2.

What might you learn? I hope you will learn that survivors have a great deal of resiliency. They've endured great trauma, but through persevering, getting psychotherapy, and reaching out for needed support, they came through feeling hopeful, healthier, and, in many cases, even stronger, because they now have much more inner strength and a sense of pride and determination. I hope you will learn that you are not alone in the suffering you have experienced, even though it may be painful to know that someone else suffered as you did.

Self-Care Time:
Relaxation Breathing and Gauging Your Reactions

After you read each story, I include a reminder to take some self-care time. Remember, this is not a race or a competition. Recovery is a long process, and each step of the way, each time you honor your feelings and honor your truth, you are taking steps to heal.

The following are my suggestions for how to use this time to be compassionate and gentle with yourself:

- Take some slow, deep, healing breaths and let yourself know that it's okay to feel whatever you are feeling.

- Revisit the meditation where you breathe in healing energy from the center of the earth, or perhaps just practice Paul Linden's six-directions breathing (review Chapter 2).

- Spend some time journaling about any aspects of the stories you relate to.

❀   ❀   ❀

To begin, you might just glance over the title of each story and perhaps its introduction, note a few titles that resonate with you, and read those stories first. You can go back to the others later.

The first story, by Rhett, reveals a fairly typical experience of male abuse by a respected person in the community, who gains the trust of his victims by offering them all sorts of special gifts in exchange for their silence. This process, as I explained earlier, is called "grooming," and often results in the survivor feeling loyal to the perpetrator for years. Often, abused men grow up in homes where there are many parental problems, including addictions, physical abuse, continuous conflict, separation, and divorce. Rhett's family didn't fit the usual profile in that regard, but he was made vulnerable by a perpetrator who groomed him. His story is graphic.

Rhett's Story: A Planted Seed

"My title references what my perpetrator did to me at a young age, and that was plant a seed. That seed would rest within me, prevented from growing because of the strength I possessed in my 20s to deliberately block out, or not tend to, what happened to me at age 12. Unfortunately, my doing this allowed the seed to anchor itself within me, only to sprout when I was 30, at which time it took hold of what little self-worth I had.

"Now, the title of my story references the seeds that I plant by telling my story to others. My hope is that I can plant more good seeds than bad, and help other men reach the point of admitting to carrying planted seeds and encourage them to plant more posi-tive ones."

I grew up at the Jersey Shore, in a very small community in Forked River. I had a stay-at-home mom and a working father, who are still married to each other to this day, and both were very active in my life. I grew up in the typical suburban, middle-class family living at the shore.

My abuser was a summertime resident who owned a shore house and came down on weekends and periods of weeks in the summer. He integrated himself into the community, and because it was small, everybody knew each other and mostly trusted one another. He began the grooming process, which con-sisted of letting kids (me included) come over to his house. He would take us to Atlantic City, let us play with his granddaugh-ter, take us out on his boat, let us have things that he planned to sell at a yard sale, and let us smoke inside his house while we played cards. Sometimes he would let us drink a little alcohol.

He then showed me where he kept his collection of porno magazines, and after a period of time, he put the moves on me by asking me if I ever messed around. He assured me that this was what guys and boys did but that we had to keep it a secret or we would get into trouble. For a period of four and a half years (from when I was ages 12 to 17), he proceeded to have me perform oral sex on him. He also performed it on me, penetrated me anally, shoved a bar of soap up my rectum, urinated on me, and made me eat his semen and mine. He would shove his dirty fingers into my mouth to help get him "hard." One time he "jerked" me off so much that he rubbed my skin raw. During this incident, his girlfriend walked in on us, and yet she never said anything. This is what I have publicly called the "double betrayal."

After I got my license at age 17, he asked me to take him for a ride in my car. He leaned over to grab me in my crotch area, his common way of demonstrating to me that he wanted to abuse me. I put my hand on his and told him that I couldn't do that stuff anymore, and that was how the abuse ended. My response came from the "double betrayal," because he had always told me that we would get in trouble if anyone found out and that never happened. I had started to think that if it were normal for guys and boys to do this, as he had said it was, then why would we get into trouble? It was from there that I found the strength to stop the abuse. But to break his emotional hold on me, I had to become much stronger later in life.

The experience of "double betrayal" is especially important to highlight, because it can make you quite confused. You know or sense that the perpetrator is doing something wrong that hurts you. Then, when someone else whom you should be able to trust to protect you finds out about the abuse and does nothing, your trust is betrayed a second time. The message you hear is that you are not being hurt or else that person would help you, yet you know that you are being hurt and that what's being done to you is wrong. You don't have the power to stop it. Rhett describes how this double betrayal actually helped him confront the lies he had been told and eventually put a stop to the abuse. As you read in his introduction and as you will read throughout this book, Rhett has worked through a great deal of his abuse so that now he can claim that he is thriving.

---ᏋᏋ---

Self-Care Time

---ᏋᏋ---

Alexander's story is graphic and emotionally disturbing, because he was prostituted by his own father and completely neglected by his mother. It's a story of abuse that was perpetrated over a very long time, from ages 3 to 18. He recalled his earliest memories during hypnosis, but unfortunately he remembers most of it because he was subjected to this suffering every weekend and, often, several times per weekend. Sometimes people don't understand why a boy would "return" to be abused. Hopefully, hearing Alexander's story will help you understand that this boy—like all victims of abuse—had no power in the situation.

Alexander's Story:
"Building Blocks, Lollipops, and Daddy's Bitch"

"The story you are about to read is the greatest inhumanity that a parent can inflict on a child. It is a story of pure horror, and you will likely find it very disturbing. It was difficult to write, let alone recall from memory. I pray to God you cannot relate to this story, but if you relate to any part of it, know that I survived this routine torture and gross neglect. Know that you, too, can overcome whatever horrors you are currently experiencing. Know that I am more powerful now in being able to speak these words and in telling you the absolute truth about what I endured for most of my childhood. Today, I am a thriver and a survivor, and I hope to inspire you so that you, too, can thrive no matter what horrors you have suffered."

Building blocks and lollipops were all that I was aware of at three years old, but I would soon learn much darker things from my biological father. As I sat in my room on a red oval, coil-rope rug playing with my ABC blocks, my father walked past my room stumbling in his drunken stupor. He looked at me in disgust and came into my room and said, "You think you something, don't you, nigger. You think you something because she loves you [referring to my mother]. Well, she is mine, and you just a little bitch. That right, you a little bitch-ass." He started taunting me as a child does a cat, saying, "Here, little bitchy, bitchy, bitchy."

Suddenly, as I tried to escape, he grasped me by the back of the neck and told me, "Come here, you little bitch mother-fucker." As I struggled to break away, my father pulled out his flaccid penis. He dug his fingernails into my cheeks and forced himself into my mouth. He told me, "If you bite me, you little faggot, I will kill you. Suck! You little bitch-ass faggot." So I did, while the stench of penis and beer filled my nose. After he ejaculated in my mouth, I was thrown into his orange Ford truck with the beige top and told, "Shut the fuck up and stop all that crying. I knew you were a faggot bitch."

As I wiped the tears away in fear for my life, we soon pulled up to a house I had never seen before. I was dragged into the house and thrown on the sofa. My father and a man I had also never seen started a conversation over why I was brought to the house. It was soon revealed that I was there as payment for my father's drug fix. My father knew that he "like them young boys, nigger. I seen you fucking with them. I'll report your ass if you don't take him." My father announced my price, just as he would for the next decade, as "a nickel bag of weed and four lines of blow," and the exchange was complete. The drug dealer took me in the back and stripped me naked. He kissed me with dead-rotten breath and licked my entire body. I felt sick and disgusted with every touch and taste. He then climbed on top of me and began to grind his rock-hard penis on me as I cried a river of tears. Once my father had finished his last line of cocaine and started smoking his first blunt, I was taken back out to the living room. The drug dealer pulled down my father's pants and started to have anal sex with him in his drugged-out state. I was grabbed by the head and forced to lick the drug dealer's anus as he screwed my father. He then flipped my father on his back, and I was, again, forcibly made to suck my father's penis as the drug dealer viciously screwed my father. Once they were done, I was put between both of them as they ejaculated on my face and head.

This was the first experience of the most horrific period of my life that lasted until I was 18 years old, when I physically left the place of my birth. You see, my father hated me because my mother loved me. He did not see me as his son but as competition for my mother's love. Therefore, he did everything in his power to belittle and degrade me in order to destroy my self-esteem and make my mother hate me. When you go through something this traumatic at such a young age, it is imprinted and burned into your mind. This is one of the hardest stories I have ever had to write in my life, and I would not wish this experience on my worst enemy.

It has been a hard road, but I have overcome so much. After years of frustration, depression, job loss, and four suicide attempts, the only thing that brought me out was the fact that transpersonal psychology, spirituality, and metaphysics were dealing with my spirit as well as my mind. For me, true healing took place through forgiveness, responsibility, and loving myself. By understanding how my mind sets itself up for failure because of the abuse, I could heal through a better understanding of my one-on-one connection with God.

This is indeed a nightmare that Alexander endured for practically his entire childhood. I call this type of abuse "torture." He was totally dependent on his father to care for him, but his father was horribly neglectful and abusive, even selling his own son to be his drug dealer's "bitch." And to make matters worse, Alexander is sure that his mother knew, and she not only did not protect him, but instead added her own physical and emotional abuse.

The long-lasting effects of abuse were amplified by the years of severe psychological problems he suffered. He nearly died in his efforts to heal. Take heart in Alexander's belief that recovery is possible for you, too, when you deal with all of the parts of you that need healing. For you, like others, that will require addressing your thought processes and the spiritual part of you that also was abused.

Self-Care Time

Several of the Silence Breakers were sexually abused by their mothers. There's a common misunderstanding in our culture that only men prey on boys, but this is far from true. Many survivors of abuse by women have struggled with shame, because in our culture, men are always supposed to control women, so for a woman to abuse a boy or man is very shameful.

SJC, whose story you will read later, told me about covert sexual abuse by his mother, or what psychotherapists call "mother-son enmeshment." In this form of sexual abuse, a mother uses her son to replace the role her husband is supposed to play. It's not unusual for a mother to engage in both covert incest, as SJC describes, and overt sexual abuse. There are a couple of other examples of this later.

There has been controversy in the media about repressed memories. Some claim that therapists plant false memories about abuse. SJC told me that he didn't recover his memories until he retired at age 60. Ken told me that he didn't recall until much later in life that he'd been abused by several uncles and family friends.

Repressed memories surface when a survivor feels safe enough to remember, usually when he has adequate emotional support and often only with the help of a trained psychotherapist. It's absolutely true that a man can repress the memories of his abuse, and for many, it's the only way they survived, because recalling the memories earlier in their lives would have been too painful. Repression is a defense mechanism that saves someone from too much pain. Most abuse survivors remember when they are psychologically ready to remember, and no experienced psychotherapist would even attempt to create traumatic memories, much less create the symptoms that typically result from experiencing such trauma.

A skilled therapist can help a survivor reclaim traumatic memories and understand them from an adult perspective. You will read in Ryan's story how he protected himself internally until he was ready. Ryan is also unique in this book in that he was raised as a Mormon, a religious tradition where rules and roles are rigidly defined, and being loyal to your family and religious authorities is of utmost importance. Because he was abused by his mother, this made confronting the truth of his abuse extremely difficult. He is also another one of our gay Silence Breakers. You will read about his partner Troy's experience later in this book.

Ryan's Story: "A Journey from Repressed Memories, Depression, and Anxiety to a Glimpse of a World Changed from Dull Gray to Technicolor"

"I'd like people to learn these things from my story: There are men out there who are recovering from abuse by a female perpetrator; you're not alone. Talking with a trusted counselor, friend, or family member is the best medicine. Fear can prevent the start of your healing process. Once you start a dialogue and get your story out into the light, much of the fearful emotion withers. During your recovery, your boundaries are always valid—no matter what."

My sexual abuse history might be considered different for a couple of reasons. One is that it's not something I grew up remembering or suffering from during childhood. In fact, I recall people telling me in my teenage years how carefree and positive I seemed. Another reason is that my perpetrator was a woman—my mother, in fact.

When I was in my mid-30s, I started to become concerned that my dating relationships with women were going nowhere. Every relationship consistently started to suffer when we began expressing normal physical affection. I grew up in a Mormon family where it was normal not to have sexual relations until marriage, and any expression of affection in a dating situation beyond a simple hug or kiss was discouraged.

Time and time again with each relationship, even the thought of holding hands or being alone with a woman when there was the potential for affection became uncomfortable for me and resulted in extreme anxiety. I'd cope with my feelings by keeping relationships as superficial as possible while avoiding situations where I'd have to be alone with my date.

At that time, I also had an uncomfortable relationship with my mother. From my teenage years onward, I don't recall any overt sexual advances on her part. I do recall feeling uneasy with the way she'd greet me with a hug, a wink, or a "love pat," as she called it. These were usually little pats on the backside, accompanied by a wink or a glance.

Her acts of affection at that point in my life never went over the line to something anyone would consider obviously inappropriate, but they felt horrible to me. I started counseling with a family therapist recommended by the bishop from my Mormon congregation. After a few weeks, my counselor and I discovered through various means that I had repressed memories of sexual abuse by my mother. I relived memories of being with my mother in her bedroom, where she was in various stages of undress and I was either encouraged or forced to look at her.

I also vividly recalled a recurring scene in which I was playing in the backyard when I was between ages six and eight. The sound of the sliding back door and the knowledge that she was coming toward me would shock me into the realization that something horrible was about to happen. When she approached me, I would "black out" and only see a gray static image similar to the noise on a TV screen with no signal. After a while, the gray static would disappear, and I'd once again see the colorful backyard scene. She would be gone, but I was left lying on the grass, feeling like a deflated beach ball sunk into the grass, exhausted and unable to move.

My counselor later explained that these memory blackouts were my mind's way of protecting me from the horror I was experiencing while the abuse was happening. Once the repressed memories came forward, I was thrust into clinical depression for the first time in my life. It required most of my energy to look normal and to hold it together. I was obsessed with worry. I was also unable to sleep more than three or four hours a night. Fortunately, I found a psychiatrist who prescribed medication that helped me function better, and regain my concentration and the ability to perform in my demanding job.

At the same time, I found the MaleSurvivor organization with the help of another gifted counselor. I was vacillating among various states of depression. Most of the time, I recall feeling as if my senses and feelings were muted. My world appeared gray. In counseling sessions, I'd describe feeling as if a locked box of horrifying emotions resided inside my chest. I felt as though any exploration of those emotions would overwhelm and destroy me.

These days, my life is free of much of the anxiety and depression of the past. For so long, I felt that the best I could do was to have a day free from anxiety. Now I'm starting to realize through continued recovery that I can have not only anxiety-free days, but also joyful days. I'm seeing glimpses of a life in which I can more frequently enjoy the present moment, marvel at the beauty of nature, reside in the love of my partner, and experience the laughter of a child.

I hope you can experience the freedom that Ryan is now experiencing in his life, and I hope that in time, you can leave much of your anxiety and depression behind you and replace it with real connections and joy. Keep in mind that Ryan needed to feel safe and secure before he could do the hard work of remembering and then risk disclosing the secrets he'd kept inside for so long.

———·\\\·———

Self-Care Time

———·\\\·———

Simon lives in Liverpool, England. His father was his sexual perpetrator, and his "mum" engaged in mother-son enmeshment. Even after he told her about the abuse, she stayed with his father and never understood its impact. Simon does share some of the graphic details.

Simon's Story: "A Father's Son"

"I grew up in a very confusing family. I was cared for in many ways by my parents, but I also was used emotionally by my mother and sexually abused by my father. My father was my hero, and he took advantage of my innocent love for him. For many years I struggled, living with a feeling of toxicity that is like an abusive presence inside of me. I didn't love the abuse, but I did love the person abusing me. Coming to terms with this confusion is a daily struggle and involves accepting the son in me for needing his parents' love but not their abuse.

"I hope my story will speak to men who struggle with similar confusion and conflict so that they can find the balance between absolute forgiveness, which amounts to denial of the abuse, and absolute hatred, which risks destroying any hope of self-respect."

My father started grooming me when I was six years old. At first it was naked wrestling games on my parents' bed when my mum was working night shifts. This introduced me in a "playful" way to his body and eventually his penis. It didn't seem scary at first, because my dad was giving me the attention I craved. He did many of the proper things dads do, but wasn't really interested in me as his son or excited by my presence until he started using me sexually. The games progressed, and one night he let me stay up late to watch <u>Hill Street Blues</u>. It was a real treat to be sitting cozily on his lap, feeling important and wanted. He smoked cigarettes and drank Bacardi and Coke, which made him feel more "alive" and helped him to transform me from a son into a toy. He wore his dressing gown that felt and smelled like my hero-father, warm and comforting. He took his penis out and said I could touch it. I felt sick in the stomach, and my hands went clammy.

I knew it was wrong, but didn't know why. I was only seven years old and had never had an erection. His penis was large, and he said that one day mine would be, too, and that I would enjoy many women with it. He coerced me to touch his penis and stroke it. It felt like a giant slug from the garden. I couldn't say no, because he was my dad.

I don't remember much else, and wonder how I must have felt going to bed alone after such an assault on my innocence. My father told me that it was natural for us to be doing this, that it was just "boys being boys." He said that there was no need to share it with my mum, because it was "our special time."

In those moments, he chose to stop being my dad. He made me feel as if I were in charge, as if I were the grown-up and therefore ultimately responsible.

112

Simon's father also abused him on camping trips they shared, and regularly took him into his bed "for comfort" when his mum was away. His mum used him by sharing inappropriate details of the sexual abuse that had occurred in her family, thereby preparing him to be the psychiatrist he became later in life. He told his mum about his father's abuse at age 13, and she believed him. His father apologized. He told his uncle at 16 and was yelled at by his father for trusting him. At 28, he confronted his parents again, but was very dissatisfied with their response.

> *I reported the abuse to the police in 2003, when I was 32. I had become increasingly concerned that there were other victims, and also I wanted society to take away my feelings of responsibility. My father pleaded guilty, receiving a sentence of two years and three months. Beyond his forced confession, I have not felt any deeper acknowledgment of the hurt he caused. My mum continued to need her husband more than her children and has been very loyal to him. No other victims were found outside the family, but my sister has told her story, which has been extremely painful for her. My father still denies her story. He served just over a year in prison and has not given me anything meaningful to aid my recovery. From prison, he wrote to tell me how well he had settled into prison life, and later came a copy of a psychology report for me to digest. I have recently received more heartfelt communication from him, only after a great deal of "coaching" from me. I suspect that in my parents' minds, I am still their parent and their psychiatrist. It hurts every day that all I wanted was to be loved as their son.*

Simon's account is another tragic story of parental abuse. He describes well the grooming his father engaged in, and the mother-son enmeshment and lack of protection from his mum. You may identify with the extreme anxiety and depression Simon describes. He didn't confront his parents until more than a decade after the abuse ended, and when that wasn't enough, he went to the police. This is a very difficult choice for any survivor, especially when the abuser is a member of your own family. Simon, like many survivors, ended up in a career that mirrors his family role while growing up. He was expected to be the family caregiver, and he grew up to become just that as a professional: a family psychiatrist.

Simon doesn't comment on it here, but it strikes me that his father received what I would regard as a very light sentence for the damage he caused Simon and his sister. I will write later in the book about confrontation and forgiveness, which come during the later stages of healing, after you have remembered, and after you have received support and help in understanding how you were abused and the effects of the traumatic events.

Self-Care Time

Jorge is one of several gay Silence Breakers, and has lived a very successful professional life. He attributes his success, in part, to the things he learned in dealing with his abuse. Success in your career or education doesn't necessary reflect success in your personal life, as his story shows. Jorge was abused by more than one person. Like many men, Jorge was abused by relatives or others whom he'd trusted, only to be betrayed by them.

Jorge came to believe early in life that he was unlovable, thus making him vulnerable to perpetrators. Jorge should have been taught that he was lovable by his parents, his extended family, his spiritual guides, and others responsible for his upbringing. It's not his fault that he felt unworthy of love. Jorge, like Rhett, also describes the process of being groomed by a perpetrator. One reason this abuse was so difficult was that the perpetrator became good friends with his mother. Her total trust in the perpetrator gave him full access to Jorge anytime he wanted it. Jorge tells his story in graphic detail.

Jorge's Story:
"From Unlovable Child to Overachieving Superstar"

"I am honored to be able to share my story with you. It is a tragedy involving many monsters who abandoned and betrayed me. I became the overachieving superstar in order to cope with the abandonment by both of my parents, and to create a 'tornado of activity' around me so that I could avoid my feelings of betrayal, shame, and guilt. Only multimodal therapy and a lot of hard work have truly helped me heal and recover. My journey is not over, but I want you to know that I am part of a large community of men who are here for you."

My childhood abuse was not a single event involving one perpetrator or even a single type of abuse. When I was ages five to six, my parents were going through a divorce, and as a result, from the time my father left during the first half of my kindergarten year at age five until I turned eight, my parents passed me back and forth like that relative no one wants. When I was eight, my father abandoned me for nine years. My mother was busy working and going to school at night. Because of these events, I believed I was an "unlovable child" and have struggled with self-esteem all my life.

Life got worse after my grandfather helped Mom buy us a house on the far-south side of Fort Worth at age six. I had neither the words nor the understanding about what would be done to me over the next three years. When I was seven, David, a neighbor in his 20s, started the grooming by trapping me with a previous victim, my best friend, Robert, who was eight, when I was playing in his backyard sandbox. First, it was just sex talk about girls and boobs. But then it moved through girly magazines, pornographic magazines, and books into teaching me masturbation, public exposure, and reciprocal oral sex. I remember thinking it was creepy from the start, yet my curiosity was piqued about this unknown world. Even as he was laying all this groundwork, David was becoming fast friends with my mother, who was only about six or seven years older than he was.

This man stalked me throughout this period. He would hang out with my mother at our house a lot, especially in the later evenings. He would come in the bathroom when I was taking my bath and molest me. He would come in my bedroom after I had gone to sleep, wake me up by touching my crotch, and comment if my penis was hard or stroke it until it was hard. To this day, I cannot be awakened by being physically touched without having a violent reaction. There was no place where I was safe from this man.

Eventually David tried his moves on a teenage boy who lived on the other side of us. That boy went home and told his mother, who then warned the other mothers, who all got in touch with the police. David was sent away for about five years. I remember very clearly when my mother interviewed me about what had transpired between David and me. I know she was probably following advice from the police by trying to make me feel comfortable enough to speak about it, but as I sat on the far side of the room, facing away from her, I never felt more alone or more ashamed, and I remember that feeling to this day.

One monster was gone but was immediately followed by a charming, intelligent, but alcoholic Texas native whom Mom met at the local junior college where she was taking classes. He delighted in torturing me as punishment for every little sin I committed. He would strip me down to just a T-shirt, stand me in the middle of my room, and then lash at me with a belt as I tried vainly to dance out of the way. He would stand in front of me and carve up my favorite toys as punishment for my curiosity that led me to take things apart and put them back together to understand how they worked. My sister recently reported things that she had observed that she has felt guilty about all her life, such as seeing him hold me off the floor against the wall by my throat. Thankfully, I don't remember these things— thank you, dissociation—though I fear that someday I will.

About the time my mother finally threw this monster out of the house, I won a scholarship to a Fort Worth day school. However, I suffered many humiliations and verbal abuses at the hands of my rich classmates and some teachers and staff.

That brought me to the summer of 1975, when I would turn 14 on July 5.

Jorge attempted suicide around this time due to his fears of returning to the day school. To provide support, his mother turned to his Boy Scouts scoutmaster, who "put the final nail in the coffin of my shattered, wretched childhood when he spent a day ceremonially raping me at his house about six weeks after my suicide attempt." Jorge has no idea how he got home that day.

Out of this was born the overachieving superstar. I made straight A's and did more activities than anyone else I knew. At one point in high school, I was president of the math club and the debate team, as well as a fixture on the tennis team, in addition to taking seven classes each term so that I could graduate in three years instead of four. In my 30s, I worked two full-time jobs, finishing my Ph.D. research in artificial-intelligence applications in medicine, while taking care of my dying partner. It wasn't until I was in my late 30s that I stopped searching for that approval I was never going to get from my parents. I was in my early 40s when I decided I didn't have to work myself to death and be perfect all the time.

Jorge's story is very difficult for even a trained psychotherapist to read, so again, please remember to take calming breaths. His story illustrates that recovering from repeated abuse could be a lifelong journey. It's tragic when a child can never feel safe in his own home. Jorge's mother had not yet learned from her tragic mistakes of associating with predatory men. Jorge never received the professional help he needed, even after the serious suicide attempt. His doctors failed to uncover the abuses he suffered, in part because he had learned not to trust anyone, especially complete strangers, with his story. His mom hoped the Boy Scout leader would help, but once again, his trust was betrayed. This pattern of trust betrayed is one of the most devastating aspects of abuse. Yet survivors can heal and learn to trust friends, therapists, fellow survivors, and intimate partners. I will provide more on this later in the book.

—⟋ⵣⵣⵡ⟍—

Self-Care Time

—⟋ⵣⵣⵡ⟍—

The tragedy in Coach's story, which follows, is that his parents knew that his perpetrator had been imprisoned twice for child molestation, but they did not protect their child. It's no surprise that Coach has struggled with his feelings toward not only his perpetrator, but also his totally neglectful parents.

Coach's Story:
"Do to Others as You Would Have Them Do to You"

"The effects of sexual abuse are devastating, much like those of a tornado, earthquake, tsunami, or financial collapse. This shakes the very foundation of one's physical, mental, emotional, social, volitional, and spiritual being. It takes extreme measures of mercy from family, friends, and community in order to help transform the male sexual abuse survivor. It's my desire that this personal story give you hope and offer you extreme mercy."

I am a 49-year-old heterosexual who has been married for 21 years. My three young children are helping me recapture what I missed in my childhood. This is what gives me meaning!

I was raped hundreds of times by my mother's younger brother, starting in early childhood and continuing through early adolescence. My uncle has a criminal history dating back to the mid-1950s. He had already served two prison sentences for sex crimes against children prior to molesting me. My sexual abuse as a child occurred in Pennsylvania. More recently (2004), my uncle was, once again, brought up on charges in

Pennsylvania for abusing two young girls. This brought up some anger in me, because the same justice system that continues to fail them failed me!

Unfortunately for society and me, the statute of limitations has run its course, and filing an official report wouldn't help my situation. I confronted my abuser face-to-face at my mother's burial service. He denied all the abuse, and the very next day, he acted out sexually on two young children and is now serving his third prison sentence.

I have come to realize that it's time to move forward. I often thought that I needed to hear an apology from my abuser in order to move further in recovery. Now I have learned to not be loyal to that dysfunction!

In my opinion, this story of Coach is one of the most tragic, because his abuse was so completely unnecessary and absolutely preventable. It's inconceivable to me that Coach's mom and dad both willingly gave his uncle what appears to be complete access to their son hundreds of times over a decade or more! What parents in their right minds would trust a babysitter who was a known child molester and had already served two prison terms? What parents would allow that same person to take their son on outings?

It is significant to me that Coach describes their neglect as more a matter of "naïveté." One of Coach's major challenges throughout his recovery is processing his feelings toward his parents and struggling to understand such profound neglect, which is another form of sexual abuse he suffered. Coach has been helped by the fact that his parents now accept full responsibility for their failure. He has stopped trying to extract an apology from his uncle, and realized that he could recover without it.

~~~∽/\\\\∽~~~

Self-Care Time

~~~∽/\\\∽~~~

Gregg, 28, had multiple abusers inside and outside of his family. He is the youngest Silence Breaker, and was abused nearly every day and, often, several times a day over a long, hellish period. He is still in the process of recovering. Yet in the midst of a lot of pain, he found the courage to be one of the men who appeared on Oprah's show with me. He has also chosen to share some of the graphic details.

Gregg's Story: "I Am a Walking Miracle"

"Like many survivors, I was abused by a number of people, including a cop, who raped me. Considering the physical, mental, and sexual abuse throughout my childhood, it's definitely a miracle that I'm doing as well as I am today. I am definitely still a work in progress, and while I may never achieve the success of someone like Tyler Perry, I hope you can hear from me that recovery is achievable, and that drugs and alcohol are not the answer. I am proud of myself for being willing to appear on the *Oprah* '200 Men' show to share part of my story, and want to offer you hope for your future."

My earliest memory of abuse was when I was about seven years old, from a female member of my family. She used to touch me and make me perform oral sex on her. This happened a few times. I'm not sure how it stopped, but it did end. When I was about age nine, my first cousin started abusing me. It started as a game: he was Dracula and used to bite my neck and grind on me. Then it progressed to my having to give him oral sex, and shortly thereafter, he had anal sex with me. This went on until I was about 15. It happened often, two to three times a day. In between the abuse I suffered from my cousin, there was also a male neighbor who not only abused me, but also hit and degraded me.

Those were the hard days when I had to go back and forth between those two people. There were also two other cousins who abused me. I felt that I was just being passed around, as if I had a scarlet letter on me. Then there was the rape in a park when I was 16—on Christmas evening by a police officer. It was violent; there was rage, blood, force, and pain.

In a nutshell, I really had nowhere to go, nor did I have parents I could talk to. Both of them beat the shit out of me on a daily basis and talked down to me. So I grew up on a diet of physical, mental, and sexual abuse.

Although I felt good about my Oprah experience, after that, I started remembering things I had forgotten, which left me pretty depressed. I think I'm just more aware of things now. I am much more aware of my bad choices in my connections with food, friends, and personal relationships. I have not lived to my full potential. But I am drug-free now and have been for a few years. Depending on how you see it, man, the ship is sailing or it's sinking. But I do have hope for a better life, and one thing I do know is that there are plenty of us out there with this same feeling.

Gregg's hope is rising through his pain and suffering. He understands that to heal, he has to be clean and sober—and he has to keep reaching out for support, which he does every time he tells his story. Each time he opens the wound and speaks the truth, it provides access to even more truth. While you may feel bad when those memories surface, in the long run, having access to the truth of your experiences helps you heal and, eventually, thrive.

—ɯɯ—

Self-Care Time

—ɯɯ—

Our most senior Silence Breaker, John Walker, is the rare survivor who feels comfortable using his real name while sharing his story. In fact, he even told it recently in a letter to *The Salt Lake Tribune*. John, whose memories of abuse were repressed until the age of 60, also is the first survivor whose story involves abuse by a clergy member, but tragically, the betrayal of trust goes beyond even that relationship.

John's Story: "It's Never Too Late"

"Age is no barrier to recovery and forgiveness, if you are willing to take advantage of the available resources. It's not easy; it's sometimes painful and requires hard work, but the result is well worth the effort."

At age 15 I was sexually abused by my father, a Protestant clergyman. I was also set up by my father to be sexually abused by one of his friends. In addition to the sexual abuse, there was emotional abuse by my father in that he treated me as an extension of himself. Nothing I did was good enough for him, not even becoming a Ph.D. scientist with an international reputation. My mother used me for emotional support, but there was no overt sexual abuse by her.

The result of all of this was that I was not loved and nurtured as a child should be, and therefore I was essentially an orphan, though living with my biological parents. My father's hold over me was so great that I completely suppressed the sexual abuse until I was in my early 60s, when the therapist with whom I was doing family-of-origin work to trace past hurts asked me if I had ever been sexually abused by my father. I exhibited the standard behaviors of those who have been abused, and the therapist picked up on it.

My recovery work went slowly, primarily because I had difficulty finding resources. Then I happened onto MaleSurvivor and attended my first Weekend of Recovery. I have attended four such weekends and two MaleSurvivor world conferences. Every one of these events made a significant contribution to my recovery.

Now, at the age of 79, I am very comfortable with my life. I have much better self-esteem, which enables me to be very open. I am emotionally alive. I have empathy and the ability to laugh and cry. In short, I feel that my inner child has been set free. I speak to groups, including men in rehab and children in treatment, about the effects of abuse on my life and about my recovery. I consider it an honor to have been one of the 200 men who stood up at the <u>Oprah</u> "200 Men" show to say "<u>Enough!</u>"

Whenever it's appropriate, I reach out with the message, "You are not alone; recovery is possible."

John is a great example of what's possible when you work at your recovery, no matter when you start. He has clearly benefited from sharing his story of abuse with other survivors, and from getting and giving support with them. When your father and mother abuse you, you learn to be loyal to all the dysfunctional messages they teach you, and in addition, such loyalty can lead to burying memories, as was the case with John. In the next chapter, I will address loyalty to dysfunction.

⸺⟋⟍⟍⸺

Self-Care Time

⸺⟋⟍⟍⸺

Bruce was abused by a trusted coach, and his story echoes the 2011 scandals at Penn State and Syracuse universities, in which trusted authority figures preyed on young men under the guise of helping them. Bruce has chosen to share some of the graphic nature of his story.

Bruce's Story: "I Could Not Be More Proud"

"It's amazing to know today that I am not alone. United, we (survivors of childhood sexual abuse and adult rape) stand together and support each other through this, and then we help new people. Shame belongs to the abusers, not us. Before I got help, I believed that vulnerability made me weak. Now, I truly believe that vulnerability makes me incredibly strong."

Hiding in the closet because of abuse just helps the predators remain active. Not very long ago, I did everything to keep my abuse secret, but I am proud to have appeared on The Oprah Winfrey Show as one of the 200 brave men, where I exposed my abusive past to millions.

I could not be more proud to be on this journey of healing from the impact of childhood sexual abuse. You can do it, too—I know it! I've been there!

I grew up in a middle-class home in a suburb of Toronto, Ontario, Canada, as the youngest of three siblings. I had an alcoholic mother and a strict physically and emotionally abusive father. I was diagnosed with ADD (attention deficit disorder), and Ritalin was prescribed. I felt like a real outcast, because most adults and kids had little patience with me. As a child, I was often depressed.

When I was 12, my parents enrolled me in basketball at the YMCA. I didn't know what to expect, but to my surprise, I was very good at basketball and was quickly elevated to a team lead position, which was a proud time for me. That first year, we won the championship, and for the first time, I felt that I fit in.

It was so great that I returned the next year. Only this time, my assistant basketball coach was Dr. Marvin Sazant, the pedophile who abused me. As my assistant coach, Marvin appeared so kind and gentle. He won my trust fairly quickly and asked me questions regarding my family challenges. He would explain to me that as a medical doctor, he completely understood about alcoholism and ADD, and he said he would help me.

Eventually, he asked me over to his home to earn money by raking leaves. This is where the sexual abuse started. This guy was twisted, and tied me up with ropes. Although I didn't want any of it, I could not say no because I was starving so much for attention; I just put up with it. He would sexually abuse me at his home, in his doctor's office, and in his car. He often visited me at school and took me to lunch, where he would allow me, unlicensed and underage, to drive his car as part of his grooming techniques.

After a few months, he started to get annoyed that I was avoiding going to his home or office, and he finally one day showed up at my school and gave me an ultimatum that if I wouldn't come over to his house, we could no longer be "friends." I told him I guessed we could no longer be friends. As I got out of his car and walked back toward school, I cried my eyes out, because I thought I had just made the biggest mistake of my life by stopping the abuse and ending the relationship.

As the years went by, I was deeply disturbed by what had happened to me. I was afraid to come forward because I figured no one would believe my story about this well-recognized doctor. My sexual identity was a nightmare. You see, prior to this abuse, I knew that I was gay. But after the abuse, I was so disgusted that I thought that if this was what gay was, then I didn't want it. I tried dating women for a while, and that didn't work, so eventually I just went to dating men. I could not truly trust anyone and went from one dysfunctional relationship to another. I also was horrified, just knowing that he was surely abusing other boys, which I later learned was true.

Bruce's story illustrates how difficult escaping abuse can be once you have been groomed. You want some of what the perpetrator is offering you, and even though you don't want to be abused, you do want the "friendship." It's never a victim's fault when abuse is repeated. It's scary and oftentimes impossible to stop an abuser.

Sometimes, a survivor can develop enough inner strength to walk away from his perpetrator, but as Bruce describes, it's very tough because it feels like a huge mistake and a major loss of a "friend." Bruce also describes the impact of the abuse on his sexual identity and how confused he became because he wanted to reject any part of him that was associated with his abuse. This type of sexual-identity confusion is common, and I will provide more information on this later in the book.

Bruce was successful in having Dr. Sazant's license to practice medicine stripped from him by the College of Physicians and Surgeons of Ontario after many years of seeking justice. He will write about that experience later in the book, too.

⌁⫴⌁

Self-Care Time

⌁⫴⌁

Jarrod, who also feels comfortable using his own name, had several abusers, including a youth minister trusted by the church community. Unfortunately, his story also mirrors the huge scandals recently rocking the Catholic Church, Penn State University, and Syracuse University. Jarrod, like other survivors, developed the defense mechanism of dissociation, which allows a survivor to forget what was done to him until later in life.

Jarrod's Story: <u>Ignis Aurum Probat, Miseria Fortes Homines</u> ("As Gold Is Tempered by Fire, So Strong Men Are Tempered by Suffering")

"When the Penn State and Syracuse child sexual abuse scandals first came to light, many people asked how this type of thing could be kept quiet for so long. Why do boys not tell? Thirty years ago, I was no exception. It was not until my own children began to mature that I was forced to face the truth of what was done to me from ages 8 to 17. I am a logical, educated, and reasoned adult. Even so, I remained trapped in shame, guilt, and fear, which became my constant companions. I feared that unnamed, terrible things would happen to me if my secret were ever exposed. The result was a state of almost-constant anxiety that took a terrible toll. I choose to tell my story now in hopes that I can bring some measure of understanding to the one in six boys who will be sexually abused before their 18th birthday. I tell my story today so that they will know they are not alone and that they did nothing wrong."

I was a lonely and vulnerable kid who desperately needed attention. When she was 12, my older sister was killed in a plane crash that left my family in disarray and shock. That night, an abuser would begin a process of grooming that ultimately led to sexual abuse, abuse that would not end until I was 17. He was a youth-group sponsor from an Episcopal church in Tulsa, Oklahoma. He was loved and trusted by most everyone who knew him, a seemingly stand-up, regular guy.

In my case, his grooming was slow but deliberate. I call it a sexual-desensitization process. It started out as teasing, horseplay, and innuendo that escalated to discussions about sex. In my young and impressionable state, I was intrigued and excited about this new, forbidden information. He also offered me something all young boys want: freedom. He had a car. Since my parents trusted him, I had many opportunities to flee the confines of my home. I would take every chance offered to go to the movies, go to church, or just go anywhere to get his special attention, because it made me feel loved.

And during sleepovers at his house, I got to stay up late, see R-rated movies, and generally feel pretty grown up. There, he'd expose himself under the pretext of taking a shower or simply changing clothes. He'd insist that there was nothing wrong with guys seeing each other naked. Eventually, he began to tell me about his exploits with women. He made himself out to be my sex educator. I recall a weekend trip when he turned up the explicit sexual talk. As an added measure, he stopped at a convenience store and purchased pornography. By the time we reached our destination, I was primed for assault.

His grooming now complete, his actions would change my life forever and lead to a long list of personal challenges that I still battle to this day. He said it wasn't gay. He said it was just guys being guys who are just really close friends. The sexuality questions raised by the assaults haunted me for years. Each time the abuse occurred, I simply wanted everything to go back to the way it was before. I wanted to forget it had happened. It never occurred to me to tell anyone. In fact, it was my hope that no one would ever find out.

Jarrod's story illustrates the loss of power a boy can feel when a perpetrator expertly grooms his victim and wins the trust of his family. The grooming Jarrod experienced fits the pattern in which the perpetrator offers "special" gifts in exchange for the vow of silence. Likewise, the perpetrator's message that what was happening was "not gay" is in direct contrast to the cultural message that it was, in fact, gay. This left Jarrod with great confusion about his sexual orientation that lasted well into adulthood. Finally, the repeated betrayal from a trusted adult damaged Jarrod's ability to trust others, creating a real sense of isolation and aloneness.

Self-Care Time

For brevity's sake, I've summarized the stories of the remaining Silence Breakers. They wanted to share them with you to further emphasize that there is always hope and that recovery is always possible.

Ken's Story: "My Memories Set Me Free"

Ken's account offers proof that you can be thriving in your life and still not have access to all of your abuse memories. Ken, like many other Silence Breakers, spent most of his life in denial of his abuse. His repressed memories began to surface as somatic, or "body," memories. *Body memories* are sensations that a survivor experiences because they are the very same body responses he experienced when he was abused or assaulted. However, as a matter of self-protection, the survivor involuntarily buries these memories in his body. When he feels safe enough, the memories can surface as these somatic experiences.

This is a common way for memories to surface. For Ken, and most people, these unexplained physical sensations can be very unsettling and puzzling, but he came to believe that these memories helped set him free.

Ken was abused numerous times by one uncle and then by another uncle, who took him on a fishing trip with family friends when Ken was just ten. He and other children on the trip were traded for sex with both male and female perpetrators. Another uncle raped him five years later.

In my late 30s, I was working in a very stressful situation. I was remodeling my master-bedroom closet, and began having memories of my great uncle sexually assaulting me in the coal bin in his basement. The memories were just flashes of thought, not detailed memories. Bits of speech, feelings of my shoulders being gripped, and pressure on my backside kept recurring. I tried to convince myself that this was anything other than a memory of being abused. I thought I was losing it, because my memory of my childhood had been idyllic. I finally spoke these memories to my wife and, with her help, located a therapist and began working on the issue. The memories are still vague but continue to surface in additional detail from time to time.

I now see myself as being in the ongoing maintenance phase of my recovery. I have acquired the tools to live a full and happy life while acknowledging the impact that abuse has had on my life. There are aspects of my life that will always bear the tagline of "survivor of sexual abuse," but that doesn't prevent me from having joy in my life.

Joe's Story: "Opening Up to Myself and to Others"

Joe had multiple abusers, both male and female, and as a result, most of his childhood was stolen from him. After the abuse started at age five, he told his mother, who did nothing to help him. Since he didn't get the protection he needed, he concluded that it wasn't so bad. He took a friend over to visit the man who was abusing him at the time, but his friend knew something was wrong and called Joe a "faggot." As an early teen, he also told a girl he was dating, and the next day, her grandmother called him "a little faggot." Three times as a child, he reached out for help, and either got none or was further shamed. Shame is the fuel of addictions, and as a teenager, he resorted to drugs and alcohol to cope. Fortunately he managed to break that cycle and find recovery once he reached adulthood. Unfortunately, after disclosing the abuse and being counseled at a treatment center, he buried the memories for 22 more years.

> *It started with "the old man down the street." Since my mother didn't appropriately address that situation, I remained vulnerable and was susceptible to being sexually abused by many others. In recovery, I have worked through my guilt, shame, and anger. I feel free to open myself up and share my experience so that I may create closer connections with, as well as help, others.*

Niall's Story: "There Is Light at the End of This Dark Tunnel"

Niall's primary abuser was his mother, who raped him twice when he was 14. She threatened to cut off his penis if he told anyone, and she also had sexually abused him from between the ages of four and seven. His father, brother, and outsiders also abused him. Like Coach, Niall attributes his faith as having played a major role in his healing.

> *I know from personal experience that healing from the terrible trauma of child abuse and incest really is possible. For me, having a solid spiritual foundation was an important component in my recovery. I am very grateful to God for all the blessings He has given me. It may seem surprising to you that I should say this, but at this point, I consider myself privileged to have experienced and learned as much as I have during my healing journey. While I wouldn't wish this pain on any human being, recovering from the abuse has molded me into the man I now am, and I very much like that man.*

SJC's Story: "You Never Know What Goes on Behind Closed Doors—'Model Families' Are No Exception"

SJC experienced covert incest from his mother and overt abuse from both his parents. He only began dealing with the effects of the abuse at age 60, similar to John's story. His life unraveled at retirement, when he could no longer use his work to hide his pain. He unfortunately went through several very unhelpful therapists before he finally found a specialist and the resources at MaleSurvivor.

I discovered, slowly but surely, what the effects of sexual abuse, not to mention emotional abuse, can have on a young child's life. It's like a cancer. It never sleeps, and sooner or later, if you don't deal with it, it will get you. Four years later, I am still on the path to recovery. I am working again, but this time it's on me. I am learning how to be empathic, how to love myself and others. Life has a whole new meaning and gets better and better as I continue to work on my healing.

Mike's Story: "Picture This: How I Put the Puzzle Pieces Together"

Mike was abused by a neighbor. His grooming included paying Mike with treats and money to do odd jobs, showing him stag films and pornography magazines, filling him with stories about his sexual exploits, showing him shoe boxes full of naked pictures, and giving him a camera. The perpetrator was so successful at grooming him that Mike was blinded to the fact that his sister was also being pulled into what his perpetrator was doing to him. He would take pictures of Mike's sister and him in different states of undress and sexual positions. This overt abuse lasted from age 8 or 9 until about age 13. His abuse led to Mike becoming a sex addict as an adult. Thankfully, he has made incredible progress in addressing this through honest communication with his wife.

I am focusing my recovery by accepting that although I can't change what happened, I can make life better for myself. I have learned that getting the truth out is the most important piece. I have found in my path to recovery—"my path to living," as I like to call it today—that I had to let those who were helping me to heal know what "we" were up against. Last year, I revealed to my wife how I was behaving. She took it as expected, but she has been strong and has stayed with me. With my wife helping me, I have not acted out since before I told her. Today, I feel that I am now in control of my life. It's still a roller coaster, but I control whether I enjoy the ride or not.

———〰〰———

Self-Care Time

———〰〰———

Chris's Story: "I'm Not Alone Anymore"

Chris was abused alongside his younger brother. His abuser was horribly shaming and emasculated him and his brother in the process. Whereas Chris has worked hard on his recovery and understands the impact of the abuse on his behavior, his brother has not reached the same place of understanding, which is a challenge for him. Whenever someone is forced to involve a sibling in abuse, it can be extremely painful, especially when the sibling is younger, as in Chris's case.

> *My guilt has been my sticking point all these 30 years. My brother has absolved me totally, but it hasn't sunk in with me and has made my recovery more difficult than if I had been abused individually. I've been as close to death as any one of us might want to be, but I've continued to push through the pain and sadness in order to create a new outlook, one that's not filled with self-doubt and destruction. I am a survivor and I'm not alone anymore.*

Christopher's Story: "The Place of No Refuge: My Journey from Brokenness to Being Loved"

Christopher struggled to understand that his abuse was significant, painful, and "bad enough" to attend a Weekend of Recovery to heal. He does know that he retreated to his neighbor's house because his parents' marriage was so chaotic. He thought he would be safe there. His perpetrator also groomed him, like many of the Silence Breakers, in this case by inviting him to wrestle WWF-style (in his underwear) with the man's son. Then on subsequent visits, the son was no longer there, so the man invited Christopher to wrestle with him instead. The abuse started from there. As for many of the Silence Breakers, his memories were hidden inside, and he is plagued because there are details of his story he simply cannot yet remember. Christopher, as is typical of survivors, remembers details of the room where he was abused by the neighbor, such as the hum of the air conditioner. After decades of struggling with depression, suicidal thoughts, and a deep-seated feeling of brokenness, he has emerged on the other side.

> *Today I am much, much better. I am remarried to an amazing, caring, loving, and supportive woman who has helped me to finally believe that I not only am worthy of being loved, but also deserve it because I am a good person. I am finally beginning to believe in myself enough to challenge myself to accomplish goals that just a few years ago I never dreamed possible. I was recently admitted to law school. I see for the first time in my life the possibility of living with pride and hope.*

Pierre's Story: "Confronting the Myth That I Would Become an Abuser, Too"

Many things prompt men to pursue recovery, and in the case of Pierre, a 44-year-old Canadian father, it was the birth of his son. Pierre had heard the myth that all survivors go on to abuse others, and this frightened him so much that he pursued therapy.

Pierre suffered stomach ulcers at the age of 11 because he lived "in quiet terror" of being abused again. His doctor failed to make the connection.

> *Today I am much more open, much happier, and truer about myself and what happened to me. I have told my story to many and found love, help, and encouragement from those with whom I have shared. I have been asked by some survivors' partners to extend my hand to their husbands, who have been living in shame alone, and that has been healing for them and me.*

Howie's Story: "This Is Not What Boys Do"

Howie was abused by his older brother. He told his parents, but nothing was done. As a parent today, Howie still struggles to understand how his mother and father could have been "so oblivious to the child's pain." He credits his wife, Debbie; our MaleSurvivor program; and many of his closest friends with helping him:

> *It all started so innocently, but it definitely wasn't innocent. Letting myself know my truth has been a major struggle, but I have had to come to terms with the truth of my abuse so that I could heal and become the healthy parent and husband I wanted to be.*
>
> *I feel freed from most of the guilt and shame I had put myself through for 30 years. Oddly enough, a lot of the issues I have now seem like "normal guy stuff." I talk to some friends who know about my past and ask them about anxiety or sexual issues. It turns out that nonabused men have the same worries. Now, that could be just the type of person I get along with, but it's nice to know that the sexual abuse isn't the cause of all of my problems.*

Rob's Story: "I Will Survive"

Rob was abused along with his sister. He suffered at the hands of a number of perpetrators and turned to drugs and alcohol for solace, much like Chris. His mother and father knew of his abuse and failed in their responsibility to protect him and his sister, which left him vulnerable to perpetrators.

> *It has taken some time to get to where I am today in my recovery. Am I well? No, not completely. Will I ever get there? It's a journey, and no one can be sure they'll arrive. I now know what it is that ails me. The power that was taken from me as a child has been returned to my hands. Now, it's up to me to use that power to be the best father, businessman, lover, and person that I can possibly strive to be. Through perseverance, dedication, and community, I will survive!*

This ends Part I of this book, and now you are ready to take steps toward thriving. The next chapter will help you examine some of the many dysfunctional messages you learned from the actions and words of your perpetrators and nonprotectors. I will help you challenge your loyalty to the people who taught you these messages, no matter how much they may have told you they loved you, so that you can be free to be disloyal to the dysfunction they taught you was "normal."

AFFIRMATIONS FOR CHAPTER 6

- *I believe I have the power now to heal and be inspired by the journeys and courage of other survivors.*
- *I have the right to tell my story—to be listened to, believed, and supported.*

✦　✦　✦　✦

PART II

MOVING FORWARD ON THE PATH TO THRIVING

"There are times in our lives when we have to address our abuse
by walking through the flames of pain and discomfort. Painful as it may be,
it is the healthiest way to move into the stage of wellness, good self-care,
and thriving." *Designer:* Rick A., Hope Springs Weekend of Recovery, 2011.

CHAPTER SEVEN

Dare to Dream You Can Be Disloyal to Dysfunction

"The T-shirt represents me at the start of the weekend when I was bound by chains of guilt, shame, and fear. The chains were broken with the help of strangers who seemed like loving, caring angels to me. I don't recall ever crying so much. It was like a peaceful release of emotions. Just to know I am no longer alone makes me feel normal. Things can only get better." *Designer:* Pepeton.

One of the most significant negative consequences of sexual victimization is that survivors learn to be "loyal to dysfunction." The goal of this chapter is to help you understand what that means and how it happens. In the chapter that follows this one, I'll offer guidance on how you can become "loyal to functionality" instead.

Your having been loyal to dysfunction means that you learned to separate from the man you were meant to be when you were born: a lovable, worthwhile person. Your personality, behaviors, thoughts, and emotions have been altered by what was done to you. Dysfunction occurs when you are unable to think and behave in a manner that would have been normal for you prior to your abuse or if you had never been abused. You can tell you are operating in a dysfunctional way if you feel unworthy, not good enough, or ashamed of yourself.

Being loyal to dysfunction means that you believe thoughts that prevent you from honoring healthy core values about yourself and the world. Being loyal to dysfunction also occurs when you listen to and follow internal messages to engage in self-destructive or self-defeating behaviors. The loyalty is generated by the trust you put in the people who then victimized you or failed to protect you after the abuse. Although you may know there are other options, your loyalty to dysfunction causes you to choose unhealthy behaviors instead of more functional ones.

EXPERIMENT WITH NEW POSSIBILITIES:
Exploring Your Patterns of Loyalty to Dysfunction

Before we go further, I'd like for you to participate in an exercise examining your patterns of loyalty to dysfunction. Use your journal to describe the dysfunctional behaviors and messages you learned in childhood. List each behavior or message, indicate in the next column who taught you to behave or think that way, and, finally, indicate the extent to which you still feel loyal to this dysfunctional behavior or message.

Choose *SL* for "Strongly loyal," *ML* for "More loyal" than you would like to be (or somewhat loyal), *NTL* for "Not too loyal" anymore, or *NWL* for "No way am I still loyal."

Example:

Dysfunctional Behavior or Message	Who Taught Me?	Degree of Loyalty
My only worth is as a sex object.	Abuser Tom	NTL

Now, make your list in your journal. I'll be covering a number of dysfunctions next, so you can peek to get some more ideas; however, it would be helpful to brainstorm here. Any examples you provide are valid and helpful to this process.

Thanks for experimenting and looking inside yourself. I believe that the more you are aware of these dysfunctional behavior and thought patterns, the more likely it is that you can become loyal to functionality. I will define this concept thoroughly in the next chapter, but for now, know that being loyal to functionality involves your being open, accepting, powerful, and confident.

Common Examples of Dysfunctional Messages

Now, I'll share some common examples of dysfunctional messages I have heard from the many men I have counseled over the years. Some of them apply to boys who were abused, and some apply to men who were sexually assaulted.

Disbelieving the Betrayal

One of the most damaging messages, and a particularly difficult one to let go, is: *My perpetrator must have loved and cared for me because he told me he did.* Even when your body is telling you that this person hurt you, you may still believe the perpetrator's words if this individual claimed to love you and care for you. Why? Perpetrators are skilled at preying on the vulnerable by treating their targets with kindness. Often those targeted come from dysfunctional homes with parental conflicts, divorce, addictive behaviors, and adults who are unable to provide the love and support that every child deserves. And often, perpetrators know this information about you.

You may have been that boy who yearned for someone to be kind and loving, to inspire you to grow up to be a healthy man, and to give you positive attention. Perpetrators groom their targets by acting kind and loving, for a while, in order to gain your trust. Once trust is established, they *betray* it.

When you were a boy, you didn't understand that you were being betrayed, and you may have become very confused. Even as an adult, you may find it difficult to believe and accept that betrayal, despite what your therapist or others tell you. Every fiber of your soul may resist the fact that the perpetrator took advantage of you, because deep down, you continue to think that the person told you that you were loved.

Here is the problem with staying loyal to any perpetrator: Because you trusted the person who groomed and then abused you—and you believed that this individual loved you as he or she claimed—you became vulnerable to believing you deserved to be abused by others. Further, you may believe that love requires being abused or even abusing others. Because of this misunderstanding of what constitutes love and trust, you may seek out partners who will mistreat you by being cruel, judgmental, self-centered, hurtful, or physically or sexually abusive. You may choose a partner who agrees to being hurt by *you*. If this physical and sexual abuse replicates the types of behaviors you suffered during your abuse experiences, this is especially problematic, because you are reaffirming that you deserved such mistreatment. Abused men may repeatedly engage in these behaviors to assert control over past experiences in which they had no control. While it's true that "choosing" to be hurt or choosing to hurt a partner may help you believe that you finally are in control, the truth is that you are not helping yourself heal.

Damaged Sense of Self

You may also grow to believe this myth: *Since I was abused, I am unlovable.*

Again, the fact is that your abuser did not love you when he or she was abusing you. But what's true of your abuser is not a reflection on your self-worth and lovability. All children born into this world are lovable just the way they are, and this includes *you.* Being wounded and hurt by your abuser doesn't change this basic fact. It may have changed how you feel and think about yourself, but it doesn't change who you are as a person.

We all are born pure, whole, and spiritual, and that part of us remembers all the experiences of our lives. No abuser can access the purest and most spiritual part of us. It is our "protector" that connects us to every other being on the planet and links us heart to heart with the purest intentions to be loving and loved, connected, caring, and cared for.

Abusers often would prefer that their victims believe there's something wrong with themselves, because that frees abusers of responsibility for their cruel actions. It's not unusual for victims to blame themselves and their flaws, imperfections, needs, and weaknesses for their having been abused. What's important for you to learn to accept is that *this perpetrator lied to you. That person lied to manipulate you, to make you feel bad, to make you feel ashamed, awful, and dirty.* That was the abuser's plan from the start: to manipulate you and control you by convincing you that you are unlovable. If you haven't accepted this truth, then you are likely to only engage in sex with people who don't care about you. Or if you believe the myth that the perpetrator who hurt you still loved you, you may not allow anyone who truly cares about you to get close enough to love you.

The "Needs" Dysfunction

Here's another pair of dysfunctional beliefs that block recovery:

- *Because I have needs, I am responsible for being abused.*

- *My needs are unimportant.*

Perpetrators are well known for teaching their victims to serve the needs of the abuser. Often, in exchange, the perpetrator provides "gifts." Any child may want the gifts, but it's absolutely untrue that it's your fault for wanting them or that you are to blame for your own abuse because you "agreed" to take the gifts. When a man is raped, he often tells himself that to survive, he should do whatever is necessary to satisfy the rapist in hopes of then being left alone. Clearly the message the rapist gives is that the victim's needs are totally unimportant. The focus is totally on the needs of the rapist. This message is also reinforced when you are abused and reach out for help only to be silenced or not believed, as Joe and Howie described in their stories. The message each received was *My needs are not important.* They were also taught that it was their job to take care of their parents' needs instead of their own.

Sexual Arousal Is Not an Indication of Guilt

Another common dysfunctional message is *Since I was sexually aroused during the abuse, I must have wanted it.* Perpetrators will do their best to manipulate the victim into believing this common myth. For physiological reasons, a male who is being abused often experiences sexual arousal. Unfortunately an erect penis is difficult to hide. The perpetrators often use that uncontrollable and involuntary physiological response as proof that you wanted the abuse and enjoyed it. Even when you experience physical pain or know inside that something is very wrong, you can still experience sexual arousal.

"All I'm Good for Is Sex"

This leads to another flawed and self-defeating belief: *Since I was sexually abused or assaulted, my only worth is as a sex object.*

Sexual victimization is not about love or caring; it's about objectifying a child, teen, or man. It's about demeaning your character and seeing you only as a sex object. The people who abused you want you to believe that being a good sex object is your only value, because then they can justify hurting you. Their thinking is that they can't hurt an object, only a human with feelings. By treating you as an object, they place the blame and guilt entirely on you. As a result, you define yourself as a sex object, rather than understanding that the perpetrator is a sexual abuser. In addition, if you feel terrible about yourself, it can be tempting to believe that being a sex object is a good thing.

If your parents were involved in your abuse, they may have set you up for further abuse by treating you as an object. For example, far too many dysfunctional parents comment on a child's bodily development. Their hurtful comments about your being inadequate or, on the other hand, their compliments about your developing muscles and good looks can lead you to think your value is measured on your physical appearance or attributes, especially if that's the sole focus of their comments to you.

For those unfortunate men whose parents comment on the size of their penises, this is especially destructive and wrong, because you have no control over the size of your penis. I've heard stories of men whose abusers told them that the reason they manipulated the victim's penis was to help make it bigger because it was too small. Or they commented about the victim's orgasm, making him feel self-conscious about how much semen he produced.

Denying the Truth of Abuse

Often, those survivors who are loyal to dysfunctional messages describe their abuse in a way that denies the truth of sexual abuse:

- *I had sex with my _____.*
  [mother, father, brother, sister, coach, and so on].

- *It happened to me when I was _____.*

In his story, Niall describes what he experienced when his mother abused him:

> *After I recalled that my mother raped me, I kept telling my-self, I had sex with my mother. I believed this on a subliminal level, because my mother always behaved more like someone my own age than my parent, leaving me to believe I was some-how co-responsible for having intercourse with her.*

The U.S. Department of Justice's newly revised definition of rape is "the penetration, no matter how slight, of the vagina or anus with any body part or object, or oral penetration by a sex organ of another person, without the consent of the victim."[1] This definition does not call it "sex," and allows for the perpetrator and victim to be of either gender for the first time since 1927. The definition includes all acts where there is no consent. These are acts of violence by forcing, coercing, or manipulating a vulnerable person to satisfy the will and desires of a perpetrator. To describe sexual abuse as "having sex" is to deny the reality of the situation. When Niall's mother raped him, she was not having "intercourse" with Niall.

If you reread the Silence Breakers' stories, you will note that many write about what "happened *to*" them. For example, Gregg describes his abuse as having "happened":

> *My earliest memory of abuse was when I was about seven years old, from a female member of my family. She used to touch me and make me perform oral sex on her. This happened a few times.*

It minimizes the fact that you were sexually abused to describe it as something that "happened to" you. Hurricanes, tsunamis, and earthquakes *happen*. People do not choose to make any of these natural phenomena occur; rather, they really do just happen. Sexual abuse is far from a "happening." It is a *choice* someone else makes to force, coerce, or manipulate his or her will onto a more vulnerable person. If I were to change Gregg's words, I'd say, "My earliest memory of abuse was when a female member of my family abused me when I was seven. She touched me inappropriately and orally raped me several times by forcing me to orally stimulate her."

Seeing Yourself as a Dangerous Perpetrator Is a Dysfunctional Belief

Another common dysfunctional belief is *I'll become just like my perpetrator, and I will be dangerous around children.*

Pierre started therapy because he believed this myth. While it's true that a small minority of men who have been sexually abused do perpetrate acts of betrayal and sexual violation against children, most survivors would find engaging in such behaviors abhorrent to their souls. Because of the difficulty of conducting such research, there are no reliable statistics on how uncommon this is, as Harvard psychology professor Jim Hopper describes on his website.[2] Yet I have worked with countless survivors who are terrified that they might perpetrate abuse. Many are fathers or teachers or men who'd like to volunteer to help kids, but are afraid they might hurt a child if they are somehow "triggered" by flashbacks to their own experiences as victims. Any man who was abused as a child can become emotionally vulnerable and anxious while around children, especially if they are the same age as the survivor was when he was abused.

Being triggered can be scary, because uncomfortable feelings and thoughts can surface. Anytime you are triggered, remember to practice the grounding skills presented in Chapter 2. Breathe deeply; feel your feet on the floor; talk compassionately to yourself; and remind yourself that what was done to you has passed, that you survived, and that this is now. Remember, too, it's always okay to reach out for support. You can manage being triggered without acting out and hurting someone else or yourself. I know that through years of experience in this field.

For Men with a History of Perpetration: The Ultimate in Loyalty to Dysfunction

Some men reading this book may have engaged in acts of sexual perpetration during childhood, adolescence, or even adulthood. If you are one of these men, I believe you can also heal and stop perpetration. You cannot do this alone, and you will need a psychotherapist to help you, or you will need to enroll in a program for perpetrators. When you go for help, you will learn about two very important aspects of recovery. First and foremost, you must take responsibility for your perpetration. If you did it during childhood or adolescence, most likely you were reacting to your abuse and trying to figure out a way to heal. You may have consciously or unconsciously believed that doing to someone else what was done to you would help change your feelings about your own abuse. If you were a perpetrator as an adult, then it's extremely important for you to take 100 percent of the responsibility for your behavior. It's not a valid excuse to say, "I was abused and didn't know what else to do."

If you engaged in perpetration as an adult, you will need to understand what led to your behaviors, including looking at how you were victimized. You will need to look at the emotional state you were in when you committed these acts of betrayal and victimization. And, you will need to learn new ways to deal with your feelings so that you will never again engage in this self-destructive and extremely hurtful behavior.

Second, you will need to develop *victim empathy,* which means understanding how you lost the ability to feel the pain and wounding you inflicted on your victims. It's also important to reconnect to the pain and wounding you suffered because of your own abuse. Most abusers who were abused have severed that connection. Some tell themselves they are abusing others to gain back control of their lives.

Many perpetrators claim to have no control over their behavior. They may well be addicted to abusive acts and unable to stop without outside intervention. Treating another person in the same cruel way that you were treated is the ultimate in loyalty to dysfunction. With this loyalty, you affirm that the perpetrator who hurt you was right, that you deserved it and are helpless to do anything but repeat the abuse done to you.

For Non-offending Survivors

Perpetrators frequently don't seem like very sympathetic people to those who have been victimized. Some may think they deserve no compassion and no help. Survivors who have never become perpetrators may believe the actions of those who rape and assault are so horrible that all they deserve is punishment and a life of suffering.

I honor whatever feelings you may be having at this time. It's normal to be so angry about what was done to you that you have no compassion for those who harmed you or others. Recovery is a process, and if this is where you are in your recovery, it's important to honor those feelings.

At another point in your recovery, you may discover that there are steps to help you move farther in the process, to a place where you can let go of that anger and other emotions that might hinder your healing. I'll discuss those steps in Chapter 12, on forgiveness. For now, rest assured that wherever you are is okay.

Challenging Emotionally Dysfunctional Messages

While we're on the topic of emotions, you might have learned to be loyal to emotionally dysfunctional messages that may inhibit your recovery. Here are some of the most common ones:

— *Boys don't cry. Crying is a weakness.* Your parents or guardians may have told you, "If you don't stop crying, I'll give you something to cry about," which meant a spanking was coming. Many boys are told to stop being a "crybaby."

If you were victimized, you were wounded and experienced both physical and emotional pain. Feeling the pain you experienced when you were abused is part of the way you learn to believe that you actually were abused. As long as you stay numb, you can pretend it didn't hurt.

Loyalty to this dysfunctional message likely means that you shut down whenever you feel like crying. Or perhaps you only cry in private and definitely never let anyone see you do so, even your psychotherapist. If you can't stop yourself from crying, then you likely feel shame and embarrassment for allowing the feelings to surface. Or you view yourself as a "wimp" because you weren't tough enough to resist.

The following is a related dysfunctional message:

— *Strength is demonstrated by showing no emotion.* There are some circumstances in which it's desirable to show no emotion. For example, if you are a soldier on a battlefield, you need to be focused, alert, and ready to protect yourself and your fellow troops. Showing emotion in the midst of a battle could easily interfere with your primary mission. But there is a difference between showing emotion and having emotions. One of the common problems that sexual abuse survivors can share with soldiers is that you might suffer from *post-traumatic stress disorder.* Simply put, this disorder occurs because you had to stuff your feelings during the abuse or combat. But when the traumatic event ends, the feelings you repressed are likely to surface and cause distress.

Managing Flashbacks and Dissociation

Flashbacks are common for abuse survivors who have experienced trauma and soldiers who have served in combat. They are caused by the resurfacing of physical and emotional memories that were repressed during the traumatic event. When you feel safe again, flashbacks are released by your unconscious, and the reliving of the memory can be very frightening, painful, and even debilitating, as some of the Silence Breakers noted in their stories.

During a traumatic experience, your mind and body shut down as a means of protecting you from the awareness of the experience. This is not something you can control. It's an involuntary survival mechanism, like the dissociation that some Silence Breakers described earlier.

As you will recall, dissociation is an elaborate defense mechanism where you separate from your body. Some people block out sights and sounds that resurface later in memory. Silence Breaker Christopher mentioned hearing the hum of the air conditioning that he'd heard during an attack. A more severe type of dissociation occurs when someone creates another personality or personalities in order to distance the conscious self from a traumatic experience. The "new" personality might even have a different voice, and you might visualize this part of you very differently than you do the core part of you. In this type of dissociation, you might typically hear inside your head the voice of the "other" you, trying to be heard and understood.

If you dissociated during your abusive experience, please understand that this survival mechanism may have saved your life and set you up to heal now. Be aware, however, that healing after this type of dissociation requires assistance from an experienced psychotherapist. Many Voices is a support group for people like you, and I've provided contact information in the Resources section at the end of this book.

Dysfunctionally Seeking Total Control of Your Emotions

As you heal, you choose whether to show your emotions. Because abuse is ultimately about losing control to a perpetrator, it's natural for you to want to take control of your life again. One way that people sometimes do that is by controlling their feelings so fiercely that they come across as entirely lacking emotion. If anyone asks about the abuse, a typical response in this case would be "It was nothing; I'm over it."

Loyalty to this dysfunctional message can hinder your healing and recovery. By blocking your feelings, you prevent any type of connection with others, even those who could help you. In addition, by denying emotions related to the abuse, you prevent others from offering you support, because you deny needing it. The biggest block to your recovery posed by shutting down emotionally is that you lose touch with your true feelings, which are a big part of who you are.

Your abuser may have been out of touch with his or her feelings, too. The perpetrator may have denied any emotional connection to you. By buying into the dysfunctional message that strength requires suppressing emotions, you are being loyal to your perpetrator. After all, you are exhibiting the same behavior, right?

The Comfort Zone as a Danger Zone

Here are other dysfunctional messages or lies that can thwart your efforts to heal. If you engage in addictive or compulsive behavior, you may be especially vulnerable to the following messages:

- *I am comfortable with my present behavior.*

- *It's better to be comfortable than risk discomfort.*

- *If I am familiar with a pattern of behavior, it's better to stay with that behavior than to risk discomfort.*

- *There's no risk in engaging in familiar behavior that makes me comfortable.*

Let me begin with an obvious observation: If you were totally comfortable with your present life choices and behaviors, it's unlikely that you would be reading this chapter or this book. Most of the times when I challenge my clients about their comfort levels, they realize that they are confusing true *comfort* with *familiarity*. They would rather not admit feeling discomfort, because it would mean having to engage in unfamiliar behaviors. It boils down to choosing a sense of "safety" over doing something that might put that sense of security at risk. It can feel risky to engage in unfamiliar behavior. There is some risk in letting go of your loyalty to a familiar behavior that may result in your feeling uncomfortable.

Yet here's the important catch: It's also risky to keep behaving in familiar ways that are dysfunctional.

Becoming an addict is a classic example of being loyal to dysfunction. A corollary of the addict's dysfunctional belief is the following:

- *Practicing my addiction keeps me safe from getting hurt by others.*

Even when you dislike the outcomes of your addiction, you may refuse to stop because you believe it keeps you "safe." It may well keep you numb; however, numbness is never safe, as I noted earlier. Experiencing your feelings and being present are necessary for healing. A survivor of abuse who becomes an addict is often trying to numb himself from that traumatic experience and the painful feelings its memories stir up. But by numbing yourself, you may minimize the impact of your abuse, just as you minimize the damage you do every time you abuse your substance of choice.

When you give yourself permission to feel discomfort, you also allow yourself to feel more joy, satisfaction, and connection, because you are expanding your ability to feel. You may be like many people in recovery, who want to skip over their pain and discomfort because they just want to feel better. However, feeling the pain and discomfort are key aspects of recovery. Feeling your discomfort and connecting with your emotions puts you on the road to embracing healing, which is also known as "being loyal to functionality."

There is more irony in believing that addictive behavior keeps you safe. How often have you heard the story of an addict who gets raped when he or she is too stoned or drunk to fight back, and then can't even remember the experience? I've had many clients say they've awakened alone in a strange bed, naked and bloody, with no idea how they got there or what was done to them. If you are one of these men, I hope you'll find the strength here to challenge this dysfunctional message.

Sexual addiction can result from loyalty to dysfunction. Psychotherapists view sex addiction as a struggle to establish an affirming or real connection with another person. Loyalty to dysfunction can lead to sex addiction or other addictions that mask one's pain. Sex addiction is most often tied to sexual abuse. Psychologist Patrick Carnes's research has proven dramatically that most sex addicts have histories of sexual, physical, and emotional abuse—and often a combination of all three types of abuse.[3] Sex addiction develops from believing the previous myth that your only worth is in being a sex object. Practicing sex addiction also temporarily helps a survivor numb his pain and have momentary control over his life.

Many survivors are addicted to sex, which definitely is not a safe behavior. They watch so much porn that they lose track of time. They may cheat on their partners or wives. They log hours on the Internet, chatting and trying to connect with, or actually connecting with, strangers. They may engage in illegal sexual behaviors like exhibitionism and voyeurism.

Eventually, most sex addicts enter treatment because of some traumatic event that exposes their addiction to people they care about. They begin therapy believing that their addiction to sex is necessary for them to cope with the stresses of life. Their addiction has become so familiar that they can barely imagine life without it. They may well lie to themselves and say they are comfortable with their sex addiction, but most of the time, that proves not to be the case when the addiction becomes known to friends and family, employers, or co-workers.

Stepping Out of the Comfort Zone into the Healing Zone

Truth: To heal and recover, it's necessary to tolerate and manage discomfort. Let me offer you a little encouragement at this point. As I tell all of my abuse-survivor clients, when you were abused, and for a long time afterward, you felt alone in your suffering, with little or no support. I hope you'll agree that this solitary suffering has gone on long enough. Now, using the tools in this book, you can declare an end to your isolation. There are people in your life who understand and know about your struggles or have the willingness to do so. You have many more resources available to you. Even if you are not yet receiving professional therapy, simply reading this book and using the tools and skills provided within its pages will provide many more resources to help you tolerate and manage your challenges and lingering pain. It's absolutely possible to learn how to tolerate and manage discomfort by tapping internal and external resources. You'll also need to learn how to be loyal to functionality, which we'll tackle in the next chapter.

The Beginning of Letting Go of Shame

One of the most painful feelings to deal with in recovery is shame, the feeling that you have been diminished by the abuse done to you. This is another dysfunctional belief you may have accepted, one that says: *I am disgraced; unworthy; not good enough, smart enough, successful enough, attractive enough, or clean enough.*

Silence Breaker Chris describes how his shame stemmed from being abused and unprotected, and how it nearly killed him:

> *The main dysfunctional message for me was that nobody cared about me. I was the number one person who looked down on me. I believed I was a dirty, blameworthy, useless, and worthless nobody that was and should be ignored. I figured that if the abuser didn't care about me as I had wished, if my family didn't protect me as I thought I deserved, and the "gods" didn't seem to be present as I had been taught, then I must be worthless. Isolation grew over time, and I slipped deeper into depression. Suicidal thoughts were rampant, and I was very close to acting on them.*

Silence Breaker Gregg wrote about his struggles with shame, especially in regard to his body. He regularly works out, pays attention to his diet, and is, by most standards, "in shape." Many survivors struggle with a condition called *body dysmorphia,* in which they have a distorted view of their actual body images. Gregg also struggles with feeling clean enough, which is a related symptom. Many male survivors are haunted by the feeling that they were "dirtied" by their abusers. Rape survivors are especially prone to this feeling, too. Gregg explains:

> *Even though I shower three times a day, I never feel clean enough: I'm bad, I'm unattractive, and I'm not fit enough or smart enough. I learned these messages from my mother and all the abusers. I had one good relationship between ages 18 and 20, but since then, the older I have become, the more I distance myself. When I try to get close, it's just one drama after another. Eventually they treat me like crap, and I'm out. When people tell me positive things about me, I don't believe them and I struggle to accept that they could be true.*

The Source of Dysfunctional Messages

At the beginning of this chapter, I asked you to make a list of the dysfunctional messages you've accepted about yourself, and then I asked you to identify the person or people who taught you those messages. Let's go back and consider those sources. I want you to think about how loyal you feel to those who have taught you dysfunctional messages and why you hold on to any degree of loyalty. Being loyal to dysfunction may mean that you choose to be loyal to people who are not worthy. Loyalty is earned. It's not a right that comes with someone's position or authority. If an individual behaves in immoral or hurtful ways, if someone deliberately hurts others by abusing their bodies, minds, and souls, you have no obligation to be loyal no matter who they are. If your religious beliefs command you to believe differently, I invite you to pray about it and to seek advice from a compassionate religious leader who understands the devastation of sexual abuse. We can choose to be compassionate with people who commit crimes, while still believing that their behavior was wrong and inexcusable.

You may struggle with ending your loyalty to a person who is in authority, especially if the individual otherwise acted in trustworthy or kind ways. If someone violated your trust and betrayed your body, it's absolutely okay to suspend your trust and respect for authority. The abuser forfeited his right to receive trust and honor by violating your rights and your body. The process of examining your loyalty to dysfunction takes time. That's why I asked you earlier to look at how much you still believe dysfunctional messages. Maybe you can find it easier to take things step-by-step. For example, if you still strongly believe a dysfunctional message, what would it take for you to move to *I am somewhat loyal to that message* instead? And if you are *somewhat loyal,* what would it take to move to *Not too loyal anymore?*

It can be immensely painful to distrust people you have trusted your whole life. It has the effect of undoing your reality as you have known it. It can make trusting anyone difficult, especially if you can't trust the people who supposedly loved you. Some men will refuse to feel this degree of pain and discomfort, because it seems "safer" to believe the old truths.

Some survivors try to live on a seesaw, believing that sometimes they can trust the people who taught them dysfunction. But sometimes, knowing the right and healthy path is to face the truth, that they manipulated or lied to you, or at least neglected your safety. This is called *feeling ambivalent*. Ambivalence is a normal response to letting go of your loyalty to dysfunction. If you recognize it as part of the process, it will help you keep moving forward. At this stage, it's important to *learn to trust people who honor your truth*. You will need the support of those men who have walked in your shoes, because they can offer you hope. Silence Breakers Bruce and Christopher shared their thoughts on this:

> *For me, knowing that there were other men (survivors) out there who also had been manipulated and fooled, as I was, helped me understand that I am not a stupid guy, and it also helped me put into perspective that when I was abused, I was an immature boy. This behavior learned over a long period of time is tricky to break away from, but with many positive reinforcements and a lot of healthy, positive support, it gets more manageable all the time. — Bruce*

> *Therapy, both individual and group, has helped me get these thoughts out of my head. I needed to be reassured by my therapist and comrades that what I grew to believe was false. What was, and still is, key was sharing, talking, and being honest with myself. I needed to confront what I'd been hiding from myself. — Christopher*

I hope you can understand that loyalty to dysfunction is not related to your intelligence, financial status, social standing, or attractiveness. This loyalty is something every survivor learns, and learns well, at the time of his abuse—and it's often reinforced by the neglect and additional abuse that frequently follow. It can hang on for a long time without intervention. Even with intervention, psychotherapy, and support, it's often a struggle to let go.

In the next chapter, I will introduce your next step: to become loyal to functionality. I am confident that your reading these two chapters together will help you take some major steps forward in your recovery and healing.

AFFIRMATIONS FOR CHAPTER 7

- *I can learn to be disloyal to dysfunction now!*
- *I can challenge the belief that I need to stay loyal to the people who abused me.*
- *Today, I can learn to place my trust in people who will honor my truth.*

CHAPTER EIGHT

Dare to Dream You Can Embrace Loyalty to Functionality

"Let the healing power of connecting with other survivors be the key to freeing that real you trapped within all your pain." *Designer:* Mike, Silence Breaker.

In the previous chapter, I described the characteristics of dysfunctional behavior and the importance of being disloyal to dysfunction. This chapter will further your recovery by helping you understand what it means to be loyal to functionality and explore ways you can practice this loyalty.

Functionality is defined for our purposes as a set of behaviors that can help you cope with the stresses of life, help you overcome the effects of your abuse, and help lead you to not only survive, but also actually heal and thrive in your life. When you are functional, you have access to a wide range of emotions, from feeling sad or angry to feeling joyful and connected. A functional man can be strong and compassionate, and powerful and sensitive at the same time. When you are loyal to functionality, anytime you are tempted to act or think in a dysfunctional way, you can challenge your beliefs and affirm your ability to make healthier choices that will empower you.

Who wouldn't want these results, right? So how do you get there?

You have already taken the first step: You have learned to identify your dysfunctional messages and behaviors. You have looked at the sources of these messages and challenged your loyalty to the people who taught them to you. You might have decided that even though you trusted these people in the past, you now feel that your trust must be earned, not given simply because someone who abused you has authority over you or claims to care for or love you.

It's likely to be uncomfortable and definitely unfamiliar for you to be loyal to functionality. Yet the more you practice a new behavior, the more comfortable you will feel. Let's look at some functional beliefs that could enhance your healing and recovery:

— *I have a right to set healthy boundaries.* What is a healthy boundary? One example is the ability to say no when you don't want to do something or when you want to stop a person whose actions make you uncomfortable. As a survivor, you probably learned that you had no right to set boundaries concerning how people treated you. You may have learned that it was your job to put the needs of others before your own. If so, you may find it challenging to assert your right for people to respect you, your needs, and your values and principles.

Experiment with New Possibilities: Exploring Your Ability to Set Healthy Boundaries

This is a list of healthy personal boundaries. Photocopy it for your journal and rate your ability to set these boundaries. Your options are "Never," "Rarely," "Sometimes," "Often," and "Always." Also list any other important boundaries.

Important Boundaries	Never	Rarely	Sometimes	Often	Always
I decide who enters my home.					
I decide what food I eat.					
I decide when I go to sleep.					
I decide when to get out of bed.					
I decide whom I date and how often.					
I decide if and when I want to commit to being monogamous with another person.					
I decide if I want to break up.					
I decide what I want to keep private.					
I decide how long someone stays with me as a guest.					
I decide if I will drink alcohol and how much.					
I decide if I will use street drugs, and how much and how often.					
I decide if I will take medicine that has been prescribed for me.					
I decide what jobs I want to apply for.					
I decide what books to read.					
I decide if I go to a social group.					
I decide if I go to a recovery group.					
I decide who touches my body.					

I decide how my body is touched.					
I decide who hugs me and how.					
I decide who will be my sex partners.					

As you complete this exercise, notice if any of these statements are rights that you have never considered to be a boundary for you. Notice how many statements you have from each category: "Never," "Always," and all those in between. Survivors struggle a lot with boundaries, because their boundaries were violated. It's okay if you have never considered that it is within your rights to set boundaries. It's okay if many of your responses are "Never" or "Rarely." You can start today!

Also notice which boundaries seem to be on the other side of the scale: "Often" or "Always." Notice what seems different about the boundaries that are easier for you to practice compared to the boundaries that are more difficult.

Most people worry about upsetting someone if they set boundaries. That may well happen, which is why you can practice establishing boundaries in a sensitive manner. Unfortunately, you cannot control how everyone will react. You can do your best to help others understand your need to be comfortable and secure. It's your right to set whatever boundaries for your body, mind, and spirit will help you feel respected and safe.

Silence Breaker Christopher wrote about the importance of understanding his right and power to set boundaries:

> *Until I began to understand that I possessed some sense of my own power, until I really owned the sense that I could set a boundary, it was impossible for me to have any boundaries, let alone healthy ones. I spent most of my life feeling severely handicapped by this sense that I had no ability to control many things in my own life.*

Silence Breakers Bruce and SJC wrote about their efforts to understand that they had the power to say no, and finally asserting their rights helped them to better care for themselves.

I had to learn to say no to people, and to learn that saying no is not rude or disrespectful. I've learned that it's a healthy boundary for my looking after myself. — Bruce

If someone is being an asshole, I have the right to walk away. I'm not sure I understood that before. I was more inclined to sit there and be the victim again. If someone is berating you, especially a family member, you, as an adult, don't have to sit there and take it. As young sexual victims, we had no choice. As adults, we really do get to decide! — SJC

— I am responsible for showing sensitivity to other people's feelings rather than being responsible for their feelings. Some of you may have learned while growing up that you are responsible for other people's feelings. The truth is that you are responsible for being sensitive to other people's feelings, which is different. Do you see the significant difference between being sensitive to feelings and being responsible for them? Sensitivity requires you to be aware that people could have some discomfort with a boundary you are setting. One way to be sensitive is to tell the person that you are aware that this boundary may be uncomfortable, but it's necessary if you are to continue your recovery. Tell the person that you mean no harm and that by setting the boundary, you hope to make it possible to grow closer to him or her—if you desire.

Your Right to Speak Your Truths

Let's look at some other aspects of being loyal to functionality:

— I have a right to speak my truth, when, where, how, and to whom I choose. This is especially important as you consider the abuse that was done to you. If you remain loyal to dysfunction and to dysfunctional people, you may be tempted to believe that

you cannot tell your truth because you will hurt the perpetrator of the abuse and make the person's life difficult. *The only person who has the right to choose when, where, and to whom you tell your truth is you.* This is your story, and it does not belong to anyone else.

The perpetrator chose to hurt you. Abuse doesn't "just happen." Since the perpetrator owns 100 percent of the responsibility for the abuse, that person also owns 100 percent of the responsibility for any consequences that befall him or her as a result of choosing to violate you. The more serious the consequences may be, the more likely it is that you will struggle, especially if the consequences could include prison time for the perpetrator.

Earlier, I presented the story of Bruce, the young man abused by a physician who was also Bruce's assistant basketball coach. The doctor groomed him, so Bruce kept silent for many years, afraid that no one would believe him. He was afraid he'd be judged, and he was worried about hurting the doctor's practice.

Bruce later learned to be loyal to functionality. He spent ten years seeking justice. Finally, a panel of the doctor's peers took his license away, and Bruce felt empowered, validated, and proud.

You, too, may be afraid to tell your story because it could hurt your abuser. But it was that person's job to protect you, and instead the perpetrator abused you. Too often, the abuser is someone in a position of authority over the victim, whether as a parent, guardian, babysitter, teacher, coach, principal, or doctor.

For some of you, especially men who were raped as adults, your abusers may likely be strangers, people who, at that time, took advantage of your vulnerability. You have the right to speak your truth as well, even though you may feel overwhelmed with shame from the false belief that you should have been able to protect yourself. Rapists pick victims they know they can overcome. It's not your fault you were not stronger at that moment. Often, rapists not only sexually assault their victims, but also physically abuse them. It's also common for them to make emotional threats to keep their victims silent. This is why it's so important to offer yourself compassion for what was done to you at a time when you could not protect yourself. Remember the story of Gregg, who was abused by a police officer? In his case, he felt it would be impossible to stand up for himself, because he'd never be believed. Although he got no justice from the police authorities, he still believes that he must speak his truth.

For those abused when they were younger, it's possible that the perpetrator who had a responsibility to protect you may feel very bad or guilty when you express your truth and define your boundaries. Still, *you have a responsibility to be sensitive to other people's feelings, but you are not responsible for their feelings.* If the perpetrator feels guilty, that's an appropriate feeling for that person to have, because he or she did share in the responsibility for your safety. While guilt is uncomfortable, everyone has the ability to heal from guilt if they accept their responsibility. By choosing to be loyal to functionality, you are choosing to let go of your own guilt and responsibility, and thus, the actual responsibility for your abuse will fall on the perpetrator and on the people who had some role in protecting you.

— *I give myself permission to cry tears of grief, sadness, joy, and happiness.* When you give yourself permission to cry, you are actually giving yourself permission to grow stronger. When you give yourself permission to feel pain and grief, you are also increasing your capacity to feel joy and happiness. Early in my recovery, when someone gave me a compliment, I cried. These were tears of sadness and tears of happiness: sadness that I waited so long to be affirmed and that my own parents were so unhealthy that they didn't know how to affirm me, and happiness that someone was telling me that I had good qualities I could be proud of.

If you were abused as an adult, crying validates the inevitable pain inside you. If you were abused as a boy, crying allows the boy inside you to let you know the pain he experienced. I invite you to proudly claim your right to cry. Know that every tear you cry validates your self-worth and gives you a great chance to be stronger and healthier today.

If you want to feel happiness and joy, then you have to also open up to pain and sadness. Think of it as expanding your "emotional muscles." Choosing to stay numb is the equivalent of doing no exercise and expecting that somehow you can get stronger and healthier. To become stronger, it's necessary to allow yourself to experience the whole range of possible feelings. When you have more emotional muscles, you will be safer, because your feelings, when combined with your intellectual understanding and insights, give you a rich place from which to understand yourself and to be present, alive, and connected with others.

— *I can let go of unhealthy shame and replace it with healthy pride.* What is unhealthy shame? As I discussed earlier, the feeling of shame occurs anytime you feel that you are not good enough. Like most survivors, you may have felt shame for a long time. You may be very uncomfortable with taking pride in your accomplishments or talents. You may have learned (yet another dysfunctional message) that people who feel pride are arrogant and, therefore, you should never admit to having good qualities. This is a recipe for a lifetime of shame and negative self-esteem, and now you are working to claim your right to a life of pride and positive self-esteem.

So what is healthy pride? It's the belief that you are good enough and have the right to claim success and recovery. Pride means you give yourself permission to be strong: emotionally, physically, intellectually, and spiritually. It means you are strong enough to stand up to those who tell you that you should feel ashamed.

When Oprah Winfrey recruited 200 men to stand in her studio on November 5 and 12, 2010, she gave them permission—and these men gave themselves and each other permission—to join forces by standing strong and feeling proud. They had survived, and they served as inspiration to others. They are proof that healing is absolutely possible.

A very important part of being loyal to functionality is the ability to feel pride. When you are in the beginning of recovery, it can be quite a struggle. As you make progress, I encourage you to practice feeling pride in yourself. Pride is a nutrient for your healthy self-esteem; allow it to take root and grow.

EXPERIMENT WITH NEW POSSIBILITIES:
Increasing Your Self-Esteem and Sense of Pride

This is an inventory of your ability to give yourself permission to increase your self-esteem and feel pride. You can photocopy it for your journal. I have listed areas of your life where you may feel worthy of pride. Check inside, and then check below how often you feel pride about these different aspects of your life. Again, your choices are "Never," "Rarely," "Sometimes," "Often," and "Always." Also list in your journal any other aspects of your character, your life, and yourself about which you feel pride.

Points of Pride	Never	Rarely	Sometimes	Often	Always
I feel proud of having survived abuse.					
I am proud that I can tell my story of my abuse and recovery.					
I am proud of my emotional strength.					
I am proud of my physical strength.					
I am proud of my body.					
I am proud of my spirituality.					
I am proud of my resiliency.					
I am proud of my ability to ask for help when I need it.					
I am proud of my ability to give help.					

I am proud of my ability to be disloyal to dysfunction.					
I am proud of my ability to be loyal to functionality.					

After you have finished the exercise and noted additional things that you are proud of, check your feelings and emotions. Be especially aware of any part of you that may be feeling uncomfortable, and remind yourself, *I have a right to claim my personal pride.* You may want to do breathing exercises to help you relax while acknowledging these truths about yourself.

Notice how many of your answers are "Never" or "Rarely," and make a commitment to yourself that in a week, you will give yourself permission to claim each truth or at least to experiment with the possibility that any of the previous statements could be true about you. Be aware of how often you wanted to add a disclaimer to the end of the statement, such as "Sometimes" or "Rarely." Even if it's "Rarely," at least you know that you can give yourself permission to feel proud, if only just a little.

If you answered "Never" to all of the previous statements, I want to offer you these two affirmations and suggest that you experiment with them this week:

- *I can learn to increase my self-esteem a little at a time.*

- *I have the right to learn to feel proud of myself, and to let go of loyalty to dysfunction, which is blocking me right now.*

Saying these statements each day, preferably while looking at yourself in a mirror, allows you to start claiming your right to a more positive self-esteem while helping you release more of your shame. Practice saying them out loud, in as firm a voice as you can muster. Even if you can only whisper these statements, start there. The child inside will hear, no matter how loud or soft you speak. I will write more about that child soon.

SILENCE BREAKERS' BEST ADVICE:
Embracing Your Pride

Now that you've completed the exercise, you might find more inspiration in this list of the things the Silence Breakers are proud of. I invite you to read over this list, remembering that every one of them has struggled like you, and if they can feel pride, I know you can, too.

I am most proud that I found the resources to get better, that I did the work, and that in doing so, have managed to help others in their recovery. — Bruce

I am proud of my perseverance and my drive to reconnect with the real me. I'm proud that I've pushed through, because I'm finally seeing the fruit of my labors. I am most proud of the fact that I believed in my boy's dreams and that I protected him, nourished him, and guided him to a way of happiness. — Chris

I'm a loyal friend. I am proud that I am letting the pain out and releasing my shame. I am proud that I am learning how to control my life. — Gregg

I am very proud that I now lead a joyous life that I had no idea existed, compared to my life before recovery. It's never too late if you are willing to do the work. I am proud that I have acquired generosity in my attitude toward others, willingness, and patience. — John

I am really proud that I am a survivor, and if I can last this long, I should be able to last to the end. As painful as it has been, I now have a much clearer understanding of who I am. — SJC

I am proud to have survived the trauma of being sexually abused as a child, but more so as an adult, when the impact of the abuse is actually more present. I am proud that I've been married for 20 years, and I'm proud of my children. I am proud of knowing how many people I have reached out to, and actually seeing the ones that I have helped and guided turn their lives around. — Rhett

> *I'm proud of my continuing trust in my Higher Power and my continuing spiritual journey. I know I'm worthy of love from others, my God, and myself. I'm proud of being able to tell my story of abuse and recovery, which has only weakened the grip and control fear has had on me. Every time I tell my story, I bounce back and feel more liberated. I am also proud of my contributions to the community of survivors through helping others. — Ryan*
>
> *I have recently become a father, which makes me feel proud and honored; I believe that I will be the father I never had to my own son. I am proud that after years of dysfunctional relationships, I have achieved a healthy and loving partnership with a woman who inspires me and believes in me; we have created the beginnings of a safe and nurturing family of our own. — Simon*

When You Struggle with Being Loyal to Functionality

Learning to be loyal to functionality is a daily challenge you will face during your recovery. Each time you embrace a functional life, you will develop more confidence and an increased ability to choose the healthier path. Despite your best efforts, you will falter. You may know what your best choice is and plan how to make that choice, and, when the time comes, choose a dysfunctional path instead. Resist the urge to stress out. Relapsing is normal in the process of recovery. You are not and never will be perfect. A healthier goal is to make the best and most functional choices as often as you can. If you do falter, make it your goal to be aware when you make unhealthy choices so that you can catch yourself and minimize the damage. If you cannot catch yourself, you have the option to learn from your mistakes and to understand what went wrong.

By engaging in this process, you have permission to be compassionate with yourself. Read what Silence Breaker Christopher has to say:

I try to remember to be kind to myself. This is sort of a "fall down seven times, get up eight" thing. I fail on a daily basis. Often, making mistakes triggers me. The difference now is that I am far better at forgiving myself than I used to be. It helps to be mindful that my dysfunctional behaviors do not truly reflect the person I am inside or the person I have the potential to become. I am not defined, limited, or predestined in any way by the dysfunctions I fight against in my world. The dysfunctions are things the acts of others created that I fell victim to. It's very difficult to hold on to this truth, because I learned very early on to see myself as a broken child.

Every time you make a healthy choice, it reinforces your commitment to functionality. You will feel better each time you make that choice. The process is very similar to working through an addiction. If you slip and relapse, instead of shaming and blaming yourself, you can choose to learn from the experience and commit to doing better next time.

Being consistent and keeping things simple can help you increase your commitment to functionality. Silence Breaker Mike advocates this and also addresses a fallacy about stress management that he learned in the military. That fallacy has not served him well in civilian life or in recovery. He has found that every small step forward reinforces his loyalty to functionality.

The biggest thing for me in this area is consistency in my overall health and activities. I eat right, maintain my medications, drink plenty of water, get the right amount of sleep, and keep things simple. If I find myself slipping, I check myself in these areas. One thing I heard in the military was to work the big items first, because they are the ones causing the most stress. I have learned that this is not true. Everything on your mind causes stress in some cases, so if you can knock out the small things, it not only eases the stress on your mind, but also builds your confidence to move forward in your other tasks and challenges.

SILENCE BREAKERS' BEST ADVICE:
Learning from Your Mistakes

When it comes to learning from your mistakes, having support is essential. Often, you may not be able to see where you went wrong, but an outsider can point out aspects that may have been hidden from you. Sometimes, supportive outsiders who are not burdened with the same traumatic history can offer constructive criticism that will help you make healthier choices. Other times, it's important to reach out to men who have walked in your path, because they will usually offer the most honest and compassionate response, yet they will challenge you, too. They know how easy it is to make excuses in your situation.

Fellow survivors can serve as a "mirror" to show you what's possible and healthy. You can look at their experience and say, *Yes, I can succeed, just as my friend has done.*

> *I let the people who matter to me (family, friends, therapist, group members) know about it so that they can support me in getting back on track without judgment.* — Bruce

> *I can always reach out to friends, my brothers through the MaleSurvivor website, or others in my support group who understand both my temptation to be dysfunctional and my desire to be functional. They get it, and can recognize and sympathize. I usually am the most honest with them, because I can trust them.* — Chris

> *When I encounter a dysfunctional relationship and unhealthy communication, rather than confront the individual, I make a choice to remove myself and seek healthier relationships. I go back to where I am centered, back to key people in my life.* — Coach

Supporters like these Silence Breakers can also help remind you that you are more than your mistakes: You are worthy and deserving of love and support, even if you made a mistake and faltered.

Silence Breaker Jarrod writes about the steps he takes to get back on "the horse":

> *I seek to acknowledge my setbacks and then put them away. Learning to be loyal to functionality means having to acknowledge when we revert back to old dysfunctional behaviors. The real victory is in not staying in that place too long and getting back on that horse. I also believe in writing it out, which is often the last thing I feel like doing. Journaling about what I am feeling usually allows me time to focus on the present moment rather than on living in and responding to the past. — Jarrod*

I often encourage my clients to carry a list in their wallets that will help provide internal support, encouragement, and motivation. Copy the following exercise, and if you are tempted to slip into dysfunctional behavior, referring to this convenient list could help you.

EXPERIMENT WITH NEW POSSIBILITIES:
Increasing Your Motivation to Stay Loyal to Functionality

I'll start you off with a few suggestions, and then I hope you will add many more of your own.

My reasons for staying loyal to functionality:

- *I will be happier.*
- *I will feel more confident.*
- *I will get the support I need.*

- _____

- _____

Take a moment to read each of your reasons aloud. Check inside and see how each one feels. If you are struggling with any particular one, try this exercise my colleague Paul Linden taught me: State the reason, and then say, "Ahhhhhhhh." Notice how saying "Ahhhhhhhh" relaxes your body. Let go of the discomfort you may feel in risking taking a more positive approach to your life. Give yourself permission to review this list every day. Keep noticing which reasons seem the most difficult to accept and believe. They may be the reasons you need to focus on.

Enjoy the following affirmations to help you keep choosing to be loyal to functionality. Next, I will explore with you how to connect with the playful, spontaneous part of you that's often connected with the boy part of you.

AFFIRMATIONS FOR CHAPTER 8

- *I have a right to set healthy boundaries.*
- *I have a right to cry tears of joy and sadness.*
- *I have a right to feel proud of my accomplishments and strengths.*
- *I choose to feel proud of myself now.*

CHAPTER NINE

Dare to Dream
You Can Connect with
the Boy Inside You

"The availability of the very small T-shirts enabled me to visualize
and express my current life project of reaching out to the hurt, molested boy
inside and to hold him with love, respect, and kindness." *Designer:* Jim Logan.

Some survivors were abused only as boys, some were abused as boys and also as men, and some were only abused as adults. If you are an adult survivor of rape, you may find this chapter totally offensive, and of course, that's not my intention. I encourage you to skip over it if you want to. You may also choose to keep an open mind, because one of the problems adult rape survivors experience is that they often have a great deal of difficulty experiencing pleasure, being spontaneous, and having fun again. They often feel so ashamed and so violated that they retreat into isolation and depression. Remember, there's a boy inside you who *did* know how to be spontaneous and how to play, and who enjoyed life before the rape.

Perhaps connecting with him may help you now. It's likely that he also felt the impact of the sexual assault on your adult body.

During the Weekends of Recovery, we play a variety of children's games, primarily because survivors often are cheated out of their childhoods and out of opportunities to be spontaneous and carefree. I had to get a bachelor's degree and a master's degree in play (well, actually my major was therapeutic recreation) to learn how important play and recreation are for us. Even men who were raped as adults find that these games give them an experience of feeling free and fun loving that's often lacking in their lives.

"Really? There's a Boy Inside Me?"

When I talk about connecting with the boy inside, most men in therapy look at me like I'm a little crazy. They sometimes say it's stupid, silly, or impossible, or just say, "Really?"

What's it like to consider the idea of a boy along with the adult you? Could you talk to the boy you? Or is that the child in you that's not interested in getting help from the adult you?

Are you ever in touch with the boy part of you? Let me give you some situations where perhaps you will be able to grasp this concept more easily.

Have you, as an adult, ever visited a playground or an amusement park, or gone sledding? Perhaps you took your son or daughter, or a niece or nephew, or you went with a group of friends. Recall how you felt being there. You may relate to feeling like a child again. You might have felt joy when you focused on the fun you were having in the moment.

Some men build elaborate train villages in their backyards or basements. Hearing those trains race around the track reminds them of being a boy. Others play board games, like *Monopoly* or *Scrabble*. Perhaps you have games on your phone, iPad, or iPod touch, or you have a Game Boy, Wii, or PlayStation? Maybe you love computer games? Have you had the experience of losing track of time while playing? That's a typical thing that happens in a healthy child's life. He gets so involved in the game he is playing that he has no idea what time it is or how much time has passed.

Do you like to sing? Ever find yourself driving and singing along to the radio or your favorite CD? You might be in tune or not; it doesn't matter, because you are just pleased to know the words or remember the tune. Boys often love to sing, as long as no one criticizes their singing.

Many men love to play sports. They enjoy the competition and the opportunity to socialize with teammates, to sweat, and to develop a sense of competency in the game. Playing sports can help you connect with the boy inside you, because that boy also loved to play.

All of these are examples of times when you may have been in touch with the boy inside you. The boy inside an abused man may have had his opportunities to enjoy his childhood severely limited, because abuse makes a boy grow up pretty fast. It may be that you participated with an abuser in some of the activities you loved. In that case, the good feelings you once had about that pastime may be tainted.

Why Connect with Your Inner Boy?

Survivors often have a hard time having fun and being spontaneous. They lose this ability because they focus so much on their abuse and recovery that having fun isn't even a consideration. Life becomes a serious challenge, and this may be truer for men who were abused as adults. In some ways, that abuse is even more devastating, because as an adult, you may believe that you *should* have been able to protect yourself. Unfortunately, this is one of the masculinity myths that many men learn in our culture, and hopefully in the last two chapters, you had an opportunity to examine the real truth about what makes men strong. The famed boxer Sugar Ray Leonard offers proof of this in his memoir, *The Big Fight: My Life In and Out of the Ring.* He describes having been sexually assaulted by his boxing coach as an adult and how his shame almost kept him from describing all the details in his book. But he said, after watching an actor on *The Oprah Winfrey Show* share his story, "I realized I would never be free unless I revealed the whole truth, no matter how much it hurt."[1] The shame of being raped as an adult can make healing a major challenge. Connecting with your boy can be a way to give yourself permission to have fun again, or at least permission to let go of all the seriousness and some of the shame.

If you were abused as a child, then connecting with your inner boy has other value. You may have disconnected from the feelings associated with your abuse. The boy inside you may know what the feelings were, but the adult part of you is disconnected. Read Silence Breaker Christopher's experience:

> Until I had attempted to make connection with my inner boy, I think I had been dealing with superficial healing. I was making some progress, but I felt that for every step forward I made, I'd eventually fall back because I hadn't dealt with the deeper issues. What I wanted to do was learn how to make the pain go away. What became clear was that the pain was emanating from that child. The little boy inside of me still hurt, and his pain was made real every day of my adult life. What's more, the child inside of me saw through his eyes the world I lived in as an adult. The adult fears that were holding me back were the fears of a boy trapped in a world of pain and darkness.

Understand what your boy learned about life from his abuse. He may have learned many dysfunctional messages. Recognizing these dysfunctional messages gives you the opportunity to challenge them and to invite yourself to be loyal to functionality instead. This is Silence Breaker SJC's challenge:

> As much as I was told how lucky I was and that our family was blessed, the cold facts were that our family was fucked up. Yes, I've led a successful life, so I've wondered if my childhood really affected me that much. Haven't I been able to rise above it? Then I realized that my false self was talking and that I never confronted all those childhood issues. When I retired, a whole bucket of issues came rifling to the surface. That inner child was one hurting soul and needed a lot of attention. I needed help to go back through all of the dysfunction, and understand what really took place and the healing I needed to address.

The Strengths of the Boy Inside

The boy inside you also has any number of strengths that may be hidden from you. He survived but, in all likelihood, with little help. Although he may have used some dysfunctional behaviors, he may also have developed some effective coping mechanisms that you could use in your adult life, if you knew about them.

Silence Breaker John describes reclaiming his authentic self:

> *I feel it has been important to connect with my inner child, because that child is the authentic me. My public persona is a facade that I built to protect myself. It succeeded to the degree that I didn't know who I was; that is, my inner child became buried. However, as an adult, this facade prevented me from being spontaneous and establishing intimate relationships. By getting in touch with my inner child, I have been able to let the real me emerge. I am now more open and spontaneous than I have been since I was a young child. I am more comfortable in my own skin, because I am now my authentic self.*

EXPERIMENT WITH NEW POSSIBILITIES: How Do You Get in Touch with Your Inner Boy?

One method for reaching the child within is dominant-nondominant handwriting, a technique described by Lucia Capacchione, the author of *Recovery of Your Inner Child*.[2] Capacchione says that when you write with your nondominant hand, you are accessing a part of the brain that's more connected to your childhood experiences. I have used this exercise with many clients, and they find it helpful and enlightening. It can be risky because your inner boy may not be pleased with you after being ignored for years. It also may be risky because what he needs to share with you will be painful to hear. This is a process, and I invite you to dialogue with your boy slowly.

If you'd like to take the challenge, let's get ready for your first session. I invite you to write your first letter to your inner boy, holding a pen in your dominant hand. I will give you a sample shortly. You might want to give yourself a few minutes to imagine yourself when you were younger. You choose the age, perhaps an age before you remember being abused.

Now imagine your boy reading the letter you wrote. If the age you are imagining is prior to your being able to read, then imagine you can get in a time machine and go back and read the letter to him. Imagine the feelings that boy is having as he reads or hears your words.

Now allow the boy to write a response. Put a pencil, a crayon, or perhaps a pen in your nondominant hand. Most likely, you'll have to print slowly.

Once he writes back, you will need to respond. It's okay to write once a week, or more often if you have the time. Here are some guidelines about responding:

- Remember what you wrote in your first letter to him.

- The most helpful thing you can do is to empathize with him; that is, tell him that you heard him, that you understand his feelings.

- You may be tempted to give advice; however, I strongly advise against it, unless he specifically asks for it.

- Refuse to judge him.

- If you don't know what to say, ask him questions about what he has shared so that you can understand his experience.

- Thank him for writing, and let him know you will keep writing and listening.

- Let him know you care about his concerns and problems.

Next, I share some examples of real letters from one survivor to his inner boy, and his inner boy's responses. My client Tom gave me permission to share these letters in the hope that they will help you connect with your inner boy. As you read them, allow yourself to be aware of any feelings you experience. Pay attention to any way you or the boy inside you can identify with what was written.

These letters were written between 61-year-old Tom and his inner boy, Tommy. Tom came to therapy because he had engaged in a lifetime of dysfunctional behavior in his marriage. He thought he was incapable of being faithful to his wife. In therapy, we uncovered that he'd been abused by his mother and father for years. He also served as his mother's emotional caretaker, which is known as *covert incest* or *mother-son enmeshment*.[3]

> *November 22, 2009*
> *Dear Tommy,*
>
> *Sorry it has been so long since I've contacted you. I hope you are well and that everything is going better for you. How are you doing? And where are you these days? I'm sorry that I've lost track of you. I feel bad that we have been out of touch with each other and that I haven't reached out to you. I really want to be your friend and become closer to you. If you need help, I want to help you. I hope that we will not lose contact again with each other and that we can be best friends.*
>
> *Love,*
> *Tom*

❀　❀　❀

> *November 22, 2009*
> *Dear Tom,*
>
> *Where have you been? I've been lost within you. No real place to fit in. Just wandering around lost for a long time. I'm lonely and always sad. Scared, too. I have no friends. Not real ones—just ones in my head. Thanks for offering to be my friend and help me, but I don't trust you. You always leave me, too.*
> *Tommy*

It's ironic that in therapy as an adult, Tom felt very lonely even though he had a loving wife. He had very few friends until he agreed to start 12-step recovery in Sex Addicts Anonymous. It was very difficult for him to believe he could trust anyone, including me and the men in his SAA group.

> *November 27, 2009*
> *Dear Tommy,*
> *I'm glad you wrote me back. It was so good to hear from you. I am sorry, however, to hear that you are so alone and in so much pain. I do hope I can be your friend and can help you. Please, tell me more about how you feel. The more I know, the more I can help. I'm sorry I left you alone for so long. I will try my best not to do that again.*
> *Love,*
> *Tom*

* * *

> *November 27, 2009*
> *Dear Tom,*
> *I didn't think you would write me back. I can't always describe how I feel. I feel ugly, fat, and never able to measure up. I'm never good enough—always alone. I feel pressure and loneliness at the same time. The friends in my head help me, and in their world, I can be a hero. Nothing feels right in my world.*
> *Tommy*

Tom is identifying the roots of his addiction, a prevailing sense of shame described by his younger self, who never felt "good enough" or "able to measure up." This degree of shame about his body is very typical of abuse survivors.

> *December 4, 2009*
> *Dear Tommy,*

Thank you so much for your honesty. I am so sorry that you are sad and lonely. I'm also sorry that you feel so pressured to be perfect and that you feel you are a disappointment to everyone. I would love to learn more about your pain. I promise I won't get mad or judge you. It seems that you are really good at your imagination. I would like to learn more about the friends in your head. Please tell me more.

Love,
Tom

❀   ❀   ❀

December 4, 2009
Dear Tom,
I'm sad because there's no joy in my house, only work. Nobody laughs. Nobody smiles. God watches everything we do, and we shouldn't disappoint Him, but I'm told I do. Mom has moved into my room now, since my sister Sue left for college. Mom watches me all the time—like God. I don't tell anyone about the friends in my head. I keep them private.

Tommy

This was the first hint to Tom that something was wrong with his relationship with his mother. The roots of his addiction are set here, as he feels condemned to a life of being bad and wrong. He has also learned how to escape, as many survivors do. As your boy feels safer, most likely he will let you know more. In June, Tommy shared more about his feelings of inferiority and the covert incest with his mother:

June 21, 2010
Dear Tom:
Part of me is afraid, because part of me thinks I'm different from other guys. I'm more sensitive and like some things most boys don't like, such as music, words, stories, and art. Other boys call me "a sissy." I just don't fit neatly into any one place. My dad

is weak, too: he's soft, never bucks Mom, and does weird art. No-
body calls him a sissy. My mom mentions to me how big his penis
is and how small mine is. That makes me feel small and inferior.
Tommy

In December, Tom suggested to Tommy that together they could create a safe place for him. Tom asked Tommy to describe what he would like his safe place to be. Tommy used all of his creativity, and over the weeks, described it:

Dear Tom:
I'm not sure where my safe place would be, but I know I would have some rules:
First, there would be no teasing and no yelling allowed. My place would be cheery, with bright, bold colors. No one would feel afraid there. It would be a place where make-believe is encouraged and not made fun of. It would have glass doors that open to a private outdoor area. I would have a big man guarding the door and only letting in whom I say. He would be scary to others but nice to me. There would be lots of creative stuff there: clay, drawing paper, sports books, stuff to build with.
Tommy

In January 2011, Tommy realized there was something missing, which is a key struggle for Tom: how to feel safe and loved at the same time. As weeks went by, he shared with Tom all of his confusion about love and how in his mind, he had to do what others wanted in order to be loved. He knew he was a disappointment to others, and he felt unlovable. Even if his parents told him they loved him, he saw them act in ways that clearly did not feel like love.

Finally, in May 2011, Tommy shared more details of the one time he made Mom happy, when the covert abuse escalated to overt abuse. This description is graphic:

May 5, 2011
Dear Tom,
The one time I can make Mom happy is if we play in Dad's bed after bath time on Saturdays. Dad and I rub powder on my mom, and we laugh. Dad and I play a game, too. Mom gets on her stomach, and we raise her nightgown and each of us rubs one half of her butt. We call it "kneading the dough," because we roll it with our hands, and then we bake the bread (pull down the nightgown). And then, after it's done, we raise the nightgown and eat the bread. By that, I mean we either kiss her butt or do "slurberts" on it. She laughs, and everyone has fun. Sometimes I get an erection. Mom makes fun of it.
Tommy

You may be shocked by what your inner boy reveals, as was the case with Tom. He'd had no conscious memory of these times. He felt responsible, because he had initiated these "play sessions" to make his mom and dad happy. Tom let Tommy know that his mother and father were wrong for putting him in their bed and involving him in their sexual pleasuring. It took many more months for Tommy to believe that he was not responsible and that it wasn't his fault for liking it.

Another Way to Visit Your Inner Boy

I cannot teach you in this book how to hypnotize yourself, but I can discuss the advantages of hypnosis as a means for "visiting" your inner boy. Although all hypnosis is "self-hypnosis," it's best done with a psychotherapist who is trained in hypnotherapy. You may have been entertained by stage hypnotists who make their subjects cluck like chickens or speak in foreign languages. Clinical hypnosis is a very different technique and a useful tool for helping survivors heal.

During hypnosis, you relax, but you can remember anything that happens during the trance. There is some controversy over whether hypnosis creates what some have called "false memories." If you are working with a psychotherapist trained in clinical hypnosis,[4] then the issue of "false memories" is impossible because the training includes many safeguards that prevent a therapist from "implanting memories." Further, such a practice would be counter-therapeutic and unethical.

It's very important to understand that no hypnotherapist can say that the memories you may recall during hypnosis are true experiences. What hypnosis is likely to help you with is discovering what images and thoughts are stored in your subconscious. These images and thoughts may be related to what you actually experienced or may be distorted images and thoughts. A hypnotherapist won't be able to tell you with any certainty whether these images and thoughts are connected to a real memory or a distorted memory. The only way to know for sure is to seek some type of corroboration of your experience, and in most cases, there are no witnesses and it's highly unlikely that the perpetrator will own up to the truth. Thankfully, healing is not dependent on knowing for sure whether your memories are real or distorted. How a memory is stored impacts how you feel about the experience, regardless of whether it's a true memory or a distorted memory. A stored memory that leads to feelings of shame and powerlessness can wreak havoc in your adult life if the boy inside feels pain about the experience. Because hypnosis helps you know what's stored inside your subconscious, it can be a useful tool in addressing buried shame and pain, as well as helpful in enhancing your internal safety.

EXPERIMENT WITH NEW POSSIBILITIES:
Creating a Safe Place for You and Your Inner Boy

I use hypnosis to help the adult man create a safe place. This is a place you can create either in a state of hypnosis or in a meditation. You read about Tommy's safe place. I invite you to review some of the skills you learned earlier in the book to create inner safety. The breathing techniques, like hypnosis, can help you create a safe place for you and your boy.

Imagine that you have an unlimited budget to create this special location. The safe place may be indoors or outdoors. It can be a place you have visited or an imaginary place. This place is yours and yours alone. You and the boy inside you are the only ones who can find it unless you both agree to allow someone else inside. Think about the age of your inner boy and what he would need in this place to feel safe and protected. You might want a comfortable bed with blankets and pillows, and an array of toys. You can include a variety of healthy food to nurture this boy. Ask what else to add for this boy, or boys as the case may be. The place may be for a 5-year-old, but also for a 10- and 15-year-old.

Picture you and your boy in this place. Be aware of how safe you feel there. Make sure that the younger part of you also has a way to reach you in case of any emergency. Remember the phone that Police Commissioner Gordon used to call Batman? All he had to do was pick up the Batphone at police headquarters, and immediately it would ring in the Batcave for Batman and Robin, and in the main house, where Alfred, the butler, could answer. You can create your inner boy's version of the Batphone. It can take any shape you like and be any color he'd like, and it calls your adult self immediately so that you are available 24/7.

Before you leave your boy in the safe place, check once more to see if anything else is needed. Would a guard at the door be a good idea? A playmate or a safe babysitter?

When you are ready, allow the image of this place to gradually fade away. How did it feel to create this safe place? Some men have difficulty visualizing the safe place. Some feel calmer, even if they haven't been able to see the place. Some see only in black and white, while others visualize in color. Some men see a younger version of themselves, while others do not.

There's no right or wrong way to do this exercise. It's meant to be an experiment. You can try it several times and notice how your experience may change each time.

Using Hypnosis to Provide
Protection for Your Inner Boy

There are two other ways that I use hypnosis with clients to protect the boy or man inside. The use of hypnosis can be helpful whether you were abused as a boy or a man. It involves traveling back in time to when you were abused. This technique, called *age regression,* should only be done with a trained psychotherapist or hypnotherapist. As I discussed previously, some therapists will say that this technique is controversial; however, with proper training it's reliable and helpful. Understand that hypnosis doesn't change the past, but it can change how you perceive it and how you feel about it once you know what memories are stored in your subconscious. Then you can provide protection for the part of you that's still carrying pain about the past, and this often creates a sense of relief and security.

Here are the steps I use after inducing a hypnotic state:

1. Create a safe place.

2. Create a time transporter.

3. Determine a time and place to visit.

4. Take yourself to that time and place in the transporter.

5. Visit the boy; observe what's important to see.

6. Provide protection.

7. Return to the present.

8. Process the experience.

There are other types of trauma therapy that have been successfully used with survivors. Christopher went to a therapist trained in eye movement desensitization and reprocessing (EMDR).[5] Here's an example of a session that Christopher experienced:

> *I worked with an EMDR-trained therapist over the course of a year and a half to allow my inner boy to have an outlet for his (my) pain. It felt very awkward at first, but over time the*

exercises became very intense and cathartic. I remember one particular session where my inner boy and I went on a trip together and found ourselves on a desert island digging up what looked like a treasure box. When I opened it, a mammoth wave of black, inky, painful darkness poured out from inside the box and overwhelmed me. I cried as years and years of buried pain were finally given a chance to be released.

Other Pathways to Your Inner Boy

Jarrod describes his fierce struggle to acknowledge his boy and his profound awareness of what was in the way: all of his shame and all of the self-blame he was carrying around. He shares the technique that finally broke through: bringing to therapy pictures of himself at various ages:

> *This idea of connecting with the boy inside me proved to be especially difficult. I didn't really know why, only that it seemed silly and I felt weak. My therapist suggested role-play, EMDR, and talking to a stuffed animal, but I stubbornly refused each suggestion. My block was the fact that I blamed the boy for all of the abuse that happened to me. He was stupid! He was ugly! He was weak! He never said no! He never told anyone! Why on earth would I ever want to connect with my inner boy?*
>
> *Finally, my therapist found the right tool. She had me bring in photos of myself from the age of 8, when the abuse began, to the age of 17, when the abuse stopped. One by one, I laid out the photos and talked about what I felt about the boy in each photo. When I got to the photo of the 14-year-old boy, I broke down in angry sobbing. It was that boy whom I blamed for everything. He was the one who could have told! He was old enough to have known better! He could have said no!*
>
> *The emotions released that day mark a watershed moment in my recovery. Only after I could forgive the young me could I truly place the blame where it was deserved. I learned that day that I did not ask to be abused. I did not ask to be lied to. I did not ask to be sexualized at age 8. I did nothing wrong. It was not my fault.*

After this day, I also wrote letters to the young me, asking what it was like for him. Was he scared? Why did he never tell? Why did he never say no? The answers were right there inside my brain. I simply had to be willing to ask the question and then, the most difficult part, listen to my own very painful answers. Now, for the first time since I was 8 years old, I can truly play.

My office is full of stuffed animals of all kinds. Typically survivors come in and say, "Why do you have all these stuffed animals?" I invite them to consider that someday, they might choose to pick one up, and if they do, they might experience a sense of comfort or perhaps even a connection with the boy inside. Listen to Chris talk about his Pooh Bear:

One way I've kept (my boy) close is to sleep with my Winnie-the-Pooh Bear. My inner child feels safe with him, and Pooh allows me to relax and find a way to sleep. He's traveled with me to workshops, and it's made a big difference at these events because when my boy feels safe and comforted, I open up more easily and share things that I need to get off my chest. I often look down toward the ground or floor to see him following me around. He's beginning to have me lift him up for a hug now, and he enjoys riding on my shoulders. He is part of me, but just happens to be invisible to others. But neither of us cares about that.

I have suggested a meditation or hypnotic-type trance you could use to connect with your boy to create a safe place for him. Next, Alexander shares a powerful meditation technique he uses to connect with not only his boy, but also his adult self and his spiritual self:

I have a meditation technique I use to speak to the boy part of me. In my mind, I go into a beautiful glade that's full of peace and serenity, complete with a waterfall, blooming flowers, sunlight, and cool breezes. In that glade is a gazebo with three different chairs, for my boy part, my adult part, and my spiritual self. We sit in the gazebo, talk, play, and enjoy each other's company. This meditation connects all aspects of my being.

EXPERIMENT WITH NEW POSSIBILITIES:
Experiencing Play as an Essential Part of Recovery

We have talked about many different ways to connect with your boy: engaging in behaviors that allow boys to connect with a sense of joy and playfulness, writing a series of letters to your younger self, establishing a dialogue, creating a safe place inside for your boy and adult selves to visit when threatened, and using hypnosis or EMDR to learn more about your truths and to provide protection so that your younger self cannot be abused again.

For this experiment, I'd like you to consider inviting a friend, male or female, to join you for an hour of play. If you cannot find a friend to join you, then imagine yourself doing the activity with your younger self. Or, if you have a pet, like a dog or a cat, you could spend this time engaging in its favorite play activity. When I need a break, I like taking my yellow Labrador for a Frisbee toss, one of his favorite forms of play. If you are playing with your cat or dog, imagine that your younger self is there, too, so that you can see the smile on his face!

Decide with your friend how you want to play. The objective is to take a break from the hard emotional work that often accompanies recovery processes. It could be any fun activity that you both enjoy.

Remember how I mentioned that we play children's games at Weekends of Recovery? One activity that most of the men enjoy is to bounce a rubber ball to the beat of lively music. When they get the hang of that, they bounce the ball to each other. Then, they form a square, and with four guys, they bounce the ball across the square until we have balls bouncing everywhere! There's no score and no penalties for dropping the ball or losing it. The goal is to let go and see what happens when you let your inner boy play without any rigid rules or expectations. This is just one idea for you.

When you are done with this experiment, check inside to see how it felt to take a break. How able were you to connect with your inner boy? How much did you let yourself smile? Did you feel any tension being released as you engaged in the activity? Hopefully, even for a little while, you allowed yourself to relax and unwind, and to connect with a younger, less troubled part of you. If you had trouble with this experiment, please refuse to judge yourself. It may take more than one attempt.

Again, I invite you to pick an affirmation to use to help you move forward in your path. In the next chapter, I will introduce you to a therapy technique I have successfully used in Weekends of Recovery to help men become unstuck from the effects of their abuse.

AFFIRMATIONS FOR CHAPTER 9

- *I can take time now to smile, laugh, relax, and unwind.*
- *I dare to dream I can connect with my younger self.*
- *I can provide protection now for the part of me that was abused and wounded.*

CHAPTER TEN

Dare to Dream You Can Sculpt Your New Path

"My T-shirt represents that hidden inside are characteristics that represent me, and others, and when you open up, you can truly see them. Likewise, when you as a survivor open up to discover yourself, you can also receive those characteristics from others." *Designer:* Rhett Hackett, Silence Breaker.

For many years, I've used a gestalt therapy technique called *sculpting* to help survivors of abuse discover what is hidden inside themselves that can help them heal.[1] *Gestalt therapy* is a type of psychotherapy that focuses on helping you be more aware of your experience in the moment. One aspect of gestalt is that, in particular, the psychotherapist invites the client to be very aware of what he is experiencing throughout his body during a session. While reading this book, you can be aware of any movement you are making, such as shaking your leg or tapping your foot. A gestalt therapist might ask, "If your foot had a voice right now, what would it be saying?"

We use sculpting at the MaleSurvivor Weekends of Recovery, and it would be most powerful to share with you if we were in the same room and I could show you. Since that's not possible, I will instead introduce this healing tool by inviting you to create pictures in your mind. Sculpting is designed to help you become unstuck from the effects of your abuse. Plug into your imagination as I describe the two-part exercise.

When you think about sculptures, you may picture Michelangelo's *David* or the Lincoln Memorial, both carved out of marble. You may be familiar with Auguste Rodin's bronze-and-marble sculpture *The Thinker* or the copper Statue of Liberty. You might have seen huge glass chandeliers blown by Dale Chihuly, or Alexander Calder's mobile sculptures. Sculptures can be made of many materials. At a WOR, a sculpture would consist of people placed around a room who could move but not speak. Since you're not at a WOR, I will help you use your mind to create your own sculpture.

Sculpting in Two Parts

When we create these sculptures during our WOR programs, all the participants, usually 28 men, play roles. One is designated as the sculptor, and several men serve as his "clay" while the majority serve as "witnesses." The various roles and viewpoints serve a purpose in understanding the impact of abuse, which is the first goal of this exercise. It is designed to show how men who have been abused often feel stuck.

When the sculpting exercise begins, the sculptor tells his clay group what they must do to create a sculpture of his experience of being stuck. Sometimes the clay doesn't move. Sometimes the clay makes faces or gestures. There may be interaction among the clay men or not. When the sculptor is ready to start, he says, "Action!" and his job is to walk around the sculpture to get a 360-degree view.

The initial goal is to create a sculpture that portrays a feeling or series of feelings related to the aftermath of the trauma. This sculpture is not a reenactment of the abuse, but rather a picture of the emotions this man feels stuck with.

I will now describe a sculpting session done at a WOR. I invite you to read the description and see if you can imagine being a witness in the room, watching this sculpture unfold.

Part I: Sculpting—Picturing Your Stuck Feeling

Take a few breaths, wiggle your toes, and be as present as you can. Imagine yourself sitting on the outside of a circle of men at a WOR. Watch as the sculptor enters the center of the circle. The sculptor tells everyone in the room that he wants to sculpt the feeling of emptiness he felt stuck with after his abuse. He describes the emptiness as if his spirit had been drained from his body. The sculptor asks five men to lie down next to each other on the floor. He gives each one an imaginary cup and fills it with water. He explains that the men represent the five different ages when he was abused. Another part of the sculpture is a sixth man, whom he describes as a shadowy figure. The sculptor asks the shadowy man to move from one person to the next while emptying each man's imaginary cup and returning it empty.

As you sit outside the circle, you hear the sculptor call, "Action!" and you see the shadowy figure move to the first man, take his cup, and drain the water into an imaginary pitcher. This first man cannot see the shadowy figure; all he knows is that his cup is taken from his grasp and returned to him empty. Then you see the shadowy figure move to each man, until he has drained the water from all five cups. He takes his pitcher full of water and walks away, leaving the men lying on the floor. You hear the sculptor say, "Stop," as he makes it all the way around the sculpture.

Take a few moments to reflect on what you felt as you imagined being in the room as a witness. Imagine, too, what you might have felt if you were one of the men on the floor. What might you have felt if you were the shadowy figure? What might it have felt like if you actually were the sculptor, walking around the room, seeing this play out in front of you, and knowing that all the men are witnessing your story enacted here?

Gestalt therapy hypothesizes that all the parts of any experience are greater than the whole, which means it's important to think about the experience of men in each part of this sculpture. Their different vantage points prompt very different feelings, thoughts, and interpretations.

If you want, write in your journal your different reactions:

- *If I were the sculptor, I might have felt or thought*

  _____.

- *If I were one of the five men lying on the floor, I might have felt or thought* _____.

- *If I were the shadowy figure, I might have felt or thought*

  _____.

- *If I were one of the witnesses, I might have felt or thought*

  _____.

In this particular exercise, the sculptor reported to us that he felt immensely sad watching the cups being drained. He felt angry at the shadowy figure, who didn't seem to care at all about the devastation he was leaving behind. The men on the floor reported feeling powerless and helpless. The men who were farther down the line and were the last ones to have their cups emptied by the shadowy figure felt guilty; they thought perhaps they should have done something to protect the first guys, since they could sense that the shadow was taking the water away from the others on the floor. They felt scared and frustrated, because they couldn't actually see the figure from their prone positions.

The witnesses told us this sculpture felt "creepy," because the shadowy figure seemed to have no feelings at all as he moved from one man to the next. When he walked away, a few witnesses felt like tackling him or going up to him and stealing the water pitcher away. Many witnesses wondered if this shadowy figure was just like any perpetrator, who didn't seem to care at all about the damage done.

After we discuss the feelings stirred by a sculpture, the next portion of the exercise begins.

Part II: Sculpting—Picturing Becoming Unstuck

Again, picture in your mind's eye that you are in the room at the WOR as a witness, and you hear this instruction from me, as the facilitator, to the sculptor: "Now imagine it's possible to transform this sculpture to one in which you can be free from the stuck feelings related to your abuse. To transform the sculpture, you are allowed to add more 'clay' [additional people] who can help with a rescue or confrontation, or both. Or the people in the sculpture may somehow get together and determine how to become unstuck."

The new sculpture starts from where the other sculpture stopped. We go through the same process as before, with the sculptor explaining to his clay what he wants for them to do in the newly transformed sculpture, and then he says, "Action!" walks around the sculpture, and says, "Stop," when he has made his way around.

Take a minute to consider: If you were the sculptor, how might you transform this sculpture? Imagine that there are 20 other guys in the room, and you can ask as many as you want to join you. They can take any role that makes you feel free. Any ideas?

I want to invite you to experience what we did at the WOR. Allow yourself to picture yourself on the outside of the circle, watching intently. You observe that the sculptor recruits ten more men. Five enter the sculpture as rescuers for each man on the floor. The other five are guards. The sculptor calls, "Action!" and you watch the guards go after the shadowy figure, back him into a corner, and demand that he give up the pitcher. They take the pitcher from his hands and "lock him up" so that he cannot escape.

The five rescuers go to the men on the floor and, one at a time, help them to gently sit up. Then the rescuers fill their cups with water. Each rescued man drinks his water and then is assisted to a standing position. You watch as, one by one, they stand until all five and their protectors are standing and holding hands in a circle. They first turn and look around the circle and feel the support you and the other witnesses are offering. Then they turn around and look at the shadowy figure, who is "locked up." They nod in approval, give a thumbs-up to the guards, and then turn back and again join hands. You hear the sculptor call, "Stop."

Imagine that the second part of the sculpture has just taken place, from the first call to action until the sculptor again says, "Stop." Although you were a witness this time, imagine the various perspectives in which you might have participated. Again, take some time to imagine this, and write your thoughts and feelings in all six roles:

- *As one of the witnesses, I felt or thought _____.*

- *If I were the sculptor, I might have felt or thought*

  _____.

- *If I were one of the men rescued from the floor, I might have felt or thought _____.*

- *If I were one of the guards, I might have felt or thought*

  _____.

- *If I were one of the rescuers, I might have felt or thought*

  _____.

- *If I were the shadowy figure, I might have felt or thought*

  _____.

In this second part of the exercise, here's what happened at the WOR:

— The sculptor felt a sense of relief and some joy that all the abused parts of him (represented by the clay men) were standing, nurtured, and protected.

— Each man on the floor reported feeling empowered and rescued. One felt some ambivalence about seeing the shadowy figure jailed, and worried whether he was okay or if he was now being neglected, just as he had been when he was lying on the ground.

— The guards generally felt powerful, having provided protection. A couple felt disappointed that they couldn't join the rest of the guys in the circle, even though they understood that the shadowy figure needed guarding.

— The rescuers generally felt pretty happy that they had saved the boy on the floor, had provided him necessary nurturing, and had helped him stand up and join the others. They liked the safety they felt when they turned around and looked at the shadowy figure, and knew that he was imprisoned.

— The shadowy figure kept himself numb so that he didn't really care what was going on with the others. He kept busy thinking of ways he could escape, since he didn't think it was fair to be jailed in the first place. This triggered some of the participants, as they had hoped the shadowy figure might feel some remorse or powerlessness.

— The witnesses had a variety of reactions. Some worried about the shadowy figure, too. They weren't sure it was realistic to lock him up forever. Some worried about the toll on the guards. Some wondered how many times the boys in the circle would have to keep turning around to be sure the shadowy figure wasn't coming back. The witnesses generally felt relief that they didn't have to spend the rest of their lives lying on the floor, feeling powerless, helpless, and unsupported. Some wished they could have learned from the guards about their roles so that they could have taken turns guarding the shadowy figure, too. They wanted to build confidence by showing they were strong enough to do this.

Some witnesses were not surprised by the shadowy figure's lack of connection with his feelings. They equated his state of mind to the perpetrator they knew, who was unfazed by being confronted. Others were angry with him for never taking responsibility. Many concluded that there's a great deal of power in being able to connect the experience of all the abused parts of you. Sharing each other's experiences and knowing they weren't alone helped their healing.

Depending on your sculpture experience and the nature of your abuse, you could have many different reactions to this exercise. It can give you permission to think about your own abuse experience in a new, unstuck way. You cannot change what was done to you; that's a fact that's important to acknowledge. However, this exercise does allow you to picture a different outcome, where you become unstuck because you are no longer that vulnerable victim. You are essentially giving yourself permission to become unstuck in your body, mind, and spirit. By directing the sculpting, or participating in or witnessing it, you orchestrate a way for you to escape or a way you can be rescued, nurtured, and protected. You may also visualize your perpetrator being prevented from ever hurting you or anyone else again. Having this experience in your mind's eye can create a sense of freedom that you deserve. Sculpting allows you to believe that it's possible for you to leave those stuck feelings behind.

I've asked two Silence Breakers to share their recollections of their sculpting exercise. You may have some intense feelings as you read these descriptions. I hope you will give yourself permission to express your feelings. Just remember to relax yourself by controlling your breathing. Again, it may be useful to imagine yourself as a witness in the room as you watch Simon's sculpture unfold.

Simon was the sculptor in his exercise, and he called it "Big Foot."

The "Big Foot" sculpture represented becoming unstuck from my feeling of isolation. I found this huge pair of costume *feet that looked like Big Bird's feet from <u>Sesame Street</u>. I put them on, and in the first part of the sculpture, I played a boy of about ten years old who was trying to join in and play with other boys who were enjoying themselves in a playground.*

As I approached them, my big feet kept stepping on their toes and kicking them by accident. I felt awkward, and the other boys got frustrated with me. I just wanted to play with them, but I felt like a freak and couldn't find a way to fit in. They ridiculed and rejected me, and I felt even lonelier.

In the second part, I approached just one boy initially, and treaded a little carefully but with more confidence. I only had to worry about how my feet might get in the way of one person. I gained his trust, and we played games using my big feet in a fun way rather than trying to ignore them or allowing any ridicule of me for having them. With him alongside as my new friend, we then joined the group, and I was accepted.

I was able to play with them all, and didn't feel like a freak for being different. The group accepted me and enjoyed how I used my big feet to make them laugh. I was accepted and valued for my uniqueness.

The big feet in my sculpture represented how the abuse made me feel different and freakish. It felt as if everyone knew my past, which I displayed as a deformity. This made me feel awkward around other people. I continually monitored the impact I was having on others, so I couldn't relax and simply join in. This anxiety made me more prone to putting people off, even those who wanted to be friendly. When social situations went badly, I felt stupid and inadequate, so I learned to isolate myself to avoid the pain of being rejected. In reality, I had a lot of social skills and things to offer, but the abuse had taken away my confidence and the joy of feeling free to just be myself.

The sculpture helped me to see the legacies of abuse (big feet) as a vulnerability that I could learn to live with and use to my advantage. In the sculpture, I needed to be aware of my feet but not so overly self-conscious that they became a disability. I

also learned to respect my vulnerability and to not rush at try-
ing to be "normal" and fit in with everyone.

A really important part of the learning process was having
Howard and the other men help me think through solutions for
the second part of the sculpture. This brought hope to me by
challenging the feeling that I have to sort out all of my problems
by myself. I learned that there was hope for me and that break-
ing isolation can be done without denying or feeling ashamed
of my past.

Before I describe the next sculpture, take some time to let
yourself be aware of what you might have experienced as you witnessed Simon's sculpture. Have you ever felt like the boy with the
big feet who just didn't fit in? What was it like to witness him feeling different and unaccepted? What was it like to witness Simon
discovering a way to be accepted and protected?

Chris describes his sculpting experience as involving a sculptor who wanted to work through his feelings about feeling stuck
because he felt unworthy. Perhaps you can imagine joining Chris
as one of the participants in the sculpture. Take a few deep breaths
before you keep reading.

I participated in a sculpture session at my first WOR. I
volunteered to help one of the members of my small group with
his sculpture. He asked one of the female facilitators to play the
role of his mother or a female figure. In the first part, she stood
aside with part of the group, who acted as "observers." Others
were asked to represent perpetrators.

My friend placed himself in the center of two circles. The
closest consisted of the perps. The second, outer circle of people
acted as observers, as if we were watching and allowing the
abuse to continue. A small "child" in the center was defense-
less and alone. The child's hands were held out in defense, as
I recall, trying to keep the closest circle from hurting him.

In the second sculpture, we circled and surrounded the
child. We asked the mother figure to come into the center with

him so that she could speak to the perpetrators and society ob-servers who watched the abuse and did nothing about it. The child asked the mother to protect him. She spoke out and said something like, "Keep your G.D. hands off of this child! You will <u>never</u> harm him again, and if you try to do so, you'll have to go through <u>me</u>!" She spoke this a couple of times while hold-ing out her hands and looking around at the circling people.

Being a participant in this exercise was a lot different from watching from my seat, as I had done in my other sculpture exercises. I was in the heart of the action this time. As she re-peated the words, I began to cry intensely. I wished my mother or another elder would have done the same for me. I ran from the room in tears, wanting so badly to have had my mom pro-tect me from my pain.

I was followed by a WOR facilitator, who helped and sup-ported me through the emotions I was experiencing. It was something I never expected to feel or to reveal in front of so many. I let myself be vulnerable so that I could be in tune with emotions that I'd hidden away until that moment. I saw that I was not alone with my wishes, and the sculpture helped me bond with everyone that weekend. "I" was becoming "we." I had "brothers" who felt what I felt and understood.

Take a few moments to allow yourself to reflect on Chris's experience with sculpting. How much do you identify with feeling unworthy? How much do you identify with knowing that there was a parent or authority figure in your life who could have stepped in to help and did nothing? What's it like to imagine through sculpting that you can invite yourself to believe that it's now possible to have the protection you always deserved but never got?

EXPERIMENT WITH NEW POSSIBILITIES:
Creating Your Own Sculpture

Now it's your turn. Most likely you don't have a crowd of people sitting around to help you create a sculpture. However, you have your mind, and you can picture creating one. Start by taking a few gentle breaths. Visualize that I am with you to help facilitate your sculpture.

Allow yourself to be aware of your body right now. Feel your breath as you slowly inhale and then exhale. Imagine that I have selected you to lead our next sculpture. I invite you now to think about the emotions that have you feeling stuck after your abuse. I've mentioned many possibilities, including feeling powerless, helpless, dirty, defective, ashamed, defenseless, angry, numb, or addicted. What feeling do you want to portray? Take your time, check inside, and, when you are ready, name the feeling.

Now imagine what your sculpture would look like. Imagine how many people it would take to fill in your picture. Imagine being the sculptor and directing all of your "clay" into whatever positions you need them to take. Imagine the instructions you would give each part. Picture yourself as you tell each person what his role is, how he should hold his body, what movements or sounds you want him to make, and how he should interact with the other parts of the sculpture and when.

When you are ready and all parts of the clay know what to do, imagine calling, *Action!* See yourself as you walk around the sculpture until you have viewed it from all vantage points. Take as much time as you need to view the entire composition and all the parts of it. When you are ready, hear yourself say *Stop.*

Take a few breaths and allow yourself to check inside concerning your own experience. What do you feel after seeing your sculpture come to life? What thoughts enter your mind as you think about its different parts?

Imagine that you are now asking each part to speak. What is each part sharing with you about your sculpture? What feelings do you identify with? Are there any feelings or reactions that surprise you?

Ask the imaginary witnesses to speak about what they saw and felt. What do you hear and feel about their reactions?

Now imagine that it's time for the second part: time to transform your sculpture and become unstuck. Imagine giving instructions now to each "part" of the sculpture about how they will change what they are doing. Be mindful of whether you need additional "clay," and if so, see additional people joining you now inside the circle.

Experience yourself as you are giving the instructions to your clay, and now you call, *Action!* You, again, walk around your sculpture as it is transformed. Allow yourself to be as present as you can be, observing all the changes and transformations you asked to see. Walk all the way around the circle, taking as much time as you need. Now call *Stop* when you are all the way around. What are you feeling and thinking as the sculptor?

What are you feeling and thinking as you check in with the different pieces of clay in your sculpture?

What are you feeling and thinking as you check in with the witnesses? What unique perspectives do they offer you?

You can do this exercise many times, especially anytime you are feeling stuck in a feeling or a behavior. It can provide you insight into how you are stuck and how you might free yourself from the painful effects of abuse. It may seem improbable; however, I have seen the power of this exercise nearly 100 times, and know that it has the power to help you feel hope and relief.

I hope you can carry this sense of hope into the next chapter, when you will read about how to bring more intimacy into your life. You will have the chance to explore what may be causing you to feel stuck in your previous efforts to pursue intimacy, and learn some more tools for increasing the likelihood that you can give yourself permission to risk more closeness and get more support.

AFFIRMATIONS FOR CHAPTER 10

- *I can use sculpting to free myself now from feeling stuck.*
- *I can benefit from seeing my abuse from a number of different perspectives.*
- *I dare to dream I can become unstuck now.*

✿ ✿ ✿ ✿

CHAPTER ELEVEN

Dare to Dream You Can Connect Safely, Intimately, and Romantically

"The most profound insight I had during my weekend was the realization that I had spent 35 years unaware of my deep personal confusion around intimacy and love because of the trauma of sexual abuse. With this newfound clarity, I was able to recognize my own commitment to intimacy and love, encourage this commitment with my new brothers in a safe and meaningful way, and then bring the joy of my discovery into my very new intimate relationship, allowing the two of us to overcome obstacles that would have been very difficult, if not impossible, to navigate in the past. It was awe-inspiring and ultimately incredibly romantic." *Designer:* Das Chapin.

Initiating, building, and maintaining intimate and romantic connections is one of the toughest challenges that survivors encounter. There are many barriers to overcome when survivors with insecurity and trust issues seek to make such intimate connections.

First, there's the critical issue of trusting someone not to hurt you after you have been so terribly betrayed in the past. It's normal for survivors of abuse to find it very difficult to trust even those they feel closest to. Some consider intimate relationships too scary to even contemplate. Yet survivors do heal, and they do have loving and trusting long-term relationships. It's possible through hard work, a willingness to take risks, and learning from mistakes.

Learning to Trust Again

How do you trust again when you have been so betrayed? Creating inner safety, which I've been coaching you on already, is one of your best tools for building relationships. Even the best romantic partner doesn't have the power to make you feel safe enough to risk emotional intimacy. You must do this yourself. The behavior of others does affect your feelings of security, which is why I had you work on analyzing relationships in terms of red, yellow, and green lights earlier. Reflect on what you learned earlier about looking for qualities that help you feel comfortable with others.

Think again about those friends and trusted acquaintances or professionals with whom you would be willing to share your story. If you have chosen to share your story with even one other person, you have already risked creating an intimate relationship.

So you've done a lot of work already on building that essential sense of security within you. As we proceed, also keep in mind the powerful stories you've been reading from the Silence Breakers. I'm sure you relate to the experiences of some, if not many, of them. You can relate also to their healing and their reborn abilities to trust and love.

To quickly review what we've covered so far, you've learned about:

- Being able to determine who is safe to get closer to
- Being willing and able to co-create trust in a relationship

- Being loyal to dysfunction, including the lie that you are unworthy of self-love and the love of others

- Replacing those dysfunctional messages with functional messages, which are keys to trusting again

- Creating and negotiating relationship boundaries

- Believing you are worthy of having a voice and speaking up for what you want and need

- Helping your inner child feel safe and worthy

- Freeing yourself from stuck feelings and thoughts connected to your abuse

Sharing Control

You may now be ready to share control, which can feel threatening for any survivor. Control was taken from you by the abuser. Many survivors become or are perceived as "control freaks" as a result of their abuse. Others respond in the opposite direction. They abdicate control entirely by becoming compliant, introverted, and reticent. The reality is that both ends of the continuum may be quite controlling, as the goal in both methods is self-protection. If at this point in your recovery, you feel a need for a lot of control, refuse to judge yourself and give yourself permission to read further.

Consider the possibility that you may be able to settle in somewhere near the middle of the continuum. You may take control in most circumstances, but you are strong enough to share control in relationships. Partners in a healthy relationship learn together how to share control, giving and taking in equal measure, because the result is mutual respect and affection.

Let's look at a simple example: You and your friend want to see a movie together. You love action movies with suspense and drama. Your friend, on the other hand, is a fan of romantic movies with happy endings. If you compromise, you may agree to alternate between your favorite genre and your friend's. You may not like romantic movies, but you do like seeing your friend enjoy them because your willingness to go to romantic movies strengthens the bonds of your relationship. This is a very simple example, but it demonstrates how sharing control through negotiation and compromise builds relationships.

Sharing experiences and feelings with each other is a critical part of being in a relationship, especially for survivors of abuse. If you want to have intimacy, you must allow your partner to talk about life challenges while you "actively listen" and respond with empathy.

Active listening is the foundation of all good psychotherapy. Therapists learn to listen intently enough to tell the speaker what they heard him say, without attaching any judgment or interpretation. *Empathic* listening is the ability to understand also the emotions being expressed when someone is speaking so that the listener relates at that level, too. Empathic listening is not offering sympathy; it is instead letting the other person know you understand how he feels, just as if you were walking in the same shoes.

EXPERIMENT WITH NEW POSSIBILITIES: Practicing Empathic and Active Listening

Pick a person in your life to whom you would like to grow closer. Pick a topic, preferably something you care about, but not something that's very serious. You might choose to talk about something you value in your life or perhaps a personal goal. You each will get a turn at practicing being the sharer and the active or empathic listener. This gives you practice in sharing control, because only one of you can be the sharer and only one can be the listener. Pay attention to how it feels to decide who will play each role. Even in this simple exercise, where each of you takes turns speaking, it still may feel awkward to ask for what you want and speak your true feelings. So check inside as you share and listen.

Before the sharer starts, I invite you both to take a few deep breaths. Be aware that both roles can be challenging. To share from your heart is to make yourself vulnerable, and merely listening can do the same, especially if you are also uncomfortable with intimacy. It can be frustrating to listen this intently, especially if you don't get it completely right. Think of this as just practicing a new skill. It's okay to make mistakes and learn from your experiences.

The sharer begins with no more than three sentences on the topic. The listener sits quietly, and when the sharer finishes, the listener reflects back to the sharer the content and the emotion expressed. When the listener is done reflecting, he asks the sharer, "Did I understand you?" If the sharer says yes, then he offers his own thoughts in one to three sentences.

The goal here is not 100 percent perfect listening. Rather, your goal as the listener is to improve your ability to more accurately hear your partner. If the listener didn't understand the sharer, then the sharer tells the listener what was right and what he missed. The listener then tells the sharer what he felt the sharer missed.

Again, the listener asks, "Did I understand you?"

If the sharer says, "Yes, you did understand; thank you," then they proceed. If not, the sharer repeats what the listener got right and what he is still missing.

Once the listener understands, the sharer offers up to three more sentences, and they repeat the process. After the sharer has spoken twice, they switch roles. Take a moment to look into each other's eyes and express thanks for listening and for sharing.

Now the listener becomes the sharer, and the process is repeated.

Before reading on, reflect what you learned about your ability to communicate and listen:

- Was it easier to share or easier to be the listener?
- Was it easier to listen to content or to listen to the feelings?

If you struggled with listening, what got in the way? For example, maybe you didn't allow yourself to be present. In other words, your body may have been present, but your mind may have been focused somewhere else. You might do this when you are uncomfortable with what the other person is sharing or because you are fearful of being closer. Dysfunctional messages you learned about yourself are likely to pop up here.

Survivors' Blocks to Intimacy

I asked the Silence Breakers to share some of their blocks to intimacy, because it's helpful to know that you are not alone and that others are also struggling. Simon admits that his biggest struggle with intimacy is feeling safe with his partner. He knows he is loved, but he questions her love and has to work hard to break the old patterns of self-protection:

> *Commitment is still a big issue, even though I'm in a loving relationship and we have started a family. The fact that survivors learn to constantly question their love and the love of others is one of the most tragic consequences of abuse. As a boy, the "family" abuse was sanctioned and tolerated by my parents. I have come a long way and learned to resist the escape fantasy that I can be free from this pain by being on my own or finding another woman.*
>
> *I desperately seek the closeness and connection, but this intimacy can also be so confusing. It can also be very hurtful for my partner to be associated with the pain of the past, so I try often to reassure her that her love is exactly what I need, even*

though I resist it. When I am overwhelmed, I have to actively remind myself that she is not the problem but in fact the most trustworthy and loving person in my life.

Christopher shares many of the same struggles as Simon, and he, too, understands how his abuse shattered his ability to trust others and himself:

The abuse shattered my willingness to trust not only other people, but also my own ability to protect myself. I didn't even realize that there was something I could do to change the way I behaved. Through much of my life, I felt intense loneliness. I was desperate for love, yet reflexively drove away anyone who wanted to get close.

In the past few years, I began to learn how to repair the emotional damage. I have found myself slowly becoming willing to trust and be open to emotional attachments. My wonderful wife takes on an active supporting role in my healing by telling me good things every day. But it's still not always easy for me to hear her when she tells me she loves me.

Confusing Sex and Intimacy

There's a lot of confusion among survivors about sex and intimacy. This section covers a number of areas of confusion. Read what Chris shares about this:

I've begun to understand that intimacy is not just sex. I see now that friends can share intimate feelings or thoughts. Intimacy can be holding hands, talking over dinner, giving a pat on the back, or smiling and nodding in understanding. Trust is my biggest struggle when it comes to intimacy. I've needed to keep others at bay because of my confusion and my previous understanding of intimacy. I can get hurt, and I can hurt others.

Romantic intimacy involves the willingness to engage in healthy sex, and for many survivors, they have never experienced the ability to be healthy and connected to their bodies while being sexual. It's no wonder after what they've experienced. At the very core of sexual abuse is the way another person chose to violate the victim's body and sexuality. You may, for example, think of your abuse as a "sexual experience." I encourage you to be clear that the act of sexual victimization is *never* a sexual experience. It is an act of someone violating you—a more vulnerable, smaller, or less powerful boy or man. Because of the way male bodies operate, you were at a significant disadvantage when you were abused.

I have heard many men talk about how their bodies "betrayed" them, because they experienced sexual pleasure and, in some cases, erections or even orgasms, which perpetrators may have used as evidence to release themselves from any responsibility for the abuse. I encourage you to be clear that it's irrelevant what, if any, pleasure you received during a perpetrator's act of violating your body when it comes to who is responsible for the abuse. The perpetrator is always 100 percent responsible, and your responsibility is zero percent.

My experience is that it's not that easy to erase the confusion or to get survivors to accept that fact. Unfortunately, this is only one aspect of erasing the confusion. Think about what your perpetrator told you or communicated to you before, during, and after the act, directly or indirectly. What messages did you hear about your body? What messages were you told about your sexual orientation? What feelings did you experience toward your own body, especially toward your genitals? All of these messages and feelings are important to acknowledge, because they may well be at the core of some of your reluctance to be sexual in an intimate way.

Niall's struggle reflects these issues of confusion:

Without a doubt, my inability to relate to my penis was my biggest block to achieving intimacy in my life. For years I didn't touch my penis, except for the practical function of urinating. I only became consciously aware of this problem several months after I started my healing journey. When I recalled the threats made by my mother to cut off my penis if I ever told anyone what she did, and other threats made by my father and my brother, I overcame this complex. Cutting off all awareness of, and contact with, my penis made me feel incomplete as a human being at every level. I now understand that my penis is my main distinguishing feature as a man.

Remember the myths I addressed earlier in this book: You may believe that the only way you can get any positive attention is through being abused. You may believe that your worth is determined only by how good you are as a sex object. You may believe that your job is to provide sexual pleasure for others and that your own needs are either unimportant or come after the needs of others.

These can be such powerful myths that you could have developed a sexual addiction as you became powerless over your pursuit of sexual pleasure. Pursuing sex may be one of the major ways that you cope with the damaged feelings from abuse.

Instead of feeling dirty and unworthy, you use sex to feel powerful and worthwhile. With sex, you've found a way to be desired that feels good to some degree, temporarily. While in some ways it feels good, it may also feel terrible because you are unable to connect with the person in any other way than as a sex object. In the process, you are also objectifying yourself. Earlier, Silence Breaker Tom couldn't stop having affairs. His wife learned of his abuse, understood what was happening, and helped him find healing for his sexual addiction. Gregg also struggles with how to have healthy sex:

My block is that I re-create a lot of the abuse. I don't know how to make love. I know how to do a quickie. I had that intimacy once with my first boyfriend, and we were together for a while. I don't tend to have tender times; for me it's just my job. I tend to be more dominant. I have done more of the repetitive abuse scenarios than I have been romantic. I don't know what to do the next day if the person spends the night; I just don't know what to talk about.

Rhett also struggles with how to make sex feel healthy:

In my adult life, I've often felt that sexual intimacy was something "to do right." Sometimes, it's felt as if there were some urgency to get it over with or to reach the goal of orgasm. I often have to

215

*remind myself that I'm now in a safe, nonjudgmental place with
my partner and that I can relax and enjoy the experience.*

Sexual Anorexia

On the opposite end of the continuum, some men are so re-pulsed by the violating experience of their abuse that they have shunned any sexual connections at all. Some may completely ab-stain from sex as a way of attempting to protect themselves from having to face the feelings of unworthiness, dirtiness, and shame. This condition is known as *sexual anorexia*, because it's similar to people "starving" themselves by not eating much. Both sexual ad-diction and anorexia are rooted in a sense of shame learned from being abused. The survivors experiencing this condition take on the shame of the perpetrator as if it were their own. You may go back and forth between both of the two extremes of sexual addic-tion and sexual anorexia.

The Use of Pornography to Regain Control

Some survivors choose masturbation and the use of pornog-raphy to help themselves feel in control. With pornography, they can take on any role within the scene depicted. In those moments, they can feel desired, in control, or controlled. They can feel at-tractive and sexy. Some survivors pick scenarios that depict the very way they were abused, and since they control the start and stop button, they may believe that watching this type of pornog-raphy is good for recovery because it helps them regain control.

While fantasy can play a healthy role in any person's sexual life, for a survivor it can also wreak havoc. Pornography can become a drug, just like alcohol or cocaine. Many survivors first get drunk or high, and then turn on pornography. My concern is that watch-ing it transforms the viewer into a sex object, thereby reinforcing the dysfunctional message that the viewer's only worth is *as* a sex object and that he deserved to be abused, in control, or controlled (versus sharing control).

❀   ❀   ❀

The solution to sex addiction and sexual anorexia is *making real connections with real people.* To heal, finding a community of men and women like you can be vitally important. Through this type of community, you can learn more about making real connections. There are several 12-step groups that address problems with sexual acting out, described in the Resources. I suggest visiting a minimum of six meetings in your community before deciding if one of these 12-step programs might be helpful to you. Most men and women who attend these meetings can identify with being a survivor of sexual abuse and assault.

Sexual Orientation Confusion

Another block to intimacy that you may be experiencing is confusion about your sexual orientation. Many factors can make it difficult for individuals to feel good about their sexuality, and sexual abuse adds considerably to this difficulty. For example, many survivors may be worried that their abuse made them gay. Others may be unable to know their true sexual orientation, because they were not given the chance to explore their sexuality without the harmful effects from the abuse. The powerful feelings generated during the abuse can be difficult to separate from one's actual sexual orientation. It's also normal for survivors to repeat the sexual behaviors of their abuse, and therefore not know if these situations indicate their true sexual orientation or are a reenactment of their abuse dynamics.

Although some may believe that sexual orientation is a choice or caused by abuse, an evolving body of research indicates that sexual orientation is determined at birth.[1] This means that your sexual orientation was determined before your abuse. However, it's normal for sexual identity, feelings, and behaviors to fluctuate for most children and adolescents during development. This may be due to their experimentation (or lack thereof) with their sexuality, the options available to explore their sexuality, and misunderstandings and prejudice about sexuality due to the stigma attached to non-heterosexuality.[2] Healthy sexual development depends on a person's ability to feel safe enough to develop his sexual curiosity and explore a wide range of sexual possibilities. This period of exploration allows the individual to know what feels right and best for him, and enhances his ability to enjoy touch and physical sensations and be present and relaxed during sexual intimacy.

For Survivors Who Are Confused

Determining what your true sexual orientation is can be very complicated, and it's important for you to know that it's your decision when and how quickly you want to proceed with exploring this issue. You can approach this in your own time. The dynamics of your abuse can cause a great deal of confusion. Some men know their sexual orientation but are terrified to acknowledge the truth. It takes time to grasp the dysfunctional quality of many of the messages you learned about your sexual orientation, sexuality, and masculinity and femininity. The more you grant yourself permission to be loyal to functionality, the easier it will be to sort out and find happiness.

Refuse to rush to a decision. If you feel uncomfortable, you will know that you've rushed. How do you know if you are really gay or bisexual or heterosexual? Men who are heterosexual will not have their sexual orientation changed by abuse, regardless of the gender of the perpetrator. But they often become very confused about sexuality. The following are some scenarios to help you understand how abuse impacts a man's sexual orientation and causes confusion.

If You Were Raped as an Adult by a Man

Sexual-orientation confusion is acute for men who were raped as adults by men. Even the most secure heterosexual man can have his world turned upside down by the experience of rape. Because of male anatomy, even if you are a heterosexual man who was raped by another man, you may experience some sexual pleasure, erection, or orgasm. You may have been "ripe for the picking" by perpetrators who chose you because you seemed vulnerable, or because your status with the perpetrator was significantly lower in rank (for example, a captain in the army violating a sergeant). Keep reminding yourself: *No one chooses to be raped.* If you could have stopped it, you would have. No matter how others may judge you, know that in refusing to be a victim, you are proving your courage and strength. By the very act of reading this book and reaching out for support, you are demonstrating that you have strength and courage far beyond what any typical macho man may claim to have.

If You Were Raped or Abused as a Boy by a Man or Older Guy

If you are heterosexual, the impact of abuse likely made you feel insecure about your masculinity. Unfortunately, in our society, doubting your masculinity has been mistakenly paired with the belief or fear that you might be gay. It's natural that a boy experiences sexual pleasure when stimulated, and a perpetrator may have pointed this out as proof that you "wanted it." Most perpetrators are skilled and cunning manipulators, so you shouldn't believe anything that person tells you to make you feel responsible for what was done to you. Male bodies naturally respond to stimulation; therefore your sexual response is unrelated to your sexual orientation.

Rhett, who now knows he is heterosexual, describes how he worked through his confusion:

> *It was a frightening thought that my abuser was a man; it would make me question my own sexual orientation and the role that I played in the sexual acts that took place. It made me feel that I was not worthy to be with a woman, because I enjoyed the pleasing part of the abuse. It made me feel that I must want to be with a man if I continued to let it happen. As I got older, and with therapy, I realized that I was becoming one of those fixated people. What I now know is that intimacy comes in all different*

*forms, and you and your partner can work toward what's inti-
mate between the two of you: a touch, a gesture, a tear, a laugh.
If it leads to having sex, then that's fine, provided you are safe
and comfortable, and if you aren't, then say so. The bottom line
is create your own intimacy and let it develop.*

Some bisexual or gay boys who were molested may wind up very
confused and insecure. If you believe you are gay (or fear that you
might be gay), you may believe that the perpetrator sensed "your
gayness" and picked you because he knew you "wanted it." *Remember, no victim of abuse "wants" to be abused.* Even if you were struggling with your same-sex attractions and seeking male attention or
affection at the time you were abused, you did not "deserve" to be
assaulted or taken advantage of because of your natural desires.

You may have interpreted your abuse experience as your "ini-
tiation" into gay sex. I have asked many gay or bisexual men about
their first sexual experiences, and often they tell me about what, to
me, is clearly an abusive experience. Many of these men think they
were "lucky" to have someone "care" enough to teach them how
to "enjoy sex," so they didn't even code it as abuse in their minds.

What about your truth? Maybe you felt no sexual attraction
toward the perpetrator, but felt obliged toward him because he was
older and perhaps portrayed himself as lonely. He may have told
you how sharing your hearts and this "special experience" would
help both of you feel better about being gay. Maybe you felt more
uncomfortable about gay sex and being gay afterward. The truth is
that the older guy only wanted what was best for himself: sexual
satisfaction and domination of you to boost his own self-esteem.

If Your Perpetrator Was a Female

You may be confused regarding your sexual orientation if a
female sexually abused you. Women perpetrate acts of sexual betrayal, violation, and rape against boys and men. If the female
is in a position of power or authority over a male, the woman
is 100 percent responsible for the abuse. Yet any male who has

been sexually betrayed, violated, or raped by a female may feel immense shame. Many men abused by women keep this secret locked inside themselves for decades.

Heterosexual males abused by females may actually be questioning their masculinity rather than their sexual orientation. This is a problem, because being secure in your masculinity is an important part of feeling secure in intimate male-female relationships.

Female perpetrators, like their male counterparts, prey on the vulnerable by winning their trust and, in the case of children, the trust of their guardians as well. Being vulnerable is something you can refuse to blame yourself for. It's an emotional condition brought on by neglect or abuse from your parents or caregivers. You may feel at fault in your heart or mind, but with time, patience, and guidance, you can discard such dysfunctional beliefs.

If you are gay or bisexual, or still searching for your sexual identity, being abused by a woman can be confusing. Especially if you experienced sexual pleasure of any kind, remind yourself that this is a normal reaction to being stimulated and is not proof of any permanent sexual proclivity one way or the other.

Silence Breaker Ryan writes about the fact that his mother's abuse caused him years of confusion in his relationships with women and questions about being gay.

Ryan describes this confusion:

> *Having been abused by my mother at a young age, the goal of my early therapy sessions was to heal my issues involving women. I thought that at some point, when I was "better," I'd find women attractive and sexually appealing. Therapy has helped me to find women to be less triggering, because I no longer feel that they all have hidden agendas or malicious intent. It's taken me a while to realize that the early abuse and my sexual orientation are unrelated. Having grown up in a conservative Mormon society, for a long time the idea of being gay was not even an option I'd allow myself to consider. When I realistically think about my history and interests, I realize that I've been attracted to men from a very early age.*

How Do You Learn How to Have Healthy Sex with Intimacy?

You can learn how to have healthy sex, even if you are not totally sure about your sexual orientation. It would help to know your orientation, because you may sabotage the intimacy and the sex if you are trying to be someone you are not. The key to healthy sex is making a real connection with another person, which means that you have to be comfortable and open, and the other person needs to feel safe enough to do the same. Disclosing enough about yourself and your history allows your partner to be sensitive toward your feelings.

Healthy sex includes:

- Honest communication regarding your boundaries and what you need from each other to feel safe

- Offering mutual and total respect, and refusing to shame or blame each other

- Expressing appreciation for any and all efforts to trust and be trustworthy

- Accepting that the other person may have insecurities, too

- Refusing to engage in sex that reenacts your abuse or your partner's abuse

- Having fun, being playful, and joking with each other

It's important that you, as a survivor of sexual abuse, be particularly careful in choosing your sexual partners. You likely won't feel safe with someone you don't know very well. You wouldn't share your story of abuse with a stranger, nor do I recommend attempting to have sex with one. Healthy sexual intimacy includes setting mutually agreeable and healthy boundaries. It's important to choose a partner who is willing to honor your boundaries and to work out mutually acceptable behaviors with you.

While "normal" guys may be able to take less care in choosing partners, the abuse you experienced and your efforts to heal require that you be more careful. Setting boundaries and communicating openly will result in much more satisfying sex for both of you. It may likely empower you to share much more intimacy than the "normal guys."

Healthy sex is also about respecting and protecting your body. That means knowing your "triggers" and vulnerabilities, and sharing them so that, for example, your partner knows not to hug you from behind because it triggers a flashback to your abuse. Once your boundaries are respected, you may eventually feel safe accepting hugs, but know that it may take time.

Anytime your partner triggers fears or hurtful memories, feel free to explain your feelings and stop the interaction. Relax your breathing and your body, and remind yourself that you are with a caring partner now and that your perpetrator is far away.

In this age of HIV/AIDS and other sexually transmitted diseases, many people negotiate healthy boundaries to protect themselves and their partners. Again, research suggests that this is another challenging area for survivors, and that an unwillingness or inability to take precautions can make them more prone to HIV infection. In fact, recent research suggests a strong link between practicing unsafe sex—specifically teen pregnancy, multiple sexual partners, and unprotected sexual intercourse—and having a history of sexual abuse.[3]

EXPERIMENT WITH NEW POSSIBILITIES:
Understanding Your Sexual and Physical Boundaries

Take a moment to breathe and check inside. Write down what you know about your sexual and physical boundaries. What behaviors will you not engage in? What do you not want someone to do to you, no matter how caring and loving he or she is? List your preferences in your journal:

- *My sexual and physical boundaries*
- *Sexual behaviors I cannot engage in and physical boundaries I need regarding being touched by an intimate partner*
- *Sexual behaviors I prefer not to be a part of*
- *Sexual behaviors and physical boundaries I want to negotiate*

How does it feel to write these boundaries? Can you give yourself permission to truthfully explain your boundaries to your partner? Know that over time, step-by-step, you can one day enjoy satisfying and rewarding sexual intimacy. Once you establish mutual respect for each other's boundaries, you may discover that some concerns and insecurities disappear.

One of the most sensitive topics for male survivors—and males in general—is sexual performance. Erectile problems have many, many causes. For survivors, they can be exacerbated by their abuse experience and lingering feelings of insecurity and fear. Refrain from making harsh judgments about yourself, if you have challenges in this arena. Be aware of any dysfunctional messages you are accepting regarding your sexual functions. Some men struggle because they were teased or criticized about penis size. It's not unusual for survivors to ejaculate quickly, because they learned during their abuse that it would end the assaults more quickly. Some were forced to perform in front of other people or while being videotaped or photographed, which was, of course, a horrible violation. I have heard traumatic stories of boys who were shamed by their abusers for their sexual performances—as if they had any control.

I hope you now have the tools to challenge those dysfunctional messages. Remember to remind yourself, whenever necessary, that healthy sex is about connecting with your partner, so find one who is willing to be patient and understanding as you work through your healing process. Keep in mind that medications you take can affect performance, too, and if so, talk with your doctor about possible remedies.

EXPERIMENT WITH NEW POSSIBILITIES:
Identifying Dysfunctional Messages
about Sexual Functioning

Think about any dysfunctional messages you learned about your penis and your sexual functioning. Whether you write them down or not, these messages are at the root of your shame.

To engage in healthy sex, I encourage you to address any dysfunctional messages you are loyal to. Dare to replace them with functional messages that support your right to engage in healthy sex. Consider what functional messages you could embrace to replace the dysfunctional messages in your head. At the top of a blank page in your journal, write the heading "Functional messages I can embrace about my sexual functioning," and list the ones that come to mind. Allow yourself to believe these functional messages, and give yourself permission to feel uncomfortable as you consider each one.

Practice the six-directions breathing method presented in Chapter 2, and give yourself permission to tune in to any current feelings. Write out any feelings you are struggling with, as well as any hopeful feelings and thoughts you are experiencing.

It's always helpful to hear others' experiences of hope and success, so next I share with you some of the positive experiences with healthy sex from three of the Silence Breakers.

SILENCE BREAKERS' BEST ADVICE:
Experiencing Healthy Sex

Christopher, Simon, and Ryan share what has worked for them in overcoming their blocks to healthy sex:

The best way for me to feel comfortable with intimate sex (as opposed to superficial tricking) is to be physically close and relaxed with my wife. The less anxiety I am feeling at any moment, the easier it is for me to be willing to be fully present and relaxed. Sometimes I have to remind myself that I don't have to put on a show or perform for anyone's benefit. I am continuing to learn to trust in the fact that my wife simply wants to be with me for no greater reason than that she loves me and truly wants to be connected to me, and that this connection is not a harmful or scary thing. — Christopher

Be present during sex and avoid dissociating through porn, drugs, and alcohol. Decide whether to disclose the abuse to your intimate partner or closest friend. Find the right time and make a conscious decision one way or another. Become more aware of the normal power dynamics that exist in every intimate relationship. Develop ways of being in control of your emotional life. Avoid controlling others or letting them control you. Be aware that the other person is vulnerable and has issues of his or her own when it comes to intimacy. Difficulties in relationships are not all about you and your abuse. Try to nurture spontaneity without being recklessly impulsive. Choose to avoid intimate situations that you are not ready to handle. — Simon

It's okay to ask for what you want or don't want. Certain kinds of touch may feel triggering or uncomfortable to you, even though you rationally think they shouldn't. It's okay to tell your partner that something is producing anxiety. A loving, caring partner will respond appropriately. Do your best to be in the present. Tune in to your senses. Observe your partner's body, the feel of his or her touch or responses to your touch. Being in the present can also mean taking your time. There's no need to be in a hurry. For me, being present in this way negates any need for me to "perform" and helps remove feelings of shame or fear that may have arisen from past experiences. — Ryan

Give yourself permission to affirm these new possibilities for you to increase the intimacy in your life. In the next chapter, I will discuss what is, no doubt, one of the most controversial topics among survivors: forgiveness. In this chapter, you will have an opportunity to understand more about what forgiveness is, and what steps you can take to achieve forgiveness for yourself and possibly for others.

AFFIRMATIONS FOR CHAPTER 11

- *I dare to dream I can remove the blocks to intimacy in my path now.*
- *I have the right to develop confidence and comfort with my own sexual orientation.*
- *I have the ability now to learn what healthy sex is.*
- *Now I can initiate, co-create, and maintain an intimate relationship.*

CHAPTER TWELVE

Dare to Dream
You Can Forgive
Yourself and Others

"I thought about what the weekend meant to me and us: being
heard and understood, a feeling of faith and hope, and the possibility
of forgiveness. A lifesaver was thrown into the sea for all of us who were
drowning in despair and shame." *Designer:* Hector L. Feliciano.

Achieving and practicing forgiveness is a possibility for all
survivors, but only in the later stages of recovery. If you are beginning your recovery, please consider that you can achieve a state
of forgiveness in your own time and at your own pace. You may
not yet be ready to even consider it if you are still dealing with
the memories of your abuse, struggling with your loyalty to dysfunction, and working on letting go of fault and self-blame. I invite you to read this chapter, knowing that it's work for you to
do in the future, and I encourage you to refuse to judge yourself
for where you are now. For some of you, this chapter could make

you very angry, and I honor those feelings. It's likely that you will identify with some of the beliefs I'll describe here that often block survivors from considering any possibility of forgiveness. You can consider being open to the words in this chapter as possibilities for you, or know that it's fine to skip it for now and read this chapter in the future, when you have made more progress.

For those of you who have made great strides in being disloyal to dysfunction, and are well on the road to being loyal to functionality, this chapter will help add another level to your recovery.

Reframing Forgiveness

Let's look at ways to reframe forgiveness that avoid the usual pitfalls that plague survivors who are seeking to move beyond blame. This is one of the most difficult concepts for most survivors to understand and accept. Bringing up the topic can lead to heated arguments between those who say, "I will never forgive my perpetrators," and those who strongly advocate for the position that "healing is impossible without forgiveness."

Consider that you could make much more progress when you are able to offer yourself forgiveness. This is the most important aspect of forgiveness. Even if you never forgive the perpetrators and nonprotectors in your life, you can still gain much from learning about self-forgiveness. For some of you, you may find that you will have extra energy for healing if you could let go of anger and resentment toward those who are responsible for your abuse and those who were responsible for your safety but failed to protect you.

Religious Beliefs about Forgiveness

The process of forgiveness has become very confusing because of the many different beliefs promoted by various religions and their traditions. It's common for survivors to hear: "God wants you to forgive," "Turn the other cheek," "Judge not lest ye be judged," or "Let him who is without sin throw the first stone." For most survivors, these messages seem to diminish the pain they have experienced. For some, talk of forgiveness can feel like a double betrayal, especially if those involved in the abuse included clergy or some other religious authority figure.

You may find that your religious beliefs can help you heal, but in some cases, survivors have felt that religious rules and teachings hindered them from healing or left them feeling conflicted. You have the right to claim loyalty to any messages that help you heal, while still considering yourself a spiritual person. If you believe in God and feel stuck around the issue of forgiveness, here's one interesting take offered by Silence Breaker Alexander:

> *People love to tell you to forgive because God forgives. This is not true. God never forgives because God always loves us at all times. God can't forgive what he never hated. God who loves us through our stuff knows nothing of forgiveness, because this is the energy of pure love. Therefore, forgiveness is the experience for man to become more like God.*

Religious issues may take some time to sort through. You may have a spiritual teacher, mentor, or clergyperson who could help you. Some may look outside of the traditions in which they were raised. Simply looking for guidance from someone other than your spiritual leader may cause you to feel that you are being disloyal to functionality. However, you may be remaining loyal to dysfunction by staying locked in your long-held religious beliefs.

Many spiritual traditions change as the world becomes a more tolerant, accepting place. Twenty years ago women were rarely allowed to lead religious services, same-gender union ceremonies were highly unusual, and gay or lesbian religious leaders were few and far between.

Many men and women have broken with the religious institutions they grew up in because of these issues and others. Hypocritical behavior by spiritual leaders who don't practice what they preach has also caused many to flee traditional religious organizations. In several high-profile cases, outspoken homophobic preachers have been discovered having sexual relationships with other men. Tragically, in nearly every faith, there have been leaders who have betrayed the trust of their followers and committed acts of sexual victimization against members of their congregations.[1]

Take your time. Hold on to any learning that might help you become a better, healthier man. I invite you to let go of any messages that don't allow you to move forward with your healing because they make you feel unworthy of love or unable to forgive yourself. If any of your religious tenets or beliefs say that you *must* forgive your perpetrators and your nonprotectors as a condition of being a spiritual person, I encourage you to consider whether they truly serve your needs as you seek to heal.

The Silence Breaker known as "Coach" has an interesting take on God and forgiveness. Coach believes that only God could empower him to practice forgiveness:

> *I believe it's not part of my human nature to offer forgiveness. Rather it has been an act of God that has occurred in my life. I did not will it to happen. It took me well over 30 years to get to the point of not wanting to end my perpetrator's life. My perpetrator violated me for over 11 years. Instead, I have needed to link to the God of the universe to empower me throughout this forgiveness process. The way I was able to recognize forgiveness is that I have been able to release my perpetrator through actions.*
>
> *This is not forgiveness of my abuser in the sense of "granting free pardon or my giving up all claims on account of an offense or debt." But it's more of a release from my being the judge, and giving the authority to God. I believe it's possible to demonstrate the actions of forgiveness (the release of anger, bitterness, resentment, retaliation, and vindication) even when your perpetrator takes no responsibility for his or her offenses against you.*

Myths That Can Block Forgiveness

Aside from religious beliefs, other myths that might block your ability to achieve a state of forgiveness include:

— *I cannot achieve forgiveness because I am unworthy: I am to blame for my abuse.* If you still believe you are unworthy of forgiveness, you are remaining loyal to your perpetrator, who would like nothing better than for you to keep blaming yourself. That way, that person can avoid taking any responsibility for his or her harmful actions. If you are stuck on that myth, I suggest reviewing Chapters 7 and 8. By treating yourself as unworthy of forgiveness, you also are cheating yourself of self-compassion.

Silence Breaker Pierre writes:

> One of my survival skills was to hold myself to a very high standard, because I believed that by being really good, no one would hurt me. This led me to see my flaws and the mistakes I make, and to be very hard on myself. The lack of self-forgiveness destroyed my confidence in myself. It made me feel worthless and unable to do anything right. When I started to be less harsh with myself, I started to forgive myself more and found more confidence in myself. I forgave myself for craving attention from my abuser because my life was so bad. This act of self-forgiveness allowed me to shed a lot of shame, the shame of having been complicit in my abuse.

Even though Pierre was not complicit in his abuse—his abuser took advantage of his vulnerability—he still needed to offer himself forgiveness for the blame he accepted at the time.

— *I cannot achieve forgiveness, because I hurt others after I was perpetrated and my destructiveness is unforgivable.* Silence Breaker SJC writes about his struggle with self-loathing because of the pain he caused others:

> To look at the destructive path I carved through myself and my family is like looking at the path of a tornado after the devastation. It takes a long time to properly rebuild. If there's an addiction involved, the struggle to rebuild is all the more difficult. I just cannot get over what I did to my wife, my children, and myself. I didn't want any part of my family of origin to leak into my adult family. I worked my whole life to build

my integrity and sense of self, and then in one bold stroke, I destroyed it. I want to learn from what I have done and all the ingredients that went into it. I still "should" myself. I know this is going to take some real work and time to get over. It's the core of my depression.

SJC knows he is making progress yet is unable to achieve forgiveness, because he can't believe he is worthy of forgiveness due to all the ways he hurt his family. Your abuse does not give you an excuse to hurt others, but it's an explanation. I believe that most survivors have chosen the path they have taken because, at the time, they had no other choice. Therefore, offering yourself compassion and forgiveness is a necessary part of this journey. To do that, you must take full responsibility for any harm you have caused to others and yourself.

If you have an addiction, you are still worthy of forgiveness. Forgiveness is a process of changing how you live today, tomorrow, and into the future. I believe that *all survivors* deserve better lives, no matter how many people they may have hurt, because I know that each has hurt himself *at least as much, if not more*. Again, it's not my intention to minimize the hurt survivors have done to others. Rather, I am acknowledging that seeking forgiveness is a necessary part of healing.

In 12-step programs designed to help people who are struggling with addictions and compulsive behaviors, forgiveness is usually part of the 8th and 9th steps. The 8th step is "Made a list of all persons we had harmed, and became willing to make amends to them all." Step 9 is "Made direct amends to such people wherever possible, except when to do so would injure them or others." The 12-step model is a good and proven tool for achieving a state of forgiveness. Typically in such programs, addicts work with a sponsor. I believe that following a process of making amends can be healing for survivors of sexual abuse, too. It can, of course, be complicated for survivors because, often, the people closest to them have been harmed due to their many challenges.

What's significant about working the 8th and 9th steps is that the outcome of taking them is not dependent on whether your forgiveness is accepted. It's the process of making amends whenever possible that's significant. If the person can forgive you, that's a wonderful gift. If that person cannot, you still can move forward in the process of forgiveness, because you have done your part.

Those you've hurt may need more time to process your request and to see if you are sincere. Some may never forgive you. This doesn't mean your actions are unforgivable.

Your responsibility is to seek forgiveness in the most humble, honest way you can. You have limited influence and no control over how others think and feel about you after you ask for forgiveness. If you ask for forgiveness and demonstrate that you've changed your behavior, it's quite possible that the person will accept your attempt to make amends.

Silence Breaker Rob writes of his experience with self-forgiveness:

> *As a direct result of my abuse, I went down the wrong path. I am an alcoholic with 15 years of sobriety. I have abused drugs. I have robbed stores, burglarized houses, and stolen cars. I've hurt and taken advantage of people, and generally been a bad seed. The key to this is that it's all past tense. I believe that I have forgiven myself, and I hope it shows in my actions and deeds. My choice is to live every day with my eyes open, be as good a father as I can be, keep my business hale and hearty, and maintain my mind and body to the best of my physical and emotional ability. I have now spent the majority of my life living on the grid: doing good things and treating people well. Today I am worthy. That's the ultimate forgiveness.*

Forgiveness and Perpetrators

Here's another myth with the potential to block you from achieving a state of forgiveness. Note that there are several different aspects of this myth relating to possible confrontations with the perpetrator in your life.

- *I cannot achieve forgiveness, because I don't have the courage to confront those who perpetrated against me.*

- *I cannot achieve forgiveness, because those who abused me won't admit it.*

- *I cannot achieve forgiveness, because I can't find the people who abused me or they refuse to talk with me.*

- *If I could just put the right combination of words together, then surely the perpetrators in my life would see the light and accept their responsibility.*

These myths can be confusing, but you can achieve a state of forgiveness, whether or not you talk with a perpetrator. It's critical to understand the truth of your abuse. It's important not to base your ability to achieve forgiveness on the opinion and behavior of any perpetrator, who may be incapable of acknowledging the truth because his or her realities are so distorted. Many perpetrators believe they were "loving" or "kind" to you, even that they did you "a favor."

Another myth you may get locked into believing is that it's your responsibility to find the right words to help perpetrators "see the light" and admit their roles in the abuse they perpetrated upon you. It's risky to believe that your words could have so much power, especially over perpetrators who cared so little about the damage they inflicted.

Healthy Confrontations with Perpetrators: One Possible Step Toward Forgiveness

Some perpetrators can heal. Some can take responsibility for their actions through effective therapy. However, remember, it's all perpetrators' responsibility to speak their own truths and to achieve their own healing. You are not responsible for helping them. Perpetrators must follow their own processes, which will likely take years. You can only influence them if they have reached a place where they are ready to be impacted by your words. If they are in the right place, your words will be powerful because they are true.

The main goal of a healthy confrontation is for you to speak your truth, which clearly states the level of your responsibility for your own abuse—that would be zero. Anyone who perpetrates is 100 percent responsible for the abuse and harm. In a healthy confrontation, you have the right to state the facts of the abuse as you know them. You have the right to clearly state how the perpetrator abused you and to make the point that your abuse didn't "just happen." You can ask the perpetrator for financial help to pay for professional help to assist with your healing. However, be aware that most won't agree to do that.

You can also have a healthy confrontation with anyone who should have protected you but failed. Again, the goal is to speak your truth and to be clear about your perceptions.

Please beware of unhealthy goals for a confrontation; they won't be successful in most cases, because they are unrealistic. They include expecting perpetrators to:

- Take responsibility for the abuse done to you.
- Agree with you on the facts, as you know them.
- Make amends with you.
- Pay you punitive damages for all the years you have suffered.

Silence Breaker Chris took an alternative way of confronting the abuser, which helped Chris forgive himself:

I've learned to transfer the power the perp had (or the power I gave him) back to myself. I gave up his name to those who have authority over him and can watch over him by keeping an eye out for other possible activities. I remain anonymous to these people, but they know my story and are advocates concerning child safety in their community. I feel safe for the first time since, well, the abuse. By releasing his name, I've, in a way, helped to forgive myself for keeping him a secret for 30 or so years. And it has helped my inner boy, too. He was waiting for me to do something to help him feel protected and worthy. I chose to do so and showed him that I would protect him, and he forgave me. I have forgiven myself in a roundabout way, boy to man.

EXPERIMENT WITH NEW POSSIBILITIES:
Opening Yourself to Forgiveness

First, I'd like you to define for yourself in your journal how you view what forgiveness is. In a moment, I'll review what I believe are important components of forgiveness, but first explore inside yourself what it means to you.

My definition of forgiveness:

Now that you've read about some typical blocks to forgiveness, I'd like you to write in your journal a list of your own blocks to forgiveness.

My blocks to forgiveness:

Last, I'd like you to identify for yourself how blocked you feel about forgiveness. I'd suggest copying this exercise in your journal, too. On the left side, list anyone you might choose to forgive, either for that person's neglect of you or his or her perpetration. I will start your list with you. In the spaces to the right, indicate how blocked you currently are by writing "NW" for "No way would I consider it," "SP" for "Slightly possible that I could forgive this person," "MP" for "Maybe it's possible," and "AP" for "Absolutely possible."

Exploring How Blocked or Open
You Are to Forgiveness

Person to Forgive	Possibility of Forgiveness
Myself	

Once you are done, remind yourself to breathe, and see how it feels to consider the possibility of forgiving any of the people on the previous list. Remember, this process is about refusing to judge yourself. Give yourself permission to honor wherever you are right now.

Four Components of Forgiveness

So far, I've addressed a number of myths and blocks that could prevent you from achieving a state of forgiveness. Through some of the Silence Breakers, you've heard how important they believe it is and how achievable it can be to reach a state of forgiveness. I have talked about what forgiveness is not. Now I want to focus on ways you can reframe forgiveness by looking at its four components:

— BUILDING BLOCK 1: **A simple definition of *forgiveness* is "the process of believing you are worthy of being loyal to functionality as fully as possible."** When you can challenge yourself each day to live in this way as fully as possible, the perpetrator will no longer have real power over you. Each day you will choose a path that's quite opposite from any the perpetrator would choose for you. This is what Chris does by advocating for his inner boy. This is what Rob does by living his life "on the grid."

Revisit the dysfunctional beliefs you used to hold. Remind yourself that these are all the messages the perpetrators and non-protectors in your life taught you. You have every right to live free of dysfunction. Also, affirm the healthy beliefs you've chosen over the dysfunctional messages. These are the keys to self-forgiveness.

— BUILDING BLOCK 2: **Your ability to achieve a state of forgiveness resides in your hands, in your mind, in your spirit.** When I appeared on *The Oprah Winfrey Show* in November 2010, she offered a definition of forgiveness from a previous guest that speaks to this point:

Forgiveness is giving up on the hope that what the past was could have been any different. It's accepting the past for what it was, and using this moment and this time to help yourself move forward.

As you see, this definition has nothing to do with confronting perpetrators with your truth. Rather, this definition puts the responsibility for achieving a state of forgiveness in your hands. It's also a reminder that being present in this moment, as I discussed in the chapter on mindfulness, will allow you to move forward as you leave the effects of the past behind you.

Silence Breaker Alexander quotes his wise old grandmother, who also empowered him to take responsibility for his forgiveness, but she is much less gentle than Oprah:

My grandmother put it best: "Drink some spiritual prune juice and let that shit go."

The power of forgiveness in helping you move forward is so great that you cannot afford to give it to anyone else, especially the perpetrator or those who failed to protect you. You cannot afford to wait for someone who has harmed you to ease your mind. You cannot wait for some court of law to find abusers guilty and lock them behind bars.

— BUILDING BLOCK 3: **Achieving forgiveness requires stating your truth unequivocally and then believing in your truth, regardless of what others may tell you.** To state your truth, it's not necessary to know 100 percent of it. You don't have to remember every experience of abuse. You do need to know simply that any abuse you endured was wrong and it was 100 percent the responsibility of those who did it to you and those who failed to protect you or help you afterward.

You may not know your truth yet. If that's the case, you may not be able to achieve forgiveness, and that's okay. Timing is critical, and your time will come.

— BUILDING BLOCK 4: **Forgiveness comes with believing you are worthy of reaching out to a community of people who can offer you unconditional acceptance just as you are.** As the process unfolds, you allow their acceptance to enter your heart, mind, and spirit, while you offer the same degree of unconditional acceptance to each person in your community.

Forgiveness requires you to be a part of a supportive community, a brotherhood, a sisterhood, a collection of souls to whom you feel an honest connection based on speaking your truth while they speak theirs.

When I think about forgiveness in this way, I equate it with the core of spirituality. You could consider living as a spiritual person when you feel worthy to make honest connections. For me, spirituality means being part of a loving, accepting community. It's different from religion in that spirituality is not based on the teachings of any one version of the Bible, Koran, or Torah, or any one God, Goddess, rabbi, pastor, or priest. Spirituality is an awareness that you can improve the world and yourself by joining forces with others and working together. Spirituality involves trusting others to support your healing while you support theirs.

I described in the Preface how an important part of my own healing occurred as I met and shared my own struggles with other male survivors who were also psychotherapists, and helped them face their challenges. Together, in 1994 we helped found MaleSurvivor, a community of healing professionals, allies, and survivors all committed to working together in the mission of healing all men from sexual victimization.

When Oprah Winfrey, with her friend Tyler Perry, a survivor of male sexual abuse, gathered with 200 other male survivors in 2010, the television host intuitively knew she was creating another community. That experience was immensely powerful, because every man in the studio knew he was no longer alone. She talked about that show as a historic moment, a healing of the shame experienced by men all over the planet. After the show, I learned about men around the world who were reaching out for support.

Support is a necessary component of forgiveness. Let's again review its four components:

1. You must undertake the process of believing that you are worthy of being loyal to functionality.

2. The power of forgiveness must reside in your hands, in your mind, and in your spirit.

3. Achieving forgiveness also requires stating your truth unequivocally and then believing in your truth, regardless of what others may tell you.

4. Forgiveness includes believing you are worthy of reaching out to a community of people who have the ability to offer you unconditional acceptance. As the process unfolds, you allow their acceptance to enter your heart, mind, and spirit, and you offer the same degree of unconditional acceptance to each of them.

Achieving Forgiveness: Opportunities for Greater Healing

As you end this chapter, I hope you understand now that there are many benefits attached to achieving forgiveness of yourself and possibly others. Forgiveness:

- Allows you to dare to dream you can be free of self-perpetrating behaviors, which include being too hard on yourself and engaging in self-defeating and addictive or compulsive behaviors.

- Gives you the opportunity to increase your self-esteem, your self-confidence, and ultimately your level of success personally and professionally.

- Opens up opportunities to join the boy inside you so that you can find joy and happiness together.

- Allows you to achieve connections with healthy people whom you value and who value you.

- Clears the path for thriving.

Affirm for yourself your worthiness to heal. The next chapter is dedicated primarily to the partners and family members of male survivors. I invite you, as a survivor, to also read that chapter, because it's important for you to understand the support your family needs while providing you the support *you* deserve. Understanding each other's needs is a critical part of healing.

AFFIRMATIONS FOR CHAPTER 12

- *I am absolutely worthy of practicing self-forgiveness now.*
- *I offer myself forgiveness now for hurting myself by staying loyal to dysfunction.*
- *I am willing to consider healing myself and offering forgiveness to those who hurt me and did not protect me.*

CHAPTER THIRTEEN

Dare to Dream You Can Receive the Support and Love You Need in this Recovery Process as a Partner or Family Member

"With the help of the other men and facilitators at the weekend, I came to realize that my abuse kept me very tightly wound and closed, and my shame and isolation has been a shroud that has kept me from being able to show my true self and make connections with others. As I continue to develop, I am working on opening my heart. The ribbons represent other people; the white space is for the opportunities for many more connections to come as I continue to grow." *Designer:* Douglas, Kempenfelt Weekend of Recovery, 2011.

If you are a male survivor reading this chapter, I hope you'll take some time to focus on what your family needs as they support your recovery. I address this chapter to the caring people in your life, although there will be important information in here for you, too.

If you are a partner, spouse, family member, or friend of a male survivor, thank you for picking up this book. Whatever your relationship, I welcome you to these pages and thank you for the support you have already offered simply by your willingness to read about breaking the silence and empowering the male survivor you love and care for. For simplicity's sake, I will refer to you as "family" and to the survivor you care about as your "family member," unless I am specifically addressing a romantic relationship.

Being a family member of a male survivor who is in the healing process can be immensely rewarding, yet it can also be very frustrating and trying at times. My goal in this chapter is to help you with some of those challenges, while reminding you of the rewards to be reaped for doing this work.

Healthy relationships are characterized by mutuality. Both the survivor and the family member need to recognize and accept that each of you requires support. This is not a competition. It's important it's characterized by mutual respect for each other's processes and feelings.

The Importance of Having Support

Receiving support during the healing process is just as important for the survivor's family members as for survivors themselves. I know this can be difficult, because the survivor in your life may not want you to tell anyone about his struggles. He may be adamant that you not tell anyone his story. Male survivors face so many challenges that directly impact those who care about them. I recommend giving yourself permission to ask for and receive as much support as you are giving to him. It's simply unreasonable for someone to expect you to deal with these challenges alone. It's also unrealistic for you to think you can deal with these issues on your own.

Some family members may be survivors of sexual abuse themselves. In this case, the need for support is even greater, because it's likely that your recovery path impacts the man you care about as much as his recovery path impacts you. If you, too, are a survivor, you may be in a unique position to offer him support, because you know what he's going through.

Blocks to Seeking Support

One of the biggest blocks to your survivor seeking support is shame, which you may carry, too. Perhaps his shame has triggered your own. You may be having problems in the relationship that feel like failures on your part. It can be difficult to let people know how much you are struggling, because you might fear that it could reflect poorly on you or your survivor.

You may minimize your problems, because you believe that your survivor's problems are much more important than your own. However, his struggles can and often do impact your struggles. They can make you vulnerable to mental health challenges.

You may be blocked because his behaviors have caused you a great deal of pain. You may have learned to shut down or keep your suffering private. You may, on the other hand, be very angry with him because of the harm he has caused you, but because you love him, you might hesitate to "bad-mouth" him, even though you feel a need to vent.

The wife of Silence Breaker "Coach" wrote that one of her biggest blocks was figuring out whom she could talk to about her husband's story of abuse:

> *I really wish I could have learned sooner how to choose the right people to talk to about Coach's abuse. I think it's key to learn how to find friends and family whom you can safely speak with. It's important that you learn how to identify whom not to talk with about it. Then it's important to give yourself plenty of grace for the mistakes you make in talking with the wrong people. When you do, try not to take it personally when someone rejects you. This does happen, and it's only because, many times, others would rather have non-intimate friendships, and*

they fear engaging in what really matters. Just remind yourself that it's their loss if they cannot be the kind of friend you need and want.

Overcoming the Blocks to Getting the Support You Need

I'd like you to take a couple of slow, deep breaths (if you don't know how, please see Chapter 2). Then, I'd like you to say this statement out loud: "I am worthy of all the support I need."

Notice what you experience as you say it out loud. What do you notice inside your body? How comfortable or uncomfortable do you feel asserting this need? Say it a few more times and notice any changes as you affirm your need for support.

Now try this one. Breathe a few times deeply first. Then say this one sentence aloud: "I am worthy of receiving as much support as I am giving."

Notice what you experience as you say it out loud. What do you notice inside your body? How comfortable or uncomfortable do you feel asserting this need? Say it a few more times and notice any changes as you affirm the need for as much support as you are offering the man you care about. Is this one easier or more difficult? If it's easier, what do you think makes it easier? If it's harder, what do you think makes it harder?

Shame can trigger or spring from feelings of unworthiness. It's impossible to be everything your family member needs, no matter how hard you try. So if your standards are that you must always be perfectly patient, compassionate, understanding, and strong, then you are setting yourself up for failure. This sort of shame related to your feelings of inadequacy may block you from getting or asking for the support you deserve, because you'll likely tell yourself you don't deserve it.

Chapters 7 and 8 offer guidance on recovery as a process of learning to be disloyal to dysfunction and, instead, being loyal to functionality. To tell yourself that you have to be perfect and always there for your survivor is a dysfunctional message. It's likely that you already have provided much support.

So what if your family member has forbidden you from speaking about his experience as a survivor? You have the right to have an honest and open talk with him. Let him know that you need support and that you want to continue offering him all the support he needs. Let him know that this is only possible if you have at least one confidant with whom to share your challenges. Your therapist could serve in this role. You have a right to choose the confidant since you know who can help you the most.

Your survivor has the right to tell his own story in his own time. You can mutually agree that you won't share the details of his story and will give him the freedom to share it when he feels ready. You can, however, indicate to this confidant that your family member is dealing with issues of sexual victimization.

Since mutuality and respect are critical, your survivor should know this person's identity. He has a right to express his concerns. It's important to be sensitive to his concerns, so base your decision on his feelings, too. If he still forbids you from sharing his story, you can talk to him about the stress you are having and the need to have someone to talk to about it. My hope is that he will empathize with and understand your need for support, while also grasping that you can offer more support to him if you have someone to talk to. Of course, you always have the right to seek professional help with or without his approval.

Sheryl, who has been married to Silence Breaker Rhett for 20 years, offers some very important advice about reaching out for help:

> *Everyone you talk to about a problem in your own life believes they have the answers to your problem, and most often that answer is that you should walk away from your problems. Whenever I confided in certain friends who knew about my husband's abuse, I would hear: "Oh, I wouldn't put up with that if I were you," "You shouldn't have to deal with all of that," or "You should leave him; it's never going to get better."*
>
> *The very first therapist I went to for guidance regarding the intimacy issues within our marriage told me that I was never going to change him and that it was in my best interest to leave him. I admit that there were times I sought to hear those words,*

because I was feeling as if I had come to the end of my rope and believed that there was no hope for us, that he was never going to let me in, or that it was only going to get worse, not better. I made the mistake of letting these comments drag me down, believing in not believing. In the end, somehow, something would tell me not to give up. I believed that something was the love for my husband that kept me going, and it was, in part.

Later, you will read how Sheryl and Rhett are thriving. She is grateful she didn't listen to the naysayers. She admits it has been tough, but she's also very grateful for hanging in there.

Silence Breaker Ryan's partner, Troy, writes that he wishes he and Ryan could have talked about the impact of the abuse before it took such a toll on their relationship:

As my partner was healing, I felt like I was losing it. I found myself needing counseling. There was nothing wrong with the way I felt. I was alone and lost in knowing what to do. He was getting help, but I was stuck in not knowing how much it affected me. I didn't realize I needed help as much as he did in order to understand and process what he and I were both going through. In retrospect, I wish I had been able to talk to him more about the abuse. It wasn't until after the damage to our relationship had been done that I looked for help and found what I needed to cope.

Lori, who is Silence Breaker Mike's wife, shares that her struggle arose from the fact that she chose to isolate herself rather than seek therapy:

Believing that by isolating, no one can hurt me has been a part of me for some time. I have always had friends and family, but I only would let them in on the surface level. They know me as a happy-go-lucky girl—not the woman who so desperately needed to spill my guts, cry, and not be judged for staying with a man who had hurt me so many times. I only wanted our marriage to be viewed as the perfect marriage, and I didn't want to

*be hurt with cruel words toward my husband or me. But the
good news is this: through therapy, I have been able to open up;
I have talked to a few people about Mike's being abused and
how it has affected me, and it has helped. I feel as if a bit of
that heaviness is off of my back.*

Silence Breaker Jorge's partner, Richard, suggests sharing your
problems cautiously:

*Be assured that everyone has problems. Be selective about
whom you share yours with, and understand that although you
may have a steamer trunk full, it might behoove you to unload
it in carry-on–size portions. A little self-effacing humor regarding the situation can make the most heinous things more palat-
able to hear.*

Getting Support on the Internet

The Internet can be a valuable resource for finding people who
share your situation and understand your feelings and struggles.
This resource also provides anonymity if you feel you need it, so
you can share more freely. A great resource is our own MaleSurvivor website's (**www.malesurvivor.org**) chat-room area for friends
and family. There's also a bulletin board on our site called "Friends
and Family Forum," where you can post comments and questions.

Another valuable place to find support on the Internet is the
website **www.1in6.org**. This site offers information on the challenges faced by the family members of survivors. It suggests helpful books and films, and provides a 24/7 support line and other
resources.

Ryan's partner, Troy, credited resources on the Internet with
helping him deal with his sexuality and with Ryan's history of
abuse and all the challenges it posed for their relationship.

*When I started to explore my gay side, it was the chat
rooms and discussion boards that first led me to believe I wasn't*

a horrible person for feeling the way I did. I found out I was not the only one in the world who felt as I did. It was a group of men who were or are Mormon that saved my life and ultimately led me to the better place where I am now. I would suggest for anyone who's struggling and hiding something like abuse to seek out support groups and discussion boards. You will find that you are not alone. That was the biggest breakthrough that I had.

How to Emotionally Manage the Disclosure of Abuse During and Afterward

Earlier in this book, some of the Silence Breakers wrote about disclosing their stories and offered their thoughts on how to make the experience as comfortable and successful as possible. Anytime a survivor shares his story, his audience will be affected, especially if the listener is a caring, empathetic person. A person who is impacted emotionally when told of another individual's pain experiences what psychologists call *vicarious traumatization.* Anytime a survivor shares his story, those listening are likely to feel a range of emotions, which is normal. As a family member listening to the survivor, you might feel sad for him, angry at the perpetrator or the people who didn't protect him, or upset with the survivor for not telling you sooner. It's possible also that you might feel honored and touched that the survivor felt safe enough to share his painful story. You may feel the desire to protect or even overprotect him. You may feel sympathy for him, or compassion and understanding for his suffering.

Sometimes a survivor has shut down emotionally as a defense mechanism so that he may report his story to you with very little feeling. Because of this, you may feel a range of emotions, and you can ask if he's open to hearing your reaction. He may not be ready, and if so, I'd suggest honoring his feelings, but offer him the option of talking some other time.

If you are a survivor, too, you likely will identify with his pain and suffering, and may project whatever feelings and thoughts you had, which may or may not be the same as his experience. Pay attention and check with him to make sure you aren't projecting inaccurate feelings and experiences onto him.

Once your family member shares with you, you may experience a range of emotional and physical responses, including feeling sick to your stomach, denial, the sense that you never want to discuss it again, a need to discuss it more, outrage, or an urgent need to do something to help him and others like him.

You will need some time to sort out your feelings. You may have some delayed reactions that you will want to discuss with the survivor. Be careful to ask him whether he wants to hear your feedback, especially if your emotions are intense. Remember that in sharing his story, he's taking a very courageous and risky step. He is leaving the "safe bubble." He has his own feelings to sort out, and he may feel vulnerable and exposed. Please go slowly as you talk about your feelings and reactions.

Hearing Survivors' Stories

Vicky, the wife of survivor Ken, offers her thoughts on being prepared for a loved one's disclosure of abuse:

> *Ken asked me if we could talk. This approach was very atypical of him, so I realized instantly that something important was about to be discussed. He recalled his childhood abuse when he was in his 40s, and had been struggling with the memories and trying to put it all together from the snippets he recalled. He shared the fears of not knowing everything that happened to him.*
>
> *He knew I had been sexually abused as a child, and he was concerned that it would upset me to discuss it. I told him that this moment was about him, not me. We talked, and I kept encouraging him to get it out. One thing I did that was out of*

character for me was to not touch Ken during the initial telling of the story. His pain was evident, and something told me that he needed to have his personal space respected.

I asked questions that gave him the opportunity to say more. I didn't react to the horror in an emotional manner. I knew there would be a time for us to share the tears of pain together, but this moment was his time to be protected. I think it was successful. I asked if he wanted to see a counselor, and when he said yes, I encouraged him to do so as soon as possible.

My advice to the survivor is sooner is always better. Your partner or family likely knows that there's upset in your life, and not knowing can be more damaging to your relationship with them. In my case, I assumed many failings of our marriage to be my fault and have spent years trying to overcome the idea that I'm not good enough or desirable. Ask your partner to be specific with you about what he needs from you in this initial sharing.

My advice for family members is this: Believe every detail you hear. Raising one iota of doubt about the story diminishes your survivor. Remember, he will be telling you about something horrible that happened to him as a child. His words, actions, and hurts may be similar to the age of occurrence. Don't expect adult emotions about the circumstances.

Sheryl next relates a very different experience at first, when her husband, Rhett, told her about his abuse. She responded in a way that she feels good about. At the same time, she had to realize that love alone is not enough to heal your family member, even though it's a powerful force. She was put in a difficult position, because she was told she had to keep it a secret:

I have been the wife of a survivor for the last 20 years. My husband told me about his abuse before we were married and prior to our committing to any kind of relationship. On the day that he told me of his abuse, he didn't disclose a great deal of information, other than that he had been sexually abused by a neighbor when he was 12 and that he had never told anyone but me. At the time, what I felt was privileged. I also felt that he must really like me a lot if he was disclosing this dreadful part of his life to me. I did and said everything I could to make him feel that what he had just told me had no bearing on my feelings for him. I, as the partner, felt as though I would be able to provide him with the security and comfort of knowing what it felt like to have a loving relationship.

At first, I thought, <u>This may be a little difficult,</u> and that we would have to take things slowly, but I believed anything was possible because our love for each other was growing and could withstand anything. I later learned that he truly felt he had just ruined any relationship we could have had together. That was not the case, but even though I thought I had reassured him plenty, I don't think he thought anyone could love him because of what happened to him. He was still loyal to dysfunction. I believe that my consistency in reassuring him of my feelings and being understanding allowed us to continue to build our relationship.

A year and a half later, we were married. I was the only person he had told. Over the first 17 years of our marriage, I was not only asked to keep what I knew a secret, but was expected to not ask questions or bring up the abuse with my husband.

Sheryl will have more to share later in this chapter concerning how this silence impacted their intimacy, and how that's changing as Rhett now feels freer to tell others, as they talk more, and as she reaches out for support.

Troy (Ryan's partner) reminds you that listening without judgment is a very important gift for the survivor. He and Ryan also discovered that sometimes the listener and the listener's family might be more supportive than the survivor's own family:

Not long after I met Ryan, he and I sat down, and he told me about his abuse. The hardest part of his telling me was the fact that it was his mother who abused him and that she was still living. Ryan was able to talk to some of my siblings as well as his. My family and, especially, his brother and sister were very supportive of him. As for family members, they need to be able to listen no matter how hard it is. They need to be able to support and help the victim in any way possible. The simple fact of listening without judgment was the greatest help that came from talking. Sometimes you learn that your true family is not the blood or biological family, but the family that you create in your life.

Getting to Know the Survivor's Inner Child

One of the many challenges facing a survivor is sharing his inner child with others. This may apply whether he is an adult rape survivor or a child abuse survivor. If he is an adult rape survivor, some fellow survivors will find the idea of an inner child offensive; in this case, you might think about this part of him as his playful, spontaneous side. In the case of men who were abused as boys or teens, encouraging him to know his inner boy can be helpful. It's important for you to understand how difficult it may be for him to share his inner child with you. He may well have learned that life and recovery are very serious. He may not be able to access his inner child, because he locked him away a long time ago.

When a survivor can access his inner child, it's much more likely that he will become better able to be spontaneous, playful, and fun with his family. You might choose to read or reread Chapter 9, about the inner child and the man you care for. You will hear stories about how men get in touch with the inner boy, and the rewards for it. What you will learn there are some of the ways your survivor could share his inner boy with you, such as by sharing letters with you between his inner boy and adult self, participating in pleasurable and fun activities with you, or sharing pictures from his childhood. If you have access to your own inner child, it could also be worthwhile to have your inner children spend time together. They might choose to talk, walk, or play together.

You might choose to engage in some artistic or creative project together. It's important to understand that your survivor may well be reluctant and fearful about your meeting his inner boy, and he may need extra reassurance from you that you are here to support him and help him, and that you promise to never judge him.

Survivor partner Troy talks about the importance of connecting with Ryan's boy, and the fun they have had together:

> *Connection with the inner boy is very important to our relationship. It's that boy who knows how to play and relax. The boy is better at letting go of fears and learning to or allowing himself to "cut loose." My partner has always been an uptight guy. It's his boy that can have fun. In his world, the adult doesn't have time for fun. He must work and provide for everyone. It's especially nice when the boy comes out to play in the bedroom. He can laugh at himself and not take things too seriously—just relax and be present in the now. I came to the relationship with two children from a prior marriage. We have taken our two children on trips. We went to Disneyland a few years back. It's fun to see the photos from there and see the child in his eyes.*

Dealing with Your Partner's Dysfunctional Behavior or Loyalty to Dysfunction

One of the toughest challenges for partners is when the survivor is being loyal to dysfunction. How can you cope with this behavior? Richard talks eloquently about the need to not take it personally and be very mindful of your own need to control:

> *The key is to understand that this [dysfunctional] behavior has nothing to do with you. It's hard for any of us to put the ego aside, but that's exactly what's required if you intend to get through the struggle. This is about your loved one, not you. His actions are not a reflection of you, his love for you, or a statement about you. They are simply the overt coping mechanisms of a damaged psyche.*

*If you don't accept that, the battle will be lost. It's diffi-
cult enough to put up with bad behavior. If you start to accept
responsibility for it, your own identity and self-worth will fall
victim, and the relationship will crumble. This is only valid if
your partner is also "actively" trying to heal by pursuing all
available positive avenues to repair what was done to him. If
that's not the case, you do share some responsibility, because
you have become an "enabler," sitting passively by and accepting bad behavior.*

Richard makes an important point here that's worth reiterating.
Even though the dysfunctional behavior can be tough to tolerate
and accept, if you know that your survivor is actively working on
his recovery, you will likely be able to have more patience. Richard
also suggests putting your loved one's dysfunctional behavior in
context in your life and considering the real consequences to you
and him. It can help to be willing to look at your dysfunctional patterns, and you may be able to work as a team.

*Examine the behavior in light of what it really is. If you
remove yourself, is the behavior actually damaging? Regardless of the conduct—whether it's sexual promiscuity, gambling,
recreational drugs, isolationism, or whatever—what are the real
consequences of the actions? Certainly, if he's out of control and
impacting his and your life, such as he's a physical danger to
himself or others, the mortgage payment isn't made, and so on,
this is unacceptable.*

*Understand that these behaviors normally satisfy some
need for pleasure, be it risk, sex, food, or escape. Examining
your own limits, tolerances, desires, and pleasures may change
how you see things. If you can change, you may help him
change. Actions that your partner may have been ashamed to
reveal or discuss might be incorporated into pleasurable activities that you both can share. Removing or changing stigmas of
behavior from "bad" to "tolerable or acceptable" can dramatically change interactions with your partner.*

Coach's wife has also learned when to let things be and when to intervene:

> *With regard to bad relationships or dysfunctional people, I'd encourage you to trust your partner's judgment when dysfunctional relationships must end. Regarding his compulsive behaviors, I've found that it's best to let them be, because the behaviors offer a sense of empowerment. When he's flooded with negative thoughts, I've learned not to force unsolicited suggestions because that's not helpful. When I listen, it helps him own his negative thoughts. Recognizing the negative thoughts has helped him be less immobilized by them. He has struggled with overwhelmingly negative thoughts and even with a personal faith in God; these things just don't go away. I am learning to be very patient. Last, with regard to his risky behaviors, I've learned that instead of imposing my own fears on my husband's outdoor adventures, I have allowed them, and he has learned through his experiences how to regulate his risks.*
>
> *I've also found other ways to help him be loyal to functionality, including encouraging healthy nutrition and exercise, and encouraging him to develop space for his personal growth or healing. I encourage that we focus our conversations more on the present than the past. I remind my partner of my unconditional love and acceptance for him, the benefits of our journey together, and the healing that has occurred. Coach is able to be more productive in his life because of our commitment to creating greater functionality in our relationship.*

Blocks to Intimacy and Strategies for Achieving Greater Intimacy

In Chapter 11, I wrote about achieving intimacy, and I invite you to review that chapter. For now, I want to examine your role as a family member and what you can do to help the survivor achieve greater intimacy with you.

Becoming intimate with a survivor can be rewarding and challenging. For a survivor to feel trusting enough to share his story with you is a great gift, because it means that he perceives you as safe enough for him to risk being vulnerable. When you help your family member who feels helpless and hopeless overcome adversity—and when you believe in him and love him more than he dares to love himself—it can be profoundly touching.

If you are in the midst of any of those challenges, you may be experiencing anger, hurt, betrayal, distrust, or frustration. You could be feeling the same emotions your family member experienced during and after his abuse. An abuse survivor can unconsciously set others up to feel what he is unable or unwilling to experience.

Debbie, Howie's wife, shares her experience with this challenge:

> I have needed a better understanding of Howie's addictive behaviors around sex and drinking, as well as his tendency to shut me out in the past. Howie is, by no means, a sex addict or an alcoholic, but I think that's due to my presence in his life. I have worried in the past that he would give in to his desire to sabotage our relationship and cheat. I have also felt that if Howie weren't in the environment that he is in, he would have tried to escape all feelings, good or bad, with drinking. I have also felt like an easy target when it came to his blame game, which was really just his past "woe is me" game that had nothing to do with me, but rather with his coming to terms with his own demons.

You don't deserve to be hurt. You have the right to set boundaries, to say what behaviors you can and cannot accept. If you set those boundaries, you have to be ready to hold to them, otherwise your survivor may not be able to believe you. For instance, it's absolutely reasonable to ask your partner to participate in the recovery process. You don't get to choose what he does; that's his choice. You do not have the right to demand that he share details about his progress. You do have the right to ask him about his progress, because you care. If he shuts you out, do what you can to let him know that you are open to hearing about his progress and his challenges in his own time and his own way. If he continues to shut you out totally, you also have the right to tell him how this impacts you and how difficult it is to know that he's in pain but unwilling to talk about it.

Troy writes that sometimes normally "healthy" behavior may really be dysfunctional. In this case, it could have an undesirable impact on the family member even though the survivor is doing it out of a desire to be helpful. To avoid this, give your partner feedback so that he can see that he needs to learn to be loyal to functionality, and in turn you can become closer and support each other so that you can grow. Troy says:

> *Understanding the dysfunctional behavior is a key to helping your partner to overcome loyalty to it. It took me several years to see that my partner was covering up his pain and hurt with this desire to be Superman. Everything he did had to be nearly perfect. He had the strong need to save people from their struggles, and literally would swoop in and take care of everything for others and me. I have often told him, "I don't need you to fix me; I need you to listen to what I'm saying and just help me think through it." He is learning that I much prefer for him to help me solve problems than to try to solve my problems. In his job, he had the strong drive to overachieve. He lived to produce and work. Now that he has been able to identify and work through this process, his new challenge is to learn to be quiet with himself.*

Building Sexual Intimacy for Partners and Spouses

In Chapter 11, I wrote about issues that surface for survivors regarding intimacy, sexuality, and lovemaking. This is one of the most difficult areas of a survivor's life. When a man is sexually abused and subjected to pain, torture, or humiliation by someone who claims to love and care for him, it can be very difficult for him to have a clear idea of what constitutes healthy sex. Sex and love may not equate for him. He may believe he can either be a sex object, or care for you but not have loving sexual relations with you. Any man who was raped as an adult likely feels immense shame, and struggles with feeling comfortable with his masculinity, which also significantly impacts his ability to feel confident during sexual intimacy.

Your survivor may be afraid that by having sex with you, somehow he'll be abusing you or expose himself to abuse from you. In his confusion, he may ask you to behave in the same way his perpetrator did, including hurting him or abusing him. You might feel obligated to go along with that, but reenacting abuse is never therapeutic or healing.

What can you do? You can invite your partner to take some little risks with you. He may not be ready to make love, but maybe he's ready to give you a massage or receive a massage, even starting with a simple hand massage. You can keep reaffirming that you value him as a loving, caring man whom you find attractive. Every step you take to be more intimate and more romantic can help him overcome the blocks. It's important that either one of you can say "stop" at any time. If you sense that he's uncomfortable, stop and check in with him. Remind him that the goal is not an orgasm or even mutually timed orgasms; you want to make a connection. It's preferable to engage in lovemaking and sex only when both of you want to participate. You may feel that he is controlling sex, because he's the only one who can say when it's okay. He may need this control for a while, and at the same time, you can let him know that you hope to reach a place where it could be mutual.

Debbie describes how her husband shut down emotionally but had a strong desire for sex:

> Howie views sex unemotionally and is unable to feel things, because his coping wall, built as a child, is set in place. I also think he is conflicted when it comes to sex, because the same thing that caused him to lose himself also creates an obsession in him. I often think he's trying to chase away his past

by substituting those painful memories with ones that don't cause him pain. It's hard to describe how this impacts me as a wife; the topic doesn't come easily. I wonder how it inherently impacts my own desire to have sex.

Sheryl and Rhett are still struggling in the area of sexual and romantic intimacy. They are feeling more hopeful, but it's still a struggle. Blaming yourself and trying to fix yourself is tempting, but as Sheryl shares, it's not the answer. This is a couple's problem, and both partners need to work to heal the relationship. Sheryl shares some very sage wisdom: keep asking your partner to talk, even though you know it will be uncomfortable. In the end, by keeping the door open, you are creating space for the man to speak his truth, which eventually will lead to more intimacy. She writes:

Over the years, we continuously struggled with intimacy. It started with a difference of opinion on the frequency of intimacy, and then led to my feeling and expressing that he didn't love me, which led to his feeling that he needed to appease me just to prove he did, which (I found out much later) ultimately made him feel victimized all over again. However, the majority of these feelings were unspoken. For him, it would bring back too many triggers, and he never wanted to feel out of control. For me, I was too afraid to cause any more strain around what was already such a strained issue. At times we would go for six months without being intimate, and as the partner of a silent abuse victim, I believed I was doing something wrong. As time went on, I would try to modify my behavior, but I'd never know how to modify it. I'd make many mistakes, and he'd get more distant. I kept thinking that if I did things differently, maybe it wouldn't make him feel uncomfortable around me. I can say now, from experience, that this way of thinking not only destroyed my self-esteem, but also didn't benefit either of us.

If I could suggest anything to other partners of survivors, it's to continue to ask your partner what makes him feel uncomfortable, even if he doesn't want to talk about the abuse.

Keep your communication open as much as you can, and don't assume; ask.

Troy shares the progress he and Ryan have made as Ryan heals from his abuse. They've gone from having no sex to having very intimate loving connections:

> *My partner is a wonderful man. He's very loving and respectful, yet finds it hard to be intimate in several ways. He's much better since attending the Weekends of Recovery. He has learned to face his fears and challenge his intimacy issues, but he still struggles with romance.*
>
> *Having sex with my partner has taken a long time to develop. There have been times when simply my touching him would cause him to withdraw and become afraid. He often said he felt as though he needed to protect his inner child from danger. It was always the child that was afraid of sex, not the adult. It's a wonderful experience when we are able to take the time and make it special. I must take it slow and easy. There can't be any pressure to perform. Allowing him to relax and feel at ease is something I have to do. He has grown a lot over the years and has learned to accept and receive sexual affection.*

If Your Partner Is Totally Shut Down Sexually

What if your survivor partner is totally shut down sexually? What if you haven't had sex for years? I have talked with many survivors who are in that situation. I know it can be tough for both partners. You may be tempted to think of this situation as "safe," because neither of you has to risk getting closer. Some may simply accept that situation because they don't want to rock the boat with a relationship that otherwise is working. That's one possibility; however, in my experience, unless there's a medical reason for not being sexual, usually partners who abstain are not intimate in other ways. They may also have stopped saying "I love you." Or they may become less and less nurturing, or much less inclined to hug or kiss. Or one or both of them may be dealing with so much shame that they both avoid intimacy, because it would be so scary. And unfortunately, the possibility exists for some men that they are dealing with their shame by being unfaithful and seeking sexual outlets outside of the relationship.

As noted previously, a partner's shame about his abuse can cause a significant inability to be intimate until he can speak his truth. I invite you to do an honest assessment of your relationship so that you can decide whether the lack of sex is the only problem. If it's not, then the lack of sex is a symptom of much more serious underlying problems, and I recommend seeking couples counseling. I recommend going to a psychotherapist who specializes in working with abuse survivors. If your partner declines, then go alone, but tell your partner. Hopefully your willingness to seek counseling and your disclosure may convince your partner to join you. As your partner takes steps to heal his shame, he may become more intimate outside of the bedroom and during sex.

Forgiveness and Confrontation

At some point your survivor family member may want to address the topic of forgiveness. You might want to read Chapter 12, which goes into the subject in great depth. What I want to focus on here is your role as a family member. The most important part of forgiveness with a survivor is to help him forgive himself for feeling responsible for his own abuse. Sometimes you can help by assuring him that you don't hold him responsible. It can take a long time for a survivor to let go of this self-blame, so don't take it personally if he struggles to accept your support. On the other hand, your care and love can help him to become loyal to functionality and to be disloyal to the perpetrator who taught him that he was to blame.

At some point the survivor may choose to forgive his perpetrator and those who failed to protect him. This might be especially hard for you, because you may not agree. You might feel that these people are not worthy of forgiveness, because you've had to live with the consequences of their assaults, betrayals, and lies. You've had to live with a man who struggles to be close to you and has difficulty being loyal to functionality. He may act in self-defeating or self-destructive ways. You've had to listen to all the pain and suffering, all the loneliness and isolation, and all the shame and guilt he has carried around.

So how can you help if you're still angry? You can listen to your survivor family member and work to understand his desire to forgive. You can listen with the same open heart that allowed you to listen to his story. You could choose to believe that there's something meaningful to explore after joining him in his forgiveness—something that could bring you closer to him. If you feel stuck, consider the components of forgiveness presented in Chapter 12.

Sheryl describes her role in helping Rhett practice forgiveness: She listened, supported, and gave him space and time.

I believed my husband never did anything wrong, and he knew it. I supported him in taking any necessary steps to help him feel better. But he needed to believe it for himself. So I gave him the space and time he needed to take these steps. Over time he opened up. Periodically he'd tell me where he was in his recovery process, and then suddenly he told me he finally understood that he could let go of old resentments, anger, and hurt. He'd learned that this was part of what was blocking his ability to move forward in his recovery.

Coach's wife has struggled with finding the most therapeutic role to play in helping him with forgiveness. She admits to having started out on the wrong track, and over time she understood the need to take a more respectful approach—toward Coach's process and recovery schedule instead of her own. By letting go, she empowered Coach to reach forgiveness:

My initial role involved a relentless commitment to direct my husband toward the steps I felt he needed to take to forgive his perpetrator and his nonprotectors. Coach initially took my good intentions as manipulative, because he wasn't ready to forgive on my schedule. The process of recovery requires a great degree of sensitivity and empathy on behalf of all loved ones who want to help. Initially, it's tempting to become over-ly confrontational—as I did with Coach's mother—and want answers that a nonprotector is incapable of giving. One can create barriers in relationships because of the emotions that surface in a face-to-face confrontation, but this communicates judgment that you didn't intend. When one is as direct as I was with Coach's mom, it gives the nonprotector little grace to ac-cept her own negligence.

I have learned to allow Coach personal ownership of his thoughts and feelings, whatever they might be. When my per-sonal expectations changed, Coach was enabled to receive the desired outcome that I hoped for his healing. This has offered freedom from the imprisoned state of being, that lack of forgive-ness and its causes, such as anger, anxiety, and bitterness. It's most powerful to create a shared goal of forgiving the perpetrator and nonprotectors. This expression of love offers encouragement.

Rewards and Challenges of Being a Survivor's Partner

Two Silence Breaker partners share the rewards and challeng-es. First, we'll hear from Debbie, Howie's partner of 15 years:

Although Howie's abuse is and will always be a part of our relationship, it doesn't define it. With communication, the release of his secret, and the chance to make things right with his children, we have come very far. I believe his lack of insight into what he and others truly feel has been the source of most of the frustration and tears I have shed over the years. There have been many times when he has either lashed out at me for no reason or made me feel that I was asking for something unreasonable. Another aspect of our life together that has been impacted by this tragedy is that my husband doesn't know how good he is. On a positive note, Howie takes fatherhood to an entirely new level. Because of his abuse—and more importantly, the love of life that it took away from him—he is even more engaged and determined to give his children the kind of childhood that he didn't have. Another reward as a wife of a survivor is that even though what happened to him was terrible and devastating, it also led to the creation of a man I fell deeply in love with. He didn't lose his humor, his kindness, his gentleness, his intelligence, his creativity, or his goodness. When my mom first met Howie, she told me she knew Howie was special. She said he was a "mensch" (Yiddish for a great soul). And he is.

Richard describes the gifts and challenges he has faced based on two long-term relationships with male partners:

I've been blessed to have had two wonderful partners in my life. Both were abused as children and raised in less-than-ideal homes. Unfortunately, the first partner didn't survive, but some of the lessons I learned from that relationship have allowed me to be a better partner today. Twenty-five years ago, I had no idea what it would mean to be in a relationship with someone who had suffered childhood abuse. Today I realize that it forms much of the core of how these individuals see, function, behave, and relate in and to the world around them.

My partners have been among the nicest, gentlest, and most giving people I've ever known. Relationships aren't easy; they take work, like most worthwhile things, if they are to flourish. Relationships with survivors can be that much more difficult. Partners need to put ego aside and realize that frequently what happens has nothing to do with them. And they are entitled to their feelings, but they don't have to act on them. Perhaps it was their own misfortune that contributed to their exceptional caring and charitable nature. With all the love I've received, it would have been my great misfortune if I hadn't seen past their demons and into their souls.

If Your Survivor Is Just Starting the Healing Process

You have read a great deal already about things to be aware of in this process. I asked the partners of the Silence Breakers to offer you their best advice on what you can do to help. Debbie, Troy, Sheryl, and Coach's wife all want you to know that there is hope, there is help, and, in time, it will get better and you will feel grateful for hanging in there.

Oh boy, this is a tough one. All I can do is role-model a healthy spirit for him. It's as if it sticks the more I say things like, "Isn't it a beautiful day outside? Just look at your two kids playing together, and did you ever think your daughter would scream out 'I love you, Daddy' while playing with Play-Doh on the porch?" You can't rely on the pace of his healing matching your expectations. It doesn't work that way. You must have patience and push, but push gently and with loving intention. — Debbie

I wish I could say, "Hold on; it gets easier." It will in time, but there will be a lot of times when you think it's never going to end or maybe that you wish it would all end. Just hang on. There's help out there for you, too. Go find it! — Troy

We made many mistakes over these 22 years. Just when we would think it was hopeless, we would have a breakthrough. And the cycle would begin again, but each time we would understand more about each other and find "our new way." Be prepared to make changes and find new ways to meet in the middle. — Sheryl

Listen a whole lot to the survivor! It's important that you really hear and understand the needs that he may not even mention. Be as empathetic as you can. Try not to give unsolicited advice. It's important that every decision a survivor makes be his own. These kinds of decisions must be made on his time schedule, when he is ready, not you. Go directly to groups and organizations that support the network of male survivors and their families. Then seek out the kinds of people you gain the most from. — Coach's wife

Thriving for Spouses, Partners, Family Members, and Friends

I believe that every survivor can achieve the goal to thrive, and you can also achieve this goal and assist each other in the process. Thriving is a process. If you can thrive for only 10 percent of the day right now, that counts as thriving. Perhaps tomorrow it will be 11 percent. It's likely that your degree of thriving will impact your survivor family member, just as his degree of thriving can impact you. Hopefully, the more you are able to achieve a state of thriving, the more it will inspire him. And the more he can achieve a state of thriving, it will empower you to thrive more, too.

I invite you to read Chapter 15, which features stories of survivors and families who are thriving. My goal is to offer you hope that you can hold onto throughout the healing process.

Sheryl offers a reminder to get the support you need to thrive as a couple:

> *One of the most important parts of thriving as a partner is the fine line you walk in being supportive to your spouse while making sure you are taking care of yourself, giving yourself the time, space, and knowledge to get help or support if you need it.*

The following are affirmations that you, as a family member, can use to help yourself get the support you need and deserve. If you aren't sure how to use affirmations, please visit the end of Chapter 1. In the next chapter, I will introduce how some survivors choose to publicly disclose being a male survivor. The role of family members is critical to this process, so I hope you will choose to read this chapter, too. Survivors will have an opportunity in the next chapter to explore the benefits of being a public spokesperson, and how to prepare yourself and your family if you decide to take such risks.

AFFIRMATIONS FOR CHAPTER 13

- *Now I am worthy of receiving as much support as I give.*
- *I accept that I need support as I experience the challenges of living through the aftermath of my partner's abuse.*
- *I dare to dream I can reach a place of forgiveness for what was done to my family member.*

CHAPTER FOURTEEN

Dare to Dream You Can Become Empowered by Publicly Disclosing Your Abuse

"The acknowledgment and unconditional respect that I have received from other survivors has given me the courage to be seen, to be heard, and to be beautiful." *Designer:* Darrel Tremaine.

Many survivors have found power and healing in publicly disclosing their abuse. Let's look at the benefits of disclosure by reading what the Silence Breakers, as well as their families and partners, have experienced after telling their stories. Most of those featured in this book were in the audience for "200 Men" *Oprah* episodes, which were originally broadcast in November 2010. Some of the men have chosen to tell their stories in other venues as well. If you are considering disclosing your abuse publicly, the tips and guidance offered in this chapter may be useful and inspiring.

Please note that I am not suggesting that every survivor should publicly disclose his abuse. This is an important but intimidating step that should only be done once you are firmly grounded in your recovery and, ideally, well along your healing journey. Going public can leave you feeling very exposed, and what seemed like a great idea can seem like a nightmare if you are not prepared to manage a variety of responses. Most often, as you'll read, the responses are very positive, especially from those closest to you. Sometimes, though, certain people may be threatened by your disclosure, especially if they are loyal to the perpetrators or loyal to dysfunction.

Choosing to Speak Your Truth Publicly Is an Act of Loyalty to Functionality

There can be tremendous benefits to public disclosure. After Hollywood producer-director-actor Tyler Perry shared his abuse history on an earlier *Oprah* show, he reported on the "200 Men" episode that afterward, he felt "lighter, as if I had taken the weight of the world off my shoulders, and I'm hoping that in talking about it . . . it's helping a lot of other men to be free, because there are so many of us who don't say anything."

Helping others is a primary reason why many survivors choose to go public. Having lived in shame and isolation, survivors know the pain of this existence. Once they discover the benefits of being connected to and supported by the survivor community, they often want to reach out to others who are still struggling.

Men may choose to tell their stories in public because they feel that it's a necessary step to protect not only themselves, but also others. When I appeared in November 2011 on the *Dr. Phil* show to talk about the Penn State sexual abuse scandal, a man named Matt Paknis was interviewed. He wanted to speak his truth to support the eight men who had come forward with allegations. He had just heard Jerry Sandusky, the serial pedophile who has now been convicted, in an interview prior to his trial where he flatly denied having sexually abused anyone. Matt Paknis heard that and said, "Enough is enough."

Matt, who was a graduate assistant coach at Penn State with Joe Paterno and Jerry Sandusky, shared details about observing Sandusky's grooming behaviors. As a survivor himself, he felt uncomfortable about what he observed:

> *I observed Jerry mainly with the kids who were attending the summer camps and the kids who were around him from his Second Mile not-for-profit. We had close to 1,000 7th- through 12th-grade participants per week attend four to six separate weeklong summer football camps every summer. Jerry was always breaking normal boundaries by head-locking, pinching, and grabbing kids. No other coaches did this. I only had contact with a player if I was demonstrating proper technique while other players were watching. Jerry, when angry at a PSU player during practice, might lean and grind into him. This was also, clearly, breaking boundaries. Coaches might lean their heads into the face mask of a player, but I never saw one lean in like Jerry. This is memorable to me: very threatening and bullying, and borderline sexually dominating.*

Matt observed these behaviors before the first allegations of actual sexual abuse surfaced in 1998. He was very forthright on the show. Dr. Phil and I congratulated him on his courage. Matt is dedicating himself today to help make sports safer for all athletes, and has joined the MaleSurvivor Board of Directors as well to help support healing for all male survivors.

The "200 Men" Episode of <u>The Oprah Winfrey Show</u>

Gregg is one of the men who responded to an e-mail sent to the alumni of the Weekends of Recovery. The e-mail asked for survivors who would be willing to speak about their abuse on *The Oprah Winfrey Show*. More than 55 WOR alumni and a few of their partners were selected to be in the audience. Gregg was one of the men who shared parts of his story on the show. Gregg wrote about his motivations for going on the show and his experience with it:

> *My good friend Jeff said, "You have a story to tell. You've been through a lot, and no one would ever believe you are still alive." The producer, Abby, was persistent; she really reassured me that we would be safe and that a lot of people would want to know. She was right. I stopped talking about the abuse for many years, because people gave me such blank stares. Now people can understand me better after I've been on the show.*

Rhett is the other Silence Breaker who was featured on *Oprah*. Rhett didn't realize that millions of people all over the world would hear his story on the show. He has received only positive responses and has continued to tell his story in other public forums.

> *My decision to go public about my abuse came from a place that was deep within me that I found during my WOR. I didn't know at the time that I would go public in a very big way on The Oprah Winfrey Show. I had been selected to provide pre-taped footage about my abuse. For the very first time, I would detail specifics and to a very large audience. Although I was scared and nervous, I was also filled with an intense amount of pride, knowing that it would help other men. It was a sacrifice that I was willing to make, and it liberated me of the shackles that tied me down for years because of the abuse.*
>
> *Having gone public with the airing of the show, I then chose opportunities to be featured in newspapers, and on radio and television shows. Each time, it was like a jolt of electricity that passed through my body and a feeling that what I was doing was exactly what I should be doing. I continued to go public through my own social media networks. It would be the first time that the people closest to me would know. Ironically, they included my fellow classmates, the people who, at the time of*

my abuse, I was most afraid would find out for fear of what they would think about me.

What happened was a miracle and a blessing. The outpouring of support from family, friends, and acquaintances was abundant. It just kept coming by e-mail, letters, phone calls, and postings on social networks. It was as if it all came together by my simply going public. In the course of it all, I never received one negative comment, and really was shocked by that. All my fears, for all those years, were false and would lead to a real shattering of my shame. Even more rewarding was how people told me their stories, liberating themselves of their own shame, which was exactly what I wanted for them.

I would not do anything differently in going public, except to tell my story even more, and here's why: The outcome of my public testimony is one of the greatest accomplishments I could have ever made, at least for now. I continue speaking out in public forums and still get that jolt of electricity. Most recently, I participated in an off-Broadway play on the subject of childhood sexual abuse.

Sure, I've been nervous, but I have never regretted it. Occasionally I would have this overwhelming feeling of Everybody knows! I can only say, after so many years of people not knowing, how different it is for that to be the reverse. It's an adjustment to experience such a change, and it gets better with time.

Howie also volunteered to be in the *Oprah* audience, because he hoped it would help him and others to talk about their experiences:

Going on Oprah was huge for me, because I felt compelled to let everyone know that I would be on the show so that no one found out by watching the show. I was deathly afraid of sending out the e-mail letting everyone know that I would be in the audience. However, the feedback from everyone was positive. I still can't believe they all know. Going public was my hope that others could also let people know. My wife, Debbie, constantly points out any reference to it, especially when Oprah mentioned she was most proud of the "200 Men" episode.

Bruce's abuse experience was similar to the victims of coach Jerry Sandusky. He was abused by a respected coach and physician. His emotions progressed from total fear of telling anyone to finally feeling liberated from the shame and emboldened to speak his truth.

> When I started my recovery from childhood sexual abuse, I was so frightened of anyone finding out. I had significant misguided fears that my disclosure would leave others asking if I might sexually abuse because I was abused. Also, I was very worried that people wouldn't believe me over a highly regarded doctor and assistant coach. I also had fears that even if people did believe me, they would minimize what happened to me because I am a gay man.
>
> After speaking in public for a few years, I've received fantastic reactions from participants at these events, and their response has made it a great experience. Still, each time I stand up to speak, I get nervous, but it passes. When we went on <u>The Oprah Winfrey Show</u>, I had a brief, overwhelming moment of manageable anxiety, but the desire to bring the message forward to so many people was much stronger than the fear of being in public.
>
> Since the show, people have not stopped asking me what it was like and complimenting us on what we did. I really have had no negative experiences, mainly because I just set up the moments for the response to be a positive one.

Jarrod went public after his appearance on the "200 Men" show, and when the Penn State scandal surfaced, the media approached him to give a statement. A friend saw him on the news, and Jarrod was quite surprised by this interaction.

> He apologized that he didn't say anything a year ago, but said he just couldn't. He then told me I have completely changed his perspective on sexually abused children and sexually abused adults. He told me he'd had a hard time getting past the fact that I was 17 years old before the abuse ended but that now he

gets it. He told me that I am the bravest guy he knows and that I have made him a better man! You could have knocked me over with a feather. In a nod to my recovery, I simply said thank you and expressed how much his words meant to me.

Alexander, as a black man who has known the pain of others who have been raped, especially wanted to give a voice to the black experience by appearing on *Oprah:*

> *For me, it was the simple fact that so many black men are suffering in silence and refuse to do anything about it. By my giving them a voice, maybe they will seek some form of help. My guiding motivations were two brothers whom I met. They disclosed their sexual abuse to me and committed suicide on the same day. That was enough for me.*
>
> *I am tired of black men suffering in silence and the black community acting as if this doesn't happen. I am tired of brothers feeling that they are the only ones that this happens to and that they can never tell this horrible secret. Something has to be done to get black men to seek help and healing. The fear of the taboo and embarrassment of these acts has to be eradicated. I stand for the emotional and mental freedom of black men, and for the healing and wholeness of brothers everywhere. If telling my story can help at least one brother to seek help and healing, I'm glad I helped.*

Alexander sat in the front row during the *Oprah* show, and here's what he experienced:

> *This was a life-changing moment. I was shocked and surprised when they called me down to be on the first row. I felt so honored to be chosen for the show, but then to also be acknowledged and asked to sit on the first row! I was so humbled and fought back the tears and raw emotion that came from the experience. I was close enough to hug Tyler and Oprah, but I simply stood back and acknowledged them when they acknowledged me.*

Alexander reports that there were very positive outcomes of his appearance on *Oprah*, but unfortunately, with his family, it was very negative:

> *The positive aspect was that men started coming to me for help and suggestions on how to heal. Several men told me they also had been molested and raped. Many let me know that when they saw me on the show holding up my baby picture, they also saw themselves and connected with my pain. Although they would never tell their story publicly, they are seeking help, and that was my main goal.*
>
> *The negativity is the fact that my parents and family are saying that the abuse never happened. They have disowned me for the third time in my life: first when I was 13, second at the age of 23, and now at the age of 41. It's amazing how people who never speak to you for years (over 11 to be exact and 10 prior to that) now are in an uproar about how I am living my life. It was freakishly disgusting how many sad, pathetic family members (especially cousins, aunt, and uncles who had not spoken to me in over 20 years) were mad at me for making my story public.*

Being public about your abuse is risky, especially with people in your life who are unable or unwilling to acknowledge your truth. It's important to be prepared for such backlash, lining up sufficient support so that no matter what the negatives are, the positive impact will more than make up for what you may lose. Alexander knew this going into the show, and remains empowered by his decision, especially knowing how many more men he is able to help.

More Motivations for Publicly Disclosing Your Abuse

As male-survivor issues continue to be brought more into the public dialogue, there will be many more opportunities to speak about your own experience. MaleSurvivor has embarked on the "Dare to Dream" program, which is a public-awareness program where we screen documentaries, such as *Boys and Men Healing,* and then include a panel of survivors to discuss their own healing and answer questions from the audience. Many more rape-crisis centers are broadening their services for men, and they also will be sponsoring more public-awareness campaigns to help them reach men. When you feel ready to speak publicly, reach out to MaleSurvivor, because speakers are needed in every community. To help inspire you more, I've included a few more stories from survivors to give you a wide sampling of the experiences men have as they choose to go public.

Ken knew that if he were to get the support he needed in his small community, he would have to take some risks. Although initially he told his story out of desperation, he soon found many rewards and felt much more powerful and confident.

> *I needed to create a supportive environment to further my recovery, because support groups and well-trained therapists simply were not readily available in my area. Initially, my decision to go public was born more out of desperation to find resources than a desire to go public. My wife supported my decision to create the resources I needed, and encouraged me. I found that the more I spoke out, the more people wanted to hear. I also was able to break through the isolation of other survivors. Whenever I speak publicly about my abuse, I receive appreciation from someone in the crowd, either because he is also a survivor and I have offered him hope, or because the person knows a survivor and now has words for him. Speaking about this is a powerful place to be, because I get to tell the story of my life in my words and not follow the coaching of my perps to stay silent and ashamed. I am proud of who I am and what I have accomplished. Saying so publicly is a way of affirming myself.*

Ken shared a very moving story about the results of one of his speaking engagements at a public forum to promote awareness of male survivors:

> *Fortunately, I have not experienced any negative consequences for going public about my abuse. One time, a woman and a little boy came up to me afterward. The woman had tears*

in her eyes, and the boy was crying and unable to speak. The woman told me, "My son wanted to thank you. He was also abused and thought he was the only one it ever happened to. Hearing you today, he knows he isn't the only one anymore." For me, that's what speaking publicly about my abuse is all about. Too many survivors have never seen the face of another survivor. If telling my story can give even one other survivor comfort, I will continue to talk about this whenever and wherever I have the opportunity.

Hope for the Future

Sexual abuse unfortunately will continue to be perpetrated for years to come, as recent scandals attest. What gives me hope is the knowledge that society is changing. You have just read the testimonies of male survivors who have dared to go public about their sexual abuse. They have offered powerful testimony about the healing benefits they've derived from speaking publicly. They've also written that their disclosures have helped many others who had suffered in silence. These men, and all the other men and women who come forward each day to tell their stories of abuse, are helping to change society. Societal institutions are also changing, becoming more accepting and tolerant, and creating opportunities for survivors to speak.

Since Oprah's groundbreaking show on male survivors of sexual abuse, many other media outlets have created opportunities for men to speak. For example, when the Penn State scandal erupted and there was an intense focus on Coach Paterno and the administrators of Penn State, many in the media broadened their reporting beyond the victims at this one school. Some reports showed that this is not an isolated problem and how witnesses who fail to report sexual abuse are as much to blame as the perpetrators. The media is also calling on more professionals in my field to educate the public about male sexual victimization, which is necessary to counter all the myths and stereotypes described throughout this book. Those myths and stereotypes help keep survivors loyal to dysfunction. Dispelling them is making it much more possible for survivors to become loyal to functionality and to thrive. As these stories are told, there will also be more opportunities for men like you to volunteer to speak your truth when you feel ready.

Progress is being made in many parts of the world outside the United States as well, including Canada, the United Kingdom (including Wales, Ireland, and Scotland), Norway, Israel, Russia, Cambodia, Japan, New Zealand, and Australia. Visit the Resources section for author and psychotherapist Mike Lew's web address, where you'll find resources for the international organizations also addressing male sexual victimization.

Use the following affirmations to support your efforts if you are ready to help male survivors who have not yet found the courage to go public. Several times per week, I still get calls from people who saw me on *Oprah,* so I know that the impact of those 200 men appearing in the audience continues to inspire others. In the next chapter, I will address the process of thriving and hopefully inspire you to believe that thriving is absolutely possible for you in the transformation you are experiencing.

AFFIRMATIONS FOR CHAPTER 14

- *When I am ready, I can find the courage to speak my truth publicly.*
- *I have the ability to find the support I need to speak my truth publicly.*

283

CHAPTER FIFTEEN

Dare to Dream
You Can Thrive!

"For 30-plus years I asked, 'What is wrong with me?' Feeling alone
stripped me of hope. Shame, guilt, and despair hovered like a dark storm,
creating chaos of mind and heart. Meeting other survivors gave me the
strength to release my guilt and shame and a desire to help others. There
is light in the hope of growing from survivor to thriver, victim to hero:
Now I love myself. It is OK2BME." *Designer:* Bob Fredrikson.

This is the final chapter in the book, and I congratulate you
for getting here! As I prepared this concluding chapter, many of
the Silence Breakers told me that they were especially excited about
this chapter because it's absolutely about giving you permission to
feel great hope for the future. This is my invitation for you to go
far beyond surviving to "thriving." Sometimes survivors worry that
they will always be "survivors" who are always grappling with the
effects of their abuse. I assure you that this is not the case for the
great majority of men who have committed themselves to recovery.

It's possible for you to become a thriver, which means it's possible for you to successfully overcome the effects of your abuse

most hours of the day, most days of the week, and most months of the year. It might creep back at times, and you might need a little touch-up, but many survivors thrive because they work hard on recovery and eventually reap the rewards of their efforts. When the temptation to be loyal to dysfunction creeps in, they address it swiftly and choose functional behavior instead.

You may be thinking, *I am far from recovered, and I'll never get to thrive.* Consider this: Moving from being a victim to a survivor to a thriver is a process. It will take time, and it will require practicing the methods and techniques offered in this book. If today, you are only thriving for 5 or 10 percent of the day, that's terrific. That's progress from where you were when you were barely surviving at all, or seriously depressed and perhaps even contemplating suicide. You survived the worst days, and now, a day at a time, a step at a time, you can keep moving forward.

Thriving is a process. Every step you take to be safer inside leads you forward. Every step you take to reach out for support, and to join forces through connecting with other survivors and allies, will help you as you feel the power that comes from being part of a healing community. Every step you take to be less dysfunctional and more loyal to functionality is a step toward thriving. Chances are very good that if you have read this far in the book, broken your silence with at least one person, and completed the exercises, you have already made significant progress.

Every opportunity you take to increase your sense of hope by imagining, perhaps even sculpting, a new pathway out of the depths of depression will move you closer to leaving your abuse and its effects behind you. Every time you connect with the part of you that was wounded, and offer yourself compassion, understanding, and acceptance helps you thrive. Every step you take to join with other survivors in groups, workshops, and conferences will reduce your isolation and shame, and increase your pride and self-compassion. And if you feel the strength to publicly tell your story, you will likely experience an even deeper sense of thriving, just as the Silence Breakers have felt. Sharing your experience gives hope and provides healing for many others who are suffering in silence.

Thriving involves improving your self-esteem, believing you are worthy of success, connecting to others, and healing. When you can say "I am proud of myself today," you are on a path toward thriving.

Dare to Dream You Can Be Loyal to Functionality as a Way of Life

In Chapter 7, I explored the concept of being disloyal to dysfunction; in Chapter 8, you learned about being loyal to functionality. You will thrive when choosing to be loyal to functionality becomes a priority in your life. I'm not talking about perfection here, but rather setting an intention and making a commitment to be loyal to functionality as a way of life now. The possibilities are wide open for health, happiness, caring, and connecting. Being loyal to functionality is often a challenge for survivors. Thriving requires being even more vigilant and dedicated to the process of healing and to moving on. Being loyal to functionality will take the power away from any perpetrator or nonprotector. You may have chosen to confront your abuser, and no matter how the person responded, you can now feel whole because you had the opportunity to speak your truth. You may not have confronted your abuser, and that may have been a healthy choice for you. You can still confront the perpetrator's messages that have lived inside you.

Now, you have the ability to stop yourself from being loyal to dysfunction. You can choose to be loyal to functionality instead, more times than not.

Rhett describes how he believes that taking little steps and using the tools of recovery keep him loyal to functionality:

> *What I think is important to realize is that the ability to thrive doesn't have to be something so grand and overwhelming. I focus on each and every small step. Take a moment out of your day, say five minutes, and think of nothing but positive*

things in your life. You could also write down how you felt when you first started therapy, recovery, or reading your first book about recovering from childhood sexual abuse. As long as whatever you are doing is about moving forward, you are beginning to thrive. I made a personal commitment to myself, almost as if I were marrying myself. My commitment was that I truly only deserved the very best and that nothing below the best would ever do for me. Not only did I do it, but also anyone can do it. It's about little wins in our everyday lives, and with each one, you build on it until you have a stronger platform. You become an armed machine of knowledge and tools of the trade that you get to apply to your life. If you feel like you are going into the negative zone or your abuse is getting the better of you, apply these tools and turn things around.

What Does Thriving Feel Like Inside?

Perhaps you are wondering how you will know if you are experiencing a state of thriving. I have asked the Silence Breakers to describe what they experience in this state.

Alexander feels joy, freedom, and permission to do what he loves:

I feel more energetic. I am happy and smiling. I take the time to do those things that I need to do to bring about a positive outcome. I stop fretting about things. I release and let go of past hurts that are wearing me down. I love me and put myself first, because I can't help anyone if I don't help myself first. I have learned to follow my heart's desire. I ask myself these questions: <u>What am I passionate about? What do I love doing? What's the one thing I would do if I didn't have to concern myself with any bills or obligations?</u> That's what I do because that's the thing that I will thrive at doing. I just need to make sure I'm consistent in it, stay focused, and overcome the adversities.

Christopher feels open to the world without being bogged down:

> *Maybe the best way to describe it is being in a place where my self-consciousness gives way to awareness of the world around me. Instead of being too finely attuned to my emotional state (or physical suffering), I am free to both take in the world around me in all its wonder and participate without the weight of shame and self-doubt holding me back or slowing me down.*

Bruce describes thriving as feeling like genuinely himself. He especially can achieve this when he is helping others heal:

> *I feel clean and true to myself. Feeling good is fantastic, so I try to make sure I make the choice as often as possible to feel positive. I really feel like I am thriving when I am helping other men heal from the impact of childhood sexual abuse. As I do the work of helping myself heal, I feel that I am most connected as I spread the word that recovery is clearly possible and that life is great.*

Gregg, like Bruce, believes he is thriving when he is helping others by talking about his abuse, as well as when he can offer others support like that which they've given him. Gregg also shares that learning to have nonsexual relationships has been an integral part of his thriving, as well as knowing what love is and what it's not.

> *I am thriving when I'm talking about it and helping other people, when I make my sister aware that she needs to protect her sons as well as her daughters, and when I am educating others and letting them know about watching their sons and protecting them, too.*
>
> *I am slowly but surely starting to grow again. Now I have about seven friends instead of one or two. I am having relationships with men that are nonsexual, and in those moments, I am thriving. I am thriving when I don't need to be validated by another man sexually. I know I want to do better, and want*

a better life. I want all of the benefits of my hard work. I now know that I won't be in any more verbally abusive relationships. I now know that that's not love.

Chris describes thriving as when he is feeling both calm and free from past stumbling blocks, and when he is sometimes excited about a risk he is taking. Reaching this stage has been a process for him. Like Bruce, he describes thriving as being "as clean as can be."

Thriving leads to my feeling a state of calm sometimes; other times it's excitement because a new journey or situation arises. Usually my feelings of conflict and guilt are considerably reduced to where I sometimes don't recognize them. My mind isn't racing or cluttered. When I'm in the moment, my emotions and feelings are released. I thrive when my slate is as clean as can be. This state of calmness for me has only come after the hard work of expressing and understanding all that's been buried or hidden because of shame and being in conflict. Being centered or feeling a balance only comes when I'm ready for change.

Howie describes thriving as the times when he feels accepted:

I've learned that once people find out about the abuse, nothing bad happens. I am always so worried that if someone finds out about my past, they will think I'm weird, won't understand, or just not want to be around me. However, if anything, they tell me how strong I am for getting through what I have been through, and our relationship stays as good as it was before. So I think part of thriving is realizing that people who are your good friends won't judge you or leave you once they find out about your past.

Rob describes thriving as being emotional and having choices about how he experiences his emotions:

Today I thrive. . . . I consider myself blessed with a healthy son who possesses no small amount of energy, a successful and challenging business, and a predominantly healthy life and lifestyle. My emotions travel with me on a daily basis, but I get to choose whether I need to hunker down and adjust to them, or continue to push myself out to where life exists. Occasionally I need to be back there, to live in the emotions of pain, grief, betrayal, and abandonment that exist in one who was abused. But I don't live there; I only visit occasionally. I am thriving when I get to make the decisions that affect my life and myself.

SJC boils down the experience of thriving to two words: *love* and *contributing*. For him, the experience of thriving is related to how much he loves himself and the people in his life. Remaining open to others is key. He also addresses the importance of being busy and engaged, and of contributing:

I will start with love: what fills my heart with joy and passion. I know I am thriving when I am able to love my children, my spouse, and myself with all my heart and soul. I know I am thriving when I have an open heart and when I am appreciating the beautiful birds, flowers, mountains, and trees. It's a feeling that brings a smile to my face when I wake up in the morning. It's a feeling that energizes my day and allows me to sleep at night. Engaging in the world is where the thriving is. I thrive when I know I am contributing.

Jorge describes thriving as when he is in touch with his strengths and gifts, even in difficult times:

I am thankful for the things that no one can take away from me: my special gifts, my resilience, my intelligence, and my ability to stand up for others, especially when they are unable to stand for themselves. I am even more thankful for my newfound abilities: to observe myself, and how I affect and influence others; to observe others, and how they affect me and others; to take back my power, and not depend on the approval of others to feel good about me; to have empathy and compassion in the face of my own anger; and to stand up for myself, even in the face of extremely dubious circumstances.

EXPERIMENT WITH NEW POSSIBILITIES:
Solidifying Your Commitment to Healing

Let's do an exercise to help you solidify your commitment to yourself. Please make two lists in your journal. The first list is the steps you are currently taking toward thriving. Think about some of the ways in which you can work toward thriving. How many of those steps are you taking, even if the step is not finished or is perhaps even barely started? Give yourself credit for every single step along the way. For example, maybe you have told only two people, but you have identified three more people you really want to tell. Give yourself credit for the two people you have told.

Take a few deep breaths and check in. Be aware of how difficult or easy it may be to feel a sense of pride. If you are blocked, see if you can imagine yourself standing alongside the community of other men reading this book, the men who have contributed to this book, the 850-plus men who have been to a Weekend of Recovery, and the men who have publicly disclosed their abuse. Visualize this, and then take a few more deep breaths. Can you now feel pride for the steps you have taken in your journey toward thriving?

Now let's work on the second list: the rewards you believe you will receive by making this commitment to yourself. You may still have little faith that you will ever receive these rewards. Even if you are lacking faith in that regard, take the next five minutes to believe that you can make different choices in your life that will lead to the same rewards that other survivors have enjoyed. Now imagine that you can have those rewards, too. The more motivated you are to lead a different life, the more likely you are to make these healthier choices, even if they are initially uncomfortable. Again, start with a few deep breaths, and be mindful of what you are experiencing in your body as you imagine filling in this list.

Dare to Dream You Can Create a Balanced Life

Balance is a very important part of thriving, and for many survivors, it's tough to define and even tougher to create. When I started writing this chapter, I was sitting in a cabin in southeastern Ohio, about an hour from my home. I had planned this writing vacation with my partner, but I didn't plan to get a serious infection a few weeks prior to the vacation. After a week in intensive care, I listened to the message I was hearing from my Higher Power and from my body, and the message was clear: *Slow down.* I heeded that message, and as I wrote this concluding chapter, I was completely healed, grateful, and committed to slowing down.

To find balance, listen to your body. Pay attention to how your body responds to your actions. How does your body react to the amount of sleep you are getting? We are all different in terms of what's "adequate sleep," depending on our age, general health, and health challenges. But thriving requires adequate sleep! Make the lifestyle choice to get all the rest you need each and every day and night.

Thriving is about valuing your body and nurturing it with healthy foods, and eating in a mindful way so that you can taste your food, enjoy it, and feel satisfied and comfortable after the meal. How does your body react to the food you eat each day? When you eat with the intention to nurture your body, your body will respond by calmly digesting your food, leaving you satisfied and comfortable. This is a lifestyle choice you can make: to consciously slow down enough to nurture your body with healthy food choices.

Thriving also includes maintaining your physical health beyond eating and sleeping. When you are thriving, you value your physical health and regularly take steps to honor your body, to challenge your body, and to stay as fit as possible. For many survivors, this means being committed to some type of regular exercise.

What is your current commitment to regular exercise? It's important to start wherever you are. As a survivor, your body has been abused, so it's understandable that you may have devalued your body perhaps from feeling unworthy of care. If you are not exercising, I invite you to explore ways you can exercise while following your doctor's recommendations.

Once you are regularly exercising, conduct another internal check to see how you feel during and after your workout. When exercise is part of your life balance, you feel invigorated and experience increased energy, your mood is improved, and your ability to fall asleep and stay asleep is improved.

Some of you will have gone to the other extreme of compulsively exercising. I honor your commitment to fitness and, at the same time, encourage you to honestly assess whether the time you are spending exercising is out of balance with the rest of your life. Consider honestly whether the amount that you exercise has led to too many accidents from doing too much or taking unnecessary risks. If so, although it may feel uncomfortable at first, in time, by cutting back, you'll find the amount of exercise that is right for you.

In Chapter 9, I wrote about connecting with the boy inside you. Thrivers have the ability to unite with that boy and to experience that they and he are partners. Silence Breaker Rob describes ways in which he connects with the boy inside him as well as to his son. By maintaining balance between his adult self and child self, he nurtures a feeling of abundance:

> *There are innumerable activities and lifestyle choices that define who I am. Being a dad is at the top of my list. I enjoy writing and am an avid barefoot water-skier, snow skier, and cyclist. I love to scuba dive and free dive, travel anywhere, or just hang out with my son. Running my business also ranks high. All of these activities are a result of the direction I took in my life. It took time to stack them properly so that they created dimension in my life rather than space. But today, they are distributed as well as they have ever been, and this leads me to a genuine feeling of abundance the majority of the time.*

Silence Breaker Christopher recently connected with his inner boy:

> *I had this amazing experience with my kid the other day: When I woke up, my kid was playing superhero inside my head, so to speak. Normally when I wake up, I have to fight through a couple of automatic negative thoughts, but all of a sudden, my kid was playing superhero and fighting off the mean thoughts. It was almost like a video game. I could watch my own kid smacking back all the negative thoughts as they "fell from the sky," before they hit bottom and sank into my heart. And he's been doing it ever since.*

If you are a survivor of adult rape, I encourage you to be mindful of the possibility of thriving by giving yourself permission to enjoy life more and to pursue more pleasurable activities. You may not choose to connect with your inner boy; however, I do hope you will connect with playful and spontaneous people in your life who can help you find more balance.

Thriving and Intimacy

Thrivers also have the ability to listen to the people in their lives, to share with these people, and to allow themselves to care about others and be cared about. Listen for any direct and indirect messages that a change is required. Maybe your loved ones express this as a concern. Maybe they express it as a request to spend more time with you or as a complaint that they aren't enjoying enough quality time with you. Pay attention to how you are responding to these messages. Are you listening? Do you feel defensive? Chances are your life is out of balance, and you have choices to make.

Survivors often grow up in intense and dysfunctional home environments. Once you believe you have the ability and the willingness to thrive, you can regularly reject any draw to dysfunction, and instead choose a life that honors functionality.

Silence Breaker SJC knows that he's thriving when he examines his roles as a marital partner and a parent:

I also thrive when I am in marital harmony: when I know I am interacting in an honest, open, forthright manner, and my spouse is reciprocating in like manner. Thriving in a marriage means that both partners need to have similar outlooks on life and act as a team. I thrive as a parent when I know that I am unconditionally loving and communicating with my adult children. It's important to me that they know how much I love them every single day.

Another important aspect of balanced relationships is examining what you do when there are problems. Thrivers make it a priority to resolve relationship problems as soon as they can. With every relationship problem is shared responsibility between both partners in the relationship. Do another internal check to examine the importance you are placing on improving your relationship problems.

Learning to be engaged in healthy, balanced relationships is another aspect of thriving. You can choose to take time each day to value the people in your life, to express your caring for them, and to be open to their caring for you. And when you do have problems in those relationships, I encourage you to make resolving those problems a priority, instead of escaping into other activities to avoid the conflict and the intimacy.

Remember, if you are single, intimacy is still a gift you can receive from friends and allies. You can be a thriver no matter what your relationship status is.

Spirituality and Thriving

Spirituality is another aspect of balance. Think about your spiritual practices in terms of balance in your life. Spirituality is being connected to others, valuing your life, and allowing others to value your life. It can also include allowing yourself to relate to any force outside of yourself, including nature.

Coach eloquently shares his experience of thriving through nature:

> *I relate to thriving best by using the analogy of the growth rate of the bristlecone pine tree. This tree, the oldest known species, is also one of the slowest-growing trees in North America. It grows best at high elevations, in poor soil, and with a minimum amount of moisture. There it becomes gnarled and sculpted into unique shapes and forms. Its growing season is less than two months per calendar year. It seems to me that these extreme conditions create a misshapen piece of beauty. Thriving, for me, has to do with reclaiming a sense of self and purpose. I thrive when my close friends remind me of and validate me about the progress and growth I have made. This helps me to accept and value the unique shapes and forms I have evolved into through the extreme neglect and suffering I encountered.*

Coach is among those Silence Breakers with strong religious beliefs, but he admits to having had to struggle with trusting God. And yet, he believes that it's God who offers him a sense of purpose, which is necessary for him to thrive:

> *When I am participating in meaningful activities, I am able to thrive, because God often infuses me with purpose. It's at that point that I'm depending on God to transform me from within. Since my abuse began at such an early age and continued through early adolescence, it has been difficult to depend on God or discover the self-esteem he created for me to have and thrive in. I recognize that I may be further along than what my mind is capable of believing about myself. I am learning to give myself latitude to progress without a performance rating.*

The practice of spirituality may start with your ability to be present. For many people, that includes regular meditation or mind-body awareness exercises. Once you are present, then you can give yourself permission to be included in your community in a way that allows you to give to others, to care about others, and to be involved in helping others with their problems and concerns.

I am referring to ways that you can spend your time investing in others, in addition to the time you spend on your own recovery.

Creating a balanced life is a choice. Thrivers choose to be aware of themselves, and involved and connected with others for the purpose of enriching their lives, finding a sense of purpose, and experiencing the joys of helping and caring for others.

SILENCE BREAKERS' BEST ADVICE:
Keep Striving Toward Thriving

Although the Silence Breakers vary tremendously in the extents to which they thrive, they offer you hope for your efforts to thrive. You may feel that you are thriving only 5 to 10 percent of the time at first, but over time that will increase as you progress in your healing.

John believes he thrives about 90 percent of the time, but it has taken years for him to reach that level. He writes:

Develop your own boundaries, and respect the boundaries of others. When you react to a situation with anger, resentment, withdrawal, or anything that takes you out of the moment, look to your past for a trigger that has ignited your reaction. Practice being nonjudgmental and empathetic. I have found that practicing these things evokes generosity, patience, and tolerance, all of which contribute greatly to my sense of thriving. After several years of work, I now put my thriving at somewhere around or above 90 percent. — John

When you have doubts about being able to thrive, it's really helpful to put your recovery in perspective. Think back to before you started the recovery process, and then consider where you are now. Simon and Christopher offer their perspectives:

When I feel that progress is slow or nonexistent, I find it helpful to look back to a year ago. When I compare how I was feeling or reacting to situations then, more often than not, I can see definite movement. Recovery is a shifting of tectonic plates but without the earthquakes! — Simon

> *In five years, I've gone from feeling suicidal and battling to keep myself afloat in the wake of a failed marriage to remarrying and feeling a sense of possibility and hope. I have developed a new sense of self and a stronger foundation to build the rest of my life on. All that, and today I'd honestly say I'm only thriving 40 to 50 percent of the time. But that's a sign of how bad things were before and how you don't need to get to 90 percent thriving to live a far better life than you might think possible now. I think the great change that comes before thriving is learning how to stop self-destructing. I don't yet know how to stop myself from feeling anxiety, but I do know how to stop my self-destructive behaviors and emotions from driving me into downward spirals of depression, anxiety, and hopelessness. To me, that's what being disloyal to dysfunction looks like. I have tools for dealing with the anxiety, which makes all the difference in the world. I have managed to build a life with genuine happiness as my reward, which I didn't think was possible.* — Christopher

Christopher reminds you to keep using all the recovery tools you have learned. Have confidence that they will protect you and help you move forward. Thriving also will require you to draw on your resilience, which is your ability to persist even in the toughest of times.

Bruce, whose resilience has helped him battle cancer along with his abuse experiences, keeps his advice very straightforward and encourages you to be persistent and positive. Joe agrees that you can transform negative energy into positive energy. Niall adds that it's absolutely possible to heal completely:

> *Never give in. This is very achievable and feels just amazing.* — Bruce

> *It is possible to change negativity from the past into positivity for the present and future.* — Joe

> *There really is light at the end of the dark tunnel of abuse. I know from experience that with time and patience, healing—complete healing—from child sex abuse really is possible. Hang in there, man! You can do it! And your life can be beyond your wildest dreams!* — Niall

Chris and Mike want you to know that you can achieve thriving, a step at a time, sometimes with baby steps and sometimes with longer steps:

> *It takes time. It takes dedication, energy, and focus. But it can be done. Baby steps are always first. You can relearn. You will begin to trust yourself and others. As you practice and relearn skills, you will begin to thrive a little at a time. Some things will come quicker, and others may take years, but you can thrive. We are proof of this process. I am thriving right now. I can't say that I am thriving all the time, but recognizing when I am leads me to be loyal to functionality. This will continually increase my percentage of thriving time. And you can do the same. — Chris*

> *I was nearing zero very fast. I prayed for help, and it came to me through the MaleSurvivor.org website. From there I began learning that I wasn't alone, and I saw others thriving who once were not. That was encouraging. The biggest thing for me was recognizing that this is an illness, and to treat it as such. Like when you have the stomach flu, when you finally feel as though you can put food in your mouth again, you might start with crackers first and then work your way up to an apple or something. Recovery as a survivor is no different; it takes time. Know in your heart that it will get better; if it's just for 20 minutes more each week, that's growth. — Mike*

SJC believes the most important thing in thriving is to stay focused and aware, believing in yourself and staying connected:

> *The enemy of us all is ourselves. Whether we thrive or not, whether it's 10 percent or 90 percent, depends on us. Recognizing and dealing with our demons is a huge part of the battle. Some days may be 20 percent, and others 90 percent. But we can all aim for an average we put out there for ourselves. The old adage "one day at a time" is more than helpful. I like waking up and saying I am going to hit 90 percent today. And for the most part I do. I control what kind of day I'm going to have. I have the power to survive and thrive, and to set goals for myself. Attitude is key. Isolation and idle do-nothing-ism is a dreadful disease. — SJC*

Gregg encourages you to try any activity that won't hurt you. Now he is pursuing creative activities that once nourished him. He also encourages you to be aware of life events that can motivate you to have a healthier perspective:

> *Get back to doing those one or two things that won't hurt you. I used to be an artist and designer of clothes; it hurt too much to keep doing those things. All my talents went out the window for a while. But now I am taking a longer road, and I'm going to get there a little at a time. I am back to doing art and designing.*
>
> *When I was beaten or molested, I would just lock myself in my room and draw, draw, draw. I had this big future in front of me. I don't know what it was this past year; when my friend Jeff got sick and then his mother died, I was triggered to value my life more. You can forget some of those simple things that gave you pleasure, and it's important to rediscover those things. — Gregg*

Coach suggests that his level of thriving is below 10 percent, but based on all that he has chosen to share with you, it seems likely that he is thriving at a much higher level. For example, a week before Thanksgiving in 2011, he wrote to his pastor, who was talking about abuse in faraway places but ignored what had occurred closer in the same week: the Penn State sexual abuse scandal. Coach challenged him to consider that there are male survivors in the congregation who need support. His message is especially helpful for those who are thriving only a small percentage of the time:

> *It's okay to feel that you are only thriving for a small percentage of the time. In fact when I am honest with myself, I only believe I am thriving 7 percent of the time. But that's entirely okay, because personal growth and healing for a survivor who is transitioning into a thriver is a strenuous process! — Coach*

Coach's wife describes how they have become much more functional in their marriage, another sign of significant thriving. Sometimes it takes someone outside of yourself to help you have a healthier perspective on your progress:

The more we learn to work together through the practice and process of a united purpose in our relationship, the greater our capacity to handle change and participate in the re-creation of our future together as a survivor and partner has grown. Coach and I have been able to reach this destination of a shared vision by becoming more transparent to one another. We do not withhold our fears, vulnerabilities, or weaknesses. Instead together, we open ourselves to hope and possibility. And it's there that we are able to develop realistic purposes that transform the past and re-create our future by giving greater hope to others and ourselves. — Coach's wife

Sheryl, Rhett's wife, reminds partners to hang in there, stay committed for the long haul, and know that it's possible to overcome the obstacles:

As a couple, our thriving comes from so many things that we choose to do together as partners, parents, and friends. Even when there are obstacles that hinder our state of thriving in an intimate way, we still choose to engage in all of our daily activities as a couple, regardless of how difficult times can get. I stand by his side, show him that he is not alone, and commit to take the journey with him no matter how long it takes. It doesn't matter how many times that journey leads you back to roads you've already traveled; show him that you value how he feels and understand any difficulties that cross his path. Show him that you will be there and that you value the time you spend together. — Sheryl

Rob also wants you to keep the faith, which is possible when you can set aside and manage your fear. He is thriving and believes you can, too:

Set aside the fear. Continue to move forward at every turn. Take the cues from your support group. Develop a foundation and build a life for yourself. You are worthy, you deserve this, and you can make this happen. Find your mark, whether it's 1 percent or 100 percent. Decide where you want to be in a few days, a few months, or a few years, and reach for that mark. Be realistic; set goals that are attainable and never give up. Take power from your setbacks because they will be there. Renew your focus and overcome. Your life is waiting for you. Claim it! — Rob

AFFIRMATIONS FOR CHAPTER 15

- *I absolutely have the ability now to keep moving forward in my recovery and to experience thriving a day at a time.*

- *I can achieve a life with balance and hope.*

- *I will adopt loyalty to functionality as a way of life.*

- *I can reach a state of thriving most days of the week, and I will take whatever steps are necessary to achieve it: I am worth it!*

AFTERWORD

Now that you have reached the end of this book, I want to thank you for your trust, your courage, and your willingness to join forces with the Silence Breakers and me on this journey. I hope you now know that recovery is absolutely possible for you! I hope you understand that you have the ability and the opportunity to join forces with a community of brothers who are eager to support you as you heal. I hope you act on your ability to not only survive your abuse and assaults, but also thrive. Take it one step at a time, one day at a time, until you are thriving on the majority of your days.

If you are a survivor's family member or ally, or a professional who works with male survivors and their families, I hope you realize that you are a vital part of the survivor community and that your contributions are immense gifts to all of us.

There are lots of resources in the pages that follow. They will assist you as you continue your recovery. Please do visit those pages, because many helpful organizations are listed there.

I know our paths may never cross; however, I plan on being around a long time, so I might get to meet you at a MaleSurvivor Weekend of Recovery, a MaleSurvivor conference, or some other public-awareness event. If not, know that I am grateful for the time we have been able to share through these pages. All my best to you in your next steps!

— Dr. Howard Fradkin

ENDNOTES

Introduction

1. Dube, S. R.; Anda, R. F.; Whitfield, C. L.; Brown, D. W.; Felitti, V. J.; Dong, M.; and Giles, W. H. 2005. "Long-term consequences of childhood sexual abuse by gender of victim." *American Journal of Preventive Medicine,* 28 (5): 430–438.
    Lisak, D.; Hopper, J.; and Song, P. 1996. "Factors in the cycle of violence: Gender rigidity and emotional constriction." *Journal of Traumatic Stress,* 9: 721–743.
    Finkelhor, D.; Hotaling, G.; Lewis, I. A.; and Smith, C. 1990. "Sexual abuse in a national survey of adult men and women: Prevalence, characteristics, and risk factors." *Child Abuse & Neglect,* 14: 19–28.
    Also visit **www.jimhopper.com** for a comprehensive discussion of sexual abuse statistics from across the world.

2. Lonsway, K. A.; Aschambault, J.; and Lisak, D. 2009. "False Reports: Moving Beyond the Issue to Successfully Investigate and Prosecute Non-Stranger Sexual Assault." *The Voice* 3 (1): 1–11.

3. Lisak, D. 1994. "The psychological impact of sexual abuse: Content analysis of interviews with male survivors." *Journal of Traumatic Stress,* 7: 525–548.
    Lisak, D.; Hopper, J.; and Song, P. 1996. "Factors in the cycle of violence: Gender rigidity and emotional constriction." *Journal of Traumatic Stress,* 9: 721–743.

4. Lisak, D.; Hopper, J.; and Song, P. 1996. "Factors in the cycle of violence: Gender rigidity and emotional constriction." *Journal of Traumatic Stress,* 9: 721–743.

Chapter 7

1. See U.S. Department of Justice, Office of Public Affairs, *The Justice Blog,* "An Updated Definition of Rape," January 6, 2012, **http://blogs.justice.gov/ovw/archives/1801.**

2. See Jim Hopper's website, **www.jimhopper.com/abstats/#meth,** *Child Abuse: Statistics, Research, and Resources,* "Retrospective Survey Research Methods: Tools for Critical Understanding."

3. See Patrick Carnes's *Don't Call It Love: Recovery from Sexual Addiction* (New York: Bantam Books, 1991).

Chapter 9

1. See Harvey Araton's article "In Book, Sugar Ray Leonard Says Coach Sexually Abused Him," *The New York Times,* May 17, 2011, **www.nytimes.com/2011/05/18/sports/in-book-sugar-ray-leonard-says-coach-sexually-abused-him.html?_r=1&pagewanted=all.**

2. See Lucia Capacchione's *Recovery of Your Inner Child: The Highly Acclaimed Method for Liberating Your Inner Self* (New York: Simon & Schuster, 1991).

4. See Kenneth M. Adams's *When He's Married to Mom: How to Help Mother-Enmeshed Men Open Their Hearts to True Love and Commitment* (with Alexander P. Morgan, New York: Simon & Schuster, 2007).

5. One way to find a skilled hypnotherapist is to visit the website of the National Board for Certified Clinical Hypnotherapists (NBCCH), organized in 1991 as an educational, scientific, and professional organization dedicated to professionalizing the mental health specialty of hypnotherapy: **www.natboard.com.** The NBCCH is committed to reflecting the diversity of its constituents and providing information to the public. The NBCCH requires that hypnotherapists also have a graduate degree in medicine or a mental health field, including state-licensed addictions and substance-abuse counselors, chiropractors, marriage and family therapists, mental health counselors, psychiatric nurses, physicians, psychiatrists, psychologists, school counselors, clinical social workers, and pastoral counselors who are full clinical members of the American Pastoral Counselors Association.

6. For more information on EMDR (Eye Movement Desensitization and Reprocessing), visit the website of the EMDR Institute (**www.emdr.com**).

Chapter 10

1. For more information on gestalt therapy, see Frederick S. Perls's *Gestalt Therapy Verbatim* (Lafayette, CA: Real People Press, 1969). See also Virginia Satir's *The Satir Model: Family Therapy and Beyond,* 1st ed. (Palo Alto, CA: Science and Behavior Books, 1991).

Chapter 11

1. See Simon LeVay's *Gay, Straight, and the Reason Why: The Science of Sexual Orientation* (New York: Oxford University Press, 2011).

2. See Ritch C. Savin-Williams and Geoffrey L. Ream's paper "Prevalence and Stability of Sexual Orientation Components During Adolescence and Young Adulthood," in *Archives of Sexual Behavior,* vol. 36 (3): pp. 385–394 (2007).

3. See online report by The University of British Columbia Public Affairs, "Sexually Abused Boys at Risk for More Unsafe Sex: UBC Research," in advance of the *Journal of Adolescent Health,* June issue (2012), **www.publicaffairs.ubc.ca/2012/04/04/sexually-abused-boys-at-risk-for-more-unsafe-sex-ubc-research.**

Chapter 12

1. See Mikele Rauch's *Healing the Soul after Religious Abuse: The Dark Heaven of Recovery* (Westport, CT: Praeger Publishers, 2009).

RESOURCES

Chapter 2

Resources on meditation and mindful awareness co-compiled by Jim Struve, LCSW, Salt Lake City, Utah:

Brach, Tara. 2003. *Radical Acceptance: Embracing Your Life with the Heart of a Buddha*. New York: Bantam Books.

Chödrön, Pema. 1994. *Start Where You Are: A Guide to Compassionate Living*. 1st ed. Boston: Shambhala Publications.

Gunaratana, Venerable Henepola. 2002. *Mindfulness in Plain English*. Boston: Wisdom Publications.

Hanh, Thich Nhat. 1975. *The Miracle of Mindfulness: A Manual on Meditation*. Translated by Mobi Ho. Boston: Beacon Press.

———. 1991. *Peace Is Every Step: The Path of Mindfulness in Everyday Life*. Edited by Arnold Kotler. New York: Bantam Books.

———. 2006. *Present Moment, Wonderful Moment: Mindfulness Verses for Daily Living*. Rev. ed. Berkeley, CA.: Parallax Press.

Hanh, Thich Nhat, and Lilian Cheung. 2010. *Savor: Mindful Eating, Mindful Life*. 1st ed. New York: HarperCollins.

Kabat-Zinn, Jon. 2005. *Coming to Our Senses: Healing Ourselves and the World Through Mindfulness*. New York: Hyperion.

Chapter 11

http://saa-recovery.org
The International Service Organization of Sex Addicts Anonymous, Inc., PO Box 70949, Houston, TX 77270; 1-800-477-8191.
SAA is a fellowship of men and women who share their experiences, strength, and hope with each other so that they may overcome their sexual addiction and help others recover from sexual addiction or dependency. SAA acknowledges each individual's dignity to choose his or her own concept of healthy sexuality. This is accomplished through the development of a "sex plan." Online meetings are hosted at this site.

www.sa.org
The International Fellowship of Sexaholics Anonymous, PO Box 3565, Brentwood, TN 37024; 1-866-424-8777.
SA is a fellowship of men and women who share their experience, strength, and hope with each other that they may solve their common problem and help

others to recover. SA predefines sobriety for its participants as no sex with oneself or with partners other than one's spouse. (Therefore, it may not be open to gays or bisexuals.)

www.slaafws.org

Sex and Love Addicts Anonymous is an anonymous 12-step, 12-tradition–oriented fellowship based on the model pioneered by AA. The only qualification for SLAA membership is a desire to stop living out a pattern of sex and love addiction. SLAA members don't necessarily define sobriety with the use of a defined plan, though this may be utilized as a tool of this program.

www.sca-recovery.org

Sexual Compulsives Anonymous International Service Organization, PO Box 1585, Old Chelsea Station, New York, NY 10011; 800-977-4325.

SCA is a "fellowship of men and women who share their experience, strength, and hope with each other, that they may solve their common problem and help others to recover from sexual compulsion." SCA welcomes people of differing sexual orientations. This program defines sobriety by a plan devised by the recovering person with the guidance of another recovering person in the SCA fellowship. Online meetings are available on this site.

www.s-anon.org

S-Anon International Family Groups World Service Office, PO Box 111242, Nashville, TN 37222-1242; 1-800-210-8141.

The S-Anon Family Groups are a fellowship of the relatives and friends of sexually addicted people, who share their experience, strength, and hope in order to solve their common problems. Their recovery program is adapted from AA and based on the 12 steps and 12 traditions of AA. S-Anon is a good program for partners of people who are struggling with sex addiction or sexual anorexia. Much like Al-Anon, the program helps partners to refuse to engage in behavior in which they deny the existence of the problem or minimize the consequences on their relationship. Rather, the program gives partners tools to constructively take care of themselves while holding their addicted partners responsible for the consequences and hurt they cause. To be clear, the partner of a survivor is never responsible for the behaviors their partner chooses to engage in to try to heal or to avoid or prolong the healing process. At the same time, throughout this book I have invited partners to share the ways they have learned to effectively help support their partner as they heal.

www.recovering-couples.org

Recovering Couples Anonymous, PO Box 11029, Oakland, CA 94611; 1-877-663-2317.

RCA is a fellowship of recovering couples who suffer from many different addictions and share their experience, strength, and hope with one another to help solve their common problems and help other recovering couples restore their relationship.

For a great book on intimacy for all couples, read John Gottman's *Why Marriages Succeed or Fail . . . and How You Can Make Yours Last* (New York: Simon & Schuster, 1994).

Chapter 14

www.bigvoicepictures.com

This is the website of documentary-film producers Kathy Barbini and Simon Weinberg. Big Voice Pictures produced the film *Boys and Men Healing,* a documentary about the impact of sexual abuse of boys on individuals and society, and the importance of healing and speaking out for male survivors to end the devastating effects.

www.nextstepcounseling.org

Visit this website, *The Next Step Counseling and Training,* by Mike Lew, and click "Resources" to find all of the international organizations that are addressing male sexual victimization.

Additional Self-Help Resources

International Male Survivor Websites

www.malesurvivor.org

MaleSurvivor: The National Organization Against Male Sexual Victimization is committed to preventing, healing, and eliminating all forms of sexual victimization of boys and men through support, treatment, research, education, advocacy, and activism. MaleSurvivor sponsors Weekends of Recovery; an online chat room and bulletin boards; resources for finding therapists and support groups; articles; a bookstore (a great place to find other books on this subject); and a biannual conference for psychotherapists, allies in healing, survivors, and their partners. Many more resources are available at this website.

www.1in6.org

1in6 offers a wealth of information and resources (including an online help line and a lending library) for men who have had unwanted or abusive childhood sexual experiences, and for those who care about them. The site is for men at various stages of information seeking and need, including those who don't see themselves as "survivors" or their experiences as "abuse." 1in6 also provides trainings for therapists and other professionals.

www.menthriving.org

Men Thriving is a peer-support resource offered to men who survived sexual abuse in childhood or adulthood.

http://matrixmensa.blogspot.com

This website is for male survivors in South Africa, and is run by survivors, for survivors.

http://menhealing.libsyn.com/webpage

Men Healing is a podcast of shows featuring interviews with male survivors and psychotherapists in the field. The goal of these podcasts is to bring hope to any man who has been living with the effects of sexual victimization.

General Survivor Websites

http://theawarenesscenter.blogspot.com

The Awareness Center, Inc., the International Jewish Coalition Against Sexual

Abuse/Assault (JCASA), is dedicated to addressing childhood sexual abuse in Jewish communities worldwide.

www.justdetention.org

Just Detention International seeks to end sexual violence committed against men, women, and children in all types of detention facilities.

www.manyvoicespress.com

Many Voices is a bimonthly, internationally distributed newsletter, founded in 1989, for people recovering from severe child abuse or trauma. The website features books and healing resources for people who are recovering from child abuse or severe trauma. MV readers form a community that is dedicated to healing from tragic physical, sexual, and emotional assaults. Solutions are suggested for overcoming dissociation, PTSD, flashbacks, self-injury, and other disabling symptoms from an abusive past. Knowledgeable and caring trauma-therapy specialists are featured on the therapist pages.

www.stopmilitaryrape.org

The Military Rape Crisis Center provides immediate crisis care, support, legal assistance, and hope to all survivors of military sexual trauma and their loved ones. The organization is privately funded. All services are free of charge.

www.nsvrc.org

The National Sexual Violence Resource Center is the nation's principle information and resource center concerning all aspects of sexual violence. It provides national leadership, consultation, and technical assistance by developing and providing information on sexual-violence intervention and prevention strategies. The NSVRC addresses the causes and impact of sexual violence through collaboration, prevention efforts, and distribution of resources.

www.pavingtheway.net

PAVE (Promoting Awareness, Victim Empowerment) is a national nonprofit organization using social, educational, and legislative strategies to raise public awareness about sexual violence.

www.pokrov.org

Protection of the Theotokos is a resource for survivors of abuse in the Orthodox churches.

www.rainn.org

RAINN (Rape, Abuse, and Incest National Network) is the nation's largest anti–sexual assault organization, and operates the National Sexual Assault Hotline (800-656-HOPE) in partnership with over 1,100 local rape-crisis centers across the country. The hotline has helped more than 1.4 million people since 1994. RAINN also provides programs for preventing sexual assault, helping victims, and ensuring that rapists are brought to justice.

www.safersociety.org

The Safer Society Foundation helps survivors, treatment professionals, people with sexual-behavior problems, family members, friends, policy makers, researchers, and educators to create evidence-based strategies for preventing sexual abuse, supporting people who have been abused, and managing people who have abused. Besides the website, The Safer Society Foundation provides resources through the Safer Society Press and its national database of professionals.

www.sidran.org

Sidran Institute is an international nonprofit organization that helps people understand, recover from, and treat traumatic stress (including PTSD); dissociative disorders; and co-occurring issues, such as addictions, self-injury, and suicidality.

www.soar99.org

SOAR (Speaking Out About Rape) runs national awareness, education, and prevention programs to empower survivors of sexual violence and improve public understanding and acceptance of rape victims.

www.snapnetwork.org

SNAP (Survivors Network of those Abused by Priests) is a national support group for women and men abused by religious authority figures.

www.safe4all.org

SAFE (Stop Abuse for Everyone) is a human-rights organization providing services, publications, and training for people who often fall through the cracks of domestic-violence services: straight men, LGBT victims, teens, and the elderly.

http://safe4athletes.org

Safe4athletes' mission is to advocate for athlete welfare, where every athlete is provided a safe and positive environment free of sexual abuse, bullying, and harassment.

INDEX

ACKNOWLEDGMENTS

To each of the Silence Breakers, I owe immense gratitude for your openness, trust, and willingness to help the readers on their healing journeys. Each of you deserves a standing ovation!

To all of the male and female survivors of abuse and assault who have trusted me to walk with them on their journeys, thank you for the incredible lessons and wisdom you have shared with me.

To my co-chairperson, Jim Struve, and the entire MaleSurvivor Weekends of Recovery facilitator team—Lee Beckstead, Peter Botteas, Bill Burmester, Joanna Colrain, Andy Dishman, Sandi Forti, Rob Hawkings, Mic Hunter, Sharon Imperato, Lisa Jameson, Don Laufersweiler, Paul Linden, Lynne MacDonell, Ernesto Mujica, and Mikele Rauch—I owe you tremendous gratitude for your solid support, for the incredible wisdom you have shared with me, and for inspiring me with your own struggles and the courage you have shown in overcoming those obstacles. This book is only possible because of our ability to form such an effective team; you are the best colleagues with whom any person could ever be privileged to share such important work. Special thanks to Jim, Joanna, and Paul for your help with Chapter 1; to Lee for your help with Chapter 11; to Ernesto for your editing assistance and encouragement; and to Mikele for your guidance with the Silence Breakers and your support throughout this process.

Special thanks to the present and past members of the board of directors of MaleSurvivor, including Ken Followell, Jorge Ramirez, Marc Spindelman, Richard Gartner, Murray Schane, Kit Sumner, Ken Singer, Curtis St. John, Ann Boyer, Jaye Rieser, Matt Paknis, and John Walker, who have been especially strong advocates on the board, and to Trisha Massa, the WOR Administrator and Community Outreach Director, who makes each weekend program possible. I am excited to also thank MaleSurvivor's first executive director, Chris Anderson, who has strongly taken the reins and dared to dream that our organization could become even more effective and far-reaching in our goals and mission.

Thanks, also, to Executive Director Steve LaPore and **1in6 .org** for your consistent support of the Weekends of Recovery and for joining forces with MaleSurvivor to work toward ending male sexual victimization.

To all the pioneers who have come before me and written such powerful and helpful books for male survivors, their allies, and psychotherapists, and done groundbreaking research—Mike Lew, Richard Gartner, Mic Hunter, Larry Morris, Ken Singer, Mikele Rauch, Paul Linden, Christine Courtois, Kenneth Adams, David Lisak, Jim Hopper, Ellen Bass, and Laura Davis—thank you all for your inspiration and for helping to pave the way for the writing of this book. (All of their books are available at the **www .malesurvivor.org** bookstore.) Thanks also to Simon Weinberg and Kathy Barbini for your incredible survivor documentaries and your love and support.

To Jan Miller, Shannon Marven, and the entire staff of Dupree Miller & Associates Literary Agency, I have deeply appreciated your invaluable guidance and strong support from the moment we started working together and throughout this process. Millions will benefit from your belief in me and from your help in getting out this message to the men and women who need it

To Reid Tracy, president and CEO of Hay House, thank you so much for believing in me, and for providing me with such excellent editors, especially Shannon Littrell and Alex Freemon, who treated me with such great respect and loving care, while providing excellent guidance and healthy challenges to make this work even more powerful. To Julie Davison and Christy Salinas, thank you for your beautiful and effective design and cover work. To all the other Hay House staff who joined forces with me to make this a reality, you have helped me make an incredible dream come true!

To Wes Smith, your consultation and guidance on this work has been invaluable in helping me craft my message to be even more powerful and effective.

To photographers Ray Lavoie and Mic Hunter, thank you both for you skillful eye and the wonderful, crisp images of the MaleSurvivor T-shirts; and to Jason Roth for your incredible cover photo! Thanks also to Bruce Reedy and Jason Bockis for your donation of your skillful videography for the publicity of this book.

To Oprah Winfrey and Tyler Perry, I would have never embarked on writing this book without your strong encouragement and belief in me. Thank you for giving me such strong support!

To the incredibly talented producers of *The Oprah Winfrey Show*, especially Stacy Strazis, Candi Carter, Rick Segall, Abby Silverman, Jim Kelley, and publicist Don Halcombe, thank you for all of your support before, during, and after the show for me and those incredible 200 men and their partners.

I write often in this book about the importance of support, and I needed a tremendous amount of it while creating this work. My primary supporter has been my life partner of 34 years, Pete, who has stood by my side and given me love, encouragement, and the appropriate challenges to help us maintain and develop an even healthier relationship. My sister-in-law Susan Wells has been an incredible asset as an editor and cheerleader extraordinaire. She has shown me how to say more with fewer words while still conveying my passion for helping others. Pete's family—Mom, James, Steve, Nancy, Shanti, Elizabeth and Jason, Andrew and Rachel—and my brother Steve and sisters-in-law Barbara and Carol have also been important supporters throughout this process.

To my business partner Don Laufersweiler and to my colleagues at Affirmations: A Center for Psychotherapy and Growth—Dwight Tolliver, Chad Corbley, Jim Hodnett, Craig Campbell, Chanté Meadows, Amy Pfeiffer, and Abbe Whelan—you have provided amazing support and encouragement every step of the way. Thanks, too, to my friend and colleague Barb Reardon, who has also been a consistent and loyal friend, and to David for your encouragement and support.

To the King Avenue Methodist Church pastors Rev. John Keeny, Rev. Linda Middelberg, and Rev. John Wooden, thank you for your spiritual nurturing and inspiration.

Last, to my group of friends known as "the Party of 75," you are the best friends any man could ever want, and to each of you, a huge thank you for all of your love and encouragement during this intense and rewarding time of my life! Special thanks to my longtime friends Rick and Brian, Matt and Brian, Greg and Mike, Doug and Mark, Andrew and Brad, Bruce and Brad, Matt and Steve, Bob, and Jimmy.

❧   ❧   ❧   ❧

ABOUT THE AUTHOR

Howard Fradkin received his Ph.D. in Counseling Psychology in 1980 from the University of North Carolina at Chapel Hill, and has been licensed as a psychologist in Ohio since 1982. In 1984 Dr. Fradkin co-founded Affirmations: A Center for Psychotherapy and Growth, a private multidisciplinary practice in Columbus, Ohio. Dr. Fradkin has counseled over 1,000 male survivors in individual, couples, and group psychotherapy and weekend workshops over the course of his 30-year career. He is respected as a national expert providing professional training to his colleagues in delivering effective psychotherapy for male survivors. He is one of the co-founders of the National Organization on Male Sexual Victimization (now known as MaleSurvivor), and has served as an advisory board member for MaleSurvivor since 2001.

In 2001, Dr. Fradkin became the chairperson of the Male-Survivor Weekends of Recovery program. In this role, he had the primary responsibility for developing and implementing the weekend experience, supervising staff, and overseeing the emotional experiences of all of the male survivors (and sometimes their partners) who participated in the weekend. In 2010, due to the success and growth of the program, it became necessary to share responsibilities for it, and since that time, he has served as co-chairperson. Dr. Fradkin has directed more than 40 Weekends of Recovery since 2001. His expertise was recognized by Oprah Winfrey when she invited him to be her professional guest for two 2010 shows, "200 Men," focusing on healing for male survivors of sexual abuse. Dr. Fradkin has also appeared on NPR, *Dr. Phil,* and TAALK radio as an expert in the field.

As a male survivor himself, Dr. Fradkin has learned firsthand about the struggles inherent in achieving recovery, and is able to offer significant hope and encouragement to empower men to thrive in many aspects of their lives.

Dr. Fradkin can be reached at:

Affirmations: A Center for Psychotherapy and Growth
918 S. Front St., Columbus, OH 43206
www.howardfradkin.com • **www.affirmationstherapy.com**
hfradkin@malesurvivor.org
614-445-8277, ext. 11

Notes

Notes

Notes

Notes

Notes

Notes

Notes

Notes

Notes

Notes

Notes

We hope you enjoyed this Hay House book. If you'd like to receive our online catalog featuring additional information on Hay House books and products, or if you'd like to find out more about the Hay Foundation, please contact:

Hay House, Inc., P.O. Box 5100, Carlsbad, CA 92018-5100
(760) 431-7695 or (800) 654-5126
(760) 431-6948 (fax) or (800) 650-5115 (fax)
www.hayhouse.com® • **www.hayfoundation.org**

❁ ❁ ❁

Published and distributed in Australia by:
Hay House Australia Pty. Ltd., 18/36 Ralph St., Alexandria NSW 2015
Phone: 612-9669-4299 • *Fax:* 612-9669-4144 • www.hayhouse.com.au

Published and distributed in the United Kingdom by:
Hay House UK, Ltd., 292B Kensal Rd., London W10 5BE
Phone: 44-20-8962-1230 • *Fax:* 44-20-8962-1239 • www.hayhouse.co.uk

Published and distributed in the Republic of South Africa by:
Hay House SA (Pty), Ltd., P.O. Box 990, Witkoppen 2068
Phone/Fax: 27-11-467-8904 • www.hayhouse.co.za

Published in India by:
Hay House Publishers India, Muskaan Complex, Plot No. 3, B-2, Vasant Kunj, New Delhi 110 070 • *Phone:* 91-11-4176-1620
Fax: 91-11-4176-1630 • www.hayhouse.co.in

Distributed in Canada by:
Raincoast, 9050 Shaughnessy St., Vancouver, B.C. V6P 6E5
Phone: (604) 323-7100 • *Fax:* (604) 323-2600 • www.raincoast.com

❁ ❁ ❁

Take Your Soul on a Vacation

Visit **www.HealYourLife.com**® to regroup, recharge, and reconnect with your own magnificence. Featuring blogs, mind-body-spirit news, and life-changing wisdom from Louise Hay and friends.

Visit **www.HealYourLife.com** today!

Lightning Source UK Ltd.
Milton Keynes UK
UKOW052335180113

205103UK00003B/106/P